BREAKING INTO HEAVEN

THE RISE AND FALL OF

THE STONE ROSES

Mick Middles

OMNIBUS PRESS

London/New York/Paris/Sydney/Copenhagen/Madrid/Tokyo

Cover designed by Michael Bell Design Ltd
Picture research by Nikki Russell
Front cover picture: Joe Dilworth/SIN; back cover: Marina Chavez/SIN

ISBN: 1.84609.516.6
Order No: OP51546

Exclusive Distributors
Music Sales Limited,
8/9 Frith Street,
London W1D 3JB, UK.

Music Sales Corporation,
257 Park Avenue South,
New York, NY 10010, USA.

Macmillan Distribution Services,
53 Park West Drive,
Derrimut, Vic 3030,
Australia.

To the Music Trade only:
Music Sales Limited,
8/9 Frith Street,
London W1D 3JB, UK.

Every effort has been made to trace the copyright holders of the photographs in this book but one or two were unreachable. We would be grateful if the photographers concerned would contact us.

Printed by Mackays of Chatham plc, Chatham, Kent
Typeset by Galleon Typesetting, Ipswich, Suffolk

A catalogue record for this book is available from the British Library.

Visit Omnibus Press on the web at **www.omnibuspress.com**

CONTENTS

1

ANARCHY IN TIMPERLEY

It began in Warrington, of all places – that strange, flat cusp where Manchester shades into Liverpool in a muddle of business parks and featureless housing estates; a meeting place for Manc and Scouse, Cheshire and Lancashire. Unpromising ground for a musical phenomenon perhaps, and yet it was Warrington which saw the introduction of a radical new music to the north of England, one which foreshadowed the invasion of rock'n'roll in the Fifties.[1] For it was at the local Birchwood Aerodrome, during the latter stages of World War Two, that off-duty American servicemen staged wild evenings of swing music, a magnetic maelstrom of sex, swagger and souped-up sound which drew in flocks of impressionable local girls, and frequently provoked violent confrontations with the comparatively unsophisticated local boys.

Ian George Brown, no stranger to violent confrontations himself, was born in Warrington on February 20, 1963, into an unpretentious, stable and loving family. His father, George, for whom Ian is allegedly a dead ringer, was a popular local joiner, laddish to a point but never one to lose himself in alcoholic revelry; Ian's mother, Jean, worked as a telephone receptionist. Although today Brown describes his Warrington years as 'grim', he still harbours a couple of striking memories of his birthplace. For instance, if you are looking for an early indication of his infamous arrogance, his 'punkism', you might trace it back to the day he was unwillingly made 'milk monitor' at his primary school. "They gave me this title, milk monitor, and I think I was supposed to feel proud," he recalls. "Took me about two seconds to realise that all it meant was that I had to hand all the milk out to all the other kids. I refused. Completely. Told the teacher that they should go and get their own milk. Damn right, too. I'm still quite proud of that." Also, Brown recalls ". . . lying in some grass (aged four), staring at the sky, feeling belligerent. I had been taken

[1] In the early Sixties, Warrington also sat at the dead centre of the vibrant band circuit which gave rise to Merseybeat.

out of school and this girl I was with, can't remember who she was, was telling me that I was 'bad'. I don't know if I was proud or ashamed. But, from that age, yeah, I did have a rebellious streak."

When Brown was aged just six, the family moved to leafy Timperley, in the soft underbelly of Manchester. This represented a slight social upgrading although to date, Timperley remains a curious place, where the sprawling council estate of Wythenshaw fizzles out into the plush suburbs of Altrincham. No wonder that for school children thrown in from the two social extremes – marked by big houses and little houses, gleaming BMWs and rusty Ford Escorts – the eternal jarring of class can readily give rise to conflict. Naturally perhaps, the kids from the rougher end of the scale – and Brown would fit into this category – would become the 'cool' ones, the ones driven to adorn themselves with the glittery prizes of social importance. (Which is why working-class school kids are traditionally regarded by their peers as the more stylish, the more streetwise, the more effortlessly hip.)

Brown had a younger brother, David, and a sister, Sharon, her name chosen by the young Ian in honour of Sharon McCready, the vivacious blonde from the Sixties' TV show *The Champions*, and one of his first crushes. (His sister actually prefers to be known as Louise.) Though he chose to lock himself for hours on end in his poster-lined bedroom as a child, Ian's early family life was uneventful and unproblematic, though those posters provide another clue to the Brown psyche. *All* of them featured the perfect, glowing figure of Muhammad Ali, the most charismatic sportsman of the century, a giant talent and a giant personality, a beautifully packaged dynamo with a wicked talent for wordplay. Brown adored Ali from the time when, only five years old, his young eyes first saw the great man on a television screen. The arrogance, the supreme power of self-confidence and the breathtaking style would all register and stay with Ian Brown, influencing his attitude to life and his style as a performer. He remains a boxing fan to this day.

And then there was the music. Music filled the Brown household. When he was eight, Ian's aunt presented him with a stack of well worn seven-inch discs, inspirational slabs of plastic, which he would pile on his self-stacking Dansette, and listen to over and over again, soaking in their curious magic. Every dusty scratched single was a classic: 'It's Not Unusual', Tom Jones; 'Help', The Beatles; 'Under My Thumb' and 'Get Off My Cloud', The Rolling Stones; 'The Happening' and 'Love Child' by The Supremes. Each one brilliantly evocative, an inspirational vinyl experience, the power of which is unlikely ever to translate effectively onto soulless compact discs. Incidentally, three of those singles – 'Help', 'Under My Thumb' and 'It's Not Unusual' were also stacked on the young Mick Hucknall's Dansette, seven miles away, across Manchester. This revelation, which emerged in separate interviews, should not be too surprising – the power of the pop single in the Sixties and Seventies was far greater than it is today, when the impact of a song is muddied by the diversity of versions afforded by multi-formatting and the visual distractions of video. In an earlier era of pop, it was simply a question of sitting in the corner of a room and soaking up the sound of one golden track after another; for Ian Brown, music became education and inspiration.

It was to be the same story for one of Brown's neighbours, who lived two doors down on Sylvan Avenue. John Thomas Squire was born on November 24, 1962, in Broadheath. The meeting of these two is already immersed in pop legend, as befits one of the most significant songwriting partnerships in recent memory – the location a communal sand pit where the local children could play. The event is spiced further by John's recollection that Ian was naked, save for a few patches of sand. Brown doesn't dispute this, but adds, "If that's how John remembers it, then maybe it was like that. I do recall the sand pit. Used to muck around in there a lot. I remember meeting John . . . probably quite a few times but we weren't, like, dead close, because I had my own mates from school. But I do recall his shy stare, which was quite intriguing even then. There was something about him."

They attended separate primary schools with Brown apparently the classroom joker at his. He was always the one to grab the lead role in the classroom plays, always out front, openly mimicking the teacher; indeed, his repertoire of localised impressions covered the entire teaching staff. "My best one? Mr Clarke, the maths teacher. He had a really gruff voice and when I did him I cracked everyone up," he told Q in 1998. Brown is under no illusions as to his disruptive influence on the rest of the class. "A lot of the teachers were wary of me, 'cos I was always quick to answer back," he recalls, adding tellingly, "not that I was particularly naughty, but I did have an attitude. I have never liked people telling me what to do." By contrast, John Squire's primary school life saw him skulking firmly at the back of the class, dodging away from any trace of drama, deflecting any possibility of attention. His shyness masked a considerable intellect, a fact recognised only by the more perceptive teachers at his school. He excelled in art and, on games afternoons, would be allowed to mooch about in the deserted art room, quietly pursuing his creative instincts. Drawing sessions allowed him to display a striking faculty for concentrated work, and he spent many solitary hours developing his skills with the pencil even at the expense of friendships. At primary school he made few if any lasting friends, preferring to live in a semi-permanent dream state, much to the concern of his teachers.

It wasn't until both boys reached secondary school age and joined

Altrincham Grammar School that Squire and Brown finally got to know each other, the gregarious Brown finding himself curiously attracted by Squire's distanced demeanour. As opposites, they bonded cautiously, walking to and from school together, avoiding fights, chatting about television and, inevitably, music. Brown was the more worldly, by far: by the age of thirteen he had already clocked up five years of travelling to Manchester city centre on Saturday afternoons, floating down to the Oasis coffee bar and watching the Crombie-clad legions gather on Market Street. Too young to attract serious attention, he saw the gangs of Salford, distinctively dressed in their stone-coloured parallels and cherry red Doc Martens, menacing teenage stragglers from Hyde and Stockport and, at times, he joined in with football related scuffles, pre-punk maelstroms of Northern Soulies, latterday Suedeheads and soccer thugs. Attracted, indeed, 'intoxicated' by all three youth groups, Brown readily staked his place in their ranks. He would boast about Wigan Casino as if he was a regular – he wasn't, though he did sneak into a soul 'all nighter' at Droylsden's Concorde Suite and was bowled over by the power of the music and the sheer energy of the dancing.

Significantly, around the same time, Brown began to nurture a growing wanderlust, a habit he retains to this day. His enthusiasm for travel was so strong that it infected his closest mates, and a gang of them, barely into their teens, would cruise the town centres of Leeds, York, Blackpool and Stoke-on-Trent. Brown's group were style-conscious teenagers who wore the sharpest street fashions, purchased at knock-down prices from 'Stolen From Ivor' in the infamous Underground Market: parallels £5, Harrington jackets £7.50, Levi's Stay Prest, £12.50. In the wild mid-Seventies, with soccer thuggery at its peak, and most city centres cowering at the chants from rival sets of fans on Saturday mornings, such gang travel was a dangerous occupation. But Brown's bunch were young and thirsted for a bit of adventure. They talked a good fight while generally ducking away from the real action; with luck and a spot of street suss, they got by.

Brown began to share his experience of youth cults, and life-transforming new music with the more reserved Squire. The latter's musical awakening was by now well underway courtesy of Sixties icons The Beach Boys and The Beatles, but John had as yet failed to latch onto the unparalleled swell of Northern Soul. Some achievement – Northern Soul soundtracked the lives of most teen scenesters in the north of England of the mid-Seventies. The phenomenon permeated from dance halls and nightclubs right down to the youth club disco and the Timperley Scout Hut.

At the same time, Brown was developing other passions. His Muhammad Ali posters had, by the mid-Seventies, been joined by pictures of pretty boy kung fu star Bruce Lee. Sneaking into the cinema at Sale, he had seen the double bill, *Enter The Dragon & Fists Of Fury*, two cultish, wholly over-the-top orgies of violence, featuring punches, chops and outrageous high-kicking bouts seemingly beyond the skill and speed of any human being. It was all fabulous fodder for an active thirteen-year-old brain, and Brown would return from the cinema deep in his own kung fu fantasy, feeling implausibly indestructible. Fantasy was enough for most kids, who were happy to let the kung fu dream fade as they rode the last bus home; the more pragmatic Brown ventured to the local karate class, where he undertook practical instruction in the martial art with a solemn determination. He was good, too, and even after the kung fu cult faded away he stuck at the lessons, cycling four miles to class and back, seven nights a week, from the age of eleven to eighteen, edging closer and closer to black belt supremacy. Brown's dedication was so strong that he even harboured dreams of travelling to Japan, of learning stronger, stricter disciplines under a grand master. In contrast to his often belligerent attitude at school, Brown would glean enjoyment from the sheer discipline of karate. It was a paradox that would continue through the days of The Stone Roses where their hedonistic image would be balanced by Brown's sober determination, the single-mindedness of a man on a mission to make glorious music; that single-mindedness would eventually push him through to achieving solo success in 1998. It is not difficult to imagine a young Ian Brown relentlessly practising karate kicks and chops, perpetually pushing himself towards some kind of limit, revelling in the demands of self-discipline. In the end, however, something prevented him from taking that final step, and three weeks before his black belt exam, Brown abruptly dropped karate.

His sudden decision highlighted another key personality trait – his stubborn individualism. Ian Brown wasn't born to follow. "I still regret that," he says, "I finally fell out with that discipline. I remember this kid, who was just fantastic . . . easily the best in the class. He was just awesome, but he had his own mind. He never took 'O' Levels and he just wouldn't do his karate the way they told him. I sort of fell into that way of thinking as well. A bit of a punk thing, I think. That kid never got beyond a white belt. I think I took some of his attitude off him, which is why I eventually left the club. But I do regret it. It was a stupid thing to do."

* * *

1976 proved to be a watershed year for music, with knock-on effects that would shape the futures of thousands of aspiring musicians, including Squire and Brown, though at the time they were barely into their teens. Not too far from Timperley, indeed within the scope of a half-hour schoolboy saunter, lay the moody sprawl of the Wythenshaw overspill estate. Vast and brimming with every angle of youth culture, it had provided Manchester, not just with a razor sharp music and fashion sense, but, since the onset of Merseybeat in the early Sixties, with a steady trickle of highly influential talent. True, the area was also responsible for a good deal of brainless football thuggery and drug-associated crime, but it's true to say that without Wythenshaw, the Manchester scene before and after 1976, would simply not have retained its edge. Wythenshaw provided the pullback from student domination; it gave, and still provides, the city with a slab of unpretentious edginess. And Wythenshaw remains quite unlike Salford, or Hulme, or Cheetham Hill or Moss Side; it was born from the days of slum clearance, where working-class Manchester, still gritty from the residue of the industrial age, was shunted to the edge of rural Cheshire, en masse. Its displaced, idiosyncratic atmosphere lingers.

During the early to mid-Seventies, a streak of glam lay on the peripheries of Wythenshaw's conglomerate of youth tribes. Not a teeny Marc Bolan-loving glam, but a darker, Iggy-esque strain that gradually became adopted by the more violent of football fans. It was a strange paradox to see the most glammed-up of young men dive down to The Roxy Room at Pips in the town centre on a Friday night, discussing the hooliganism of the day while applying make-up. This strange hybrid of blusher and boot boys had originally evolved from the skinhead movement of the late Sixties. (Slade, whose glam image was shot through with ballsy rock'n'roll, had briefly adopted the skinhead look, albeit only to attract attention to themselves, but the lingering image did them no harm.) Swiftly, these boys, had moved through the suedehead and soulie stages to emerge bedecked in Lurex and eye liner, blood-red Bowie hair and, by day, gold-painted Doc Martens.

From this scene emerged a bombastic, musically inept gang of pre-punk strutters known as Slaughter And The Dogs. Inarticulate, bursting with youthful arrogance and strongly connected with the area's 'controlling forces' (of which more later), the band acted as a natural magnet for all those who longed for the violent days of the skinheads to return. (Hence, the inspiration for the Dogs' mini-classic, 'Where Have All The Boot Boys Gone?') Although, strictly speaking, Slaughter And The Dogs were up and running before punk exploded, they managed to embrace the punk movement with a natural ease that escaped their fellow Manchester punksters The Drones (who had started life as a sub-Slik cabaret boy pop unit called Rockslide). Slaughter And The Dogs were much more than Buzzcocks-punk naturals.[2] And Wythenshaw knew it.

---

[2] Slaughter And The Dogs, led by volcanic motormouth, Wayne Barrett, were profoundly working class and believed, as Barrett revealed to *Shy Talk* fanzine, "that a punk is supposed to be a pauper. Buzzcocks are middle class, they have 'O' Levels and all that . . ."

And so, apparently, did Timperley. At thirteen, Ian Brown was profoundly attracted to the local mythology of Slaughter And The Dogs. He even knew some of the lesser, younger notables of the burgeoning music scene at that time, though he didn't make it to a remarkable local gig, at Wythenshaw Forum in 1976, featuring Slaughter And The Dogs and the older Wild Ram, an inane crew of rockers who would soon mutate into one of the maddest, baddest examples of full-blown lad rock that the UK has produced — the aptly named Ed Banger And The Nosebleeds. The stories of that riotous gig, however, permeated the Altrincham school yard which was, for some time, filled with tales of the strange weirdo who, in the Forum car park, tried to start a fight with local TV presenter and compere for the evening, Tony Wilson. The weirdo in question was named, for the duration of punk at least, Martin Zero; soon he would revert back to his real name of Martin Hannett.

With a foot still firmly in Northern Soul, Brown found himself drifting inexorably towards the polar extreme of punk, in particular its leading lights, The Sex Pistols, after a mate had picked up a copy of 'Anarchy In The UK' from Woolworth's for 29p.[3] Brown's memories of the first time he heard the Pistols, that mind-juddering moment when Rotten's manic chuckle leaped out of the speakers on the back of a searing stream of power chords, remain cornily vivid. As he noted, in 1985, to *Muze Magazine* writer Paula Greenwood, "That was the moment that altered everything, forever. I would do anything to be able to make a record like Anarchy." He was, however, even more enamoured with the single's extraordinary B-side, the chaotic 'I Wanna Be Me', a marvellous cross-blend of badly played Iggy and Small Faces, all wrapped up in a live production that, in its own inarticulate way, sounded the death knell for the prog rock pomposity which had held sway for so much of the musical decade so far. Howard Devoto, one of the original Buzzcocks, succeeded in getting the Pistols to play twice in Manchester in 1976, a factor which Tony Wilson believes is directly responsible for radically changing the kind of music which the city was producing.

Brown was smitten by 'I Wanna Be Me', especially by Rotten's untutored attack and the sheer daftness of the '. . . cover me in margarine . . .' lyric. Whether he realised it or not, the underlying message of both sides of this single was the classic punk DIY call-to-arms: 'If we can do it, so can you!' The same message came from Slaughter And

---

[3] A widespread bargain. Following the band's four-letter word outburst on Bill Grundy's *Today* programme, and EMI's subsequent decision to withdraw the single, 'Anarchy' was immediately dumped onto bargain bin counters across the country.

The Dogs who overcame their musical limitations by sheer ferocity of performance – indeed, by making their very ineptness a feature of that performance. By exposing raw youth to skyscraping possibilities in this way, punk delivered the perfect pop paradox. Slaughter And The Dogs' début single, 'Cranked Up Really High', a wild celebration of unbridled hedonism fuelled by speed (the punks' drug of choice) and alcohol, became an immediate and lasting influence on Ian Brown. It was a yob record more than a punk disc, a hymn to scrapping and screaming, rather closer to Northern Soul than to the boozy London R&B from which The 101ers, Joe Strummer's pre-Clash band, and Dr Feelgood emerged. In Wythenshaw, if nowhere else in the world, 'Cranked Up Really High' held the frisson of 'Anarchy In The UK'. Also, it had a big impact locally: the record was released on the Wythenshaw label, Rabid, managed by Wythenshaw gobshites Tosh Ryan and the aforementioned Martin Zero, who also produced the disc; even the Dogs' fanzine, *Manchester Rains*, was written by a local ex-hippy hanger-on called Rob Gretton. Alas, the record met with public indifference and quickly joined releases by other sub-punk no-hopers from '77 in obscurity, but Ian Brown was smitten and would acknowledge its impact on him during the press for the release of his solo album in 1998.

During the heady days of punk, his relationship with John Squire intensified considerably. Indeed, it was Brown who ushered Squire into the punk era by taking records around to his house and excitedly slapping them on Squire's Dansette. Hence, Squire's bedroom, that had been previously filled with the sounds of The Beach Boys and The Beatles, now shook to Slaughter And The Dogs, The Drones, The Sex Pistols, and The Adverts' mini-classic, 'One Chord Wonders'. Indeed, for six months, it seemed that each weekend brought a new punk classic to that turntable, with Brown making regular Saturday morning forays into Manchester's cosy hangout, Virgin Records on Lever Street, where Manchester punks would lounge, swap gossip, sell fanzines and slap Beefheartian messages onto the notice board. Brown would return from that welcoming nucleus, the antithesis of today's ice-cold Virgin Megastores, with such definitive punk statements as The Buzzcocks 'Spiral Scratch' EP, The Sex Pistols' 'God Save The Queen' or The Clash's début album, the record through which John Squire finally succumbed to punk's magnetic pull.

Squire's guitar playing, which had begun a year earlier with a hesitant run-through of 'Three Blind Mice', soon aspired to the spiky chord bursts of Mick Jones. He fell totally under the influence of The Clash: the entire Westway riot, the heavy slant to the left, the hint of dub and Rastafarianism, the hot dusty tension of Notting Hill Gate's extraordinary summer of '76, the direct appeal of the 'us and them' mentality.[4] The Clash were eventually to founder over such simplistic sloganeering, but for a good six months, in the mind of the talented, impressionable teenager John Squire, they seemed to conjure up a whole new world. Mick Jones' distinctive guitar playing – undoubtedly born from Jones' aversion to any traces of pub rock – were to be a key influence on Squire's own style. (Ironically, Strummer's 101ers, quite the archetypal pub rockers, would also influence Squire's style.) To this day, even in The Seahorses, who are not without their own pub rock leanings, traces of that first Clash album can still be glimpsed. Moreover, Jones' playing, in stark contrast to Page, Clapton, Kossoff et al, represented a sound and style that seemed attainable to a teenager with a thirty quid guitar. And that, more than anything else, was the true spirit of the punk ethos.

Squire's infatuation was absolute. Brown was astonished, one day, to wander into Squire's bedroom and find an entire wall covered by a mural that Squire had just completed, celebrating Joe Strummer. Squire's blending of art and music had begun. Consumed by these two passions, Squire would paint and play, play and paint, edging closer and closer to the standard laid down by his heroes. In such times as these, when you didn't even need a band, or even an instrument to climb on to the stage and grab punk notoriety – cf. Jon The Postman, The Negatives, John Cooper Clark – it seemed that it was only their extreme youth that was holding Squire and Brown back.

Life in Timperley, wandering to and from school, through leafy suburbia and the vast, deadening Sixties estates of Timperley and Sale, or along the endless arterial highways, wasn't exactly the most romantic backdrop for two young punks. Timperley and its big sister, Altrincham, produced little in the way of local music. As 1977 became 1978, on a good night one might find plucky local popsters, The Freshies, grasping their pink painted guitars and slashing through their inspired but generally ignored set of sardonic love songs. They were too clever to catch the attention of the music press, and too nice, perhaps, to seriously attract Brown and Squire, who searched hard for some kind of scene that might hold more interest than hopelessly parochial band nights in rustic halls. The Bowdon Vale Youth Club, might not sound (and certainly didn't look) like any kind of antidote to this predicament, but, throughout 1978, it produced a string of inspired gigs

---

[4] Occasionally, the area really did witness riots. In the summer of 1976, in front of television camera crews, the Notting Hill Carnival dissolved into a seething mess of brick-throwing, glass-smashing anarchy. Although there was little to be said for such violence *per se*, the riot did throw up a great deal of evocative imagery for intelligent onlookers such as Strummer and Jones, who accurately caught the spirit of the times.

that, although barely grabbing one line in *New Manchester Review* rock section, seem like positive stunners in retrospect. Ian Brown experienced his first live gig, on March 14, 1978, in this unprepossessing venue. He had already missed out on recent appearances by The Electric Circus, Rafters, The Squat and The Band On The Wall until, accompanied by a friend and the friend's little sister, he set forth, aged 15, to sample his first taste of live rock'n'roll. And what was it? Incredibly, it was Joy Division.[5] Not that Joy Division were particularly good that night: they weren't, they were dopey and Ian Curtis gave the impression of having listened to rather too much Throbbing Gristle but, nonetheless, to see the most important rock band on the planet at that time, in a youth club in soft plush Bowdon, was, to say the least, a unique experience. And Ian Brown, by chance, stumbled unwittingly into this extraordinary event. To this day, I doubt he realises just how privileged he was to walk into such a baptism.

The front of the stage was patrolled by Joy Division's omnipresent manager, Rob Gretton – bear-like, even then. Curtis launched into the mind-crushing intensity of 'She's Lost Control', a song which when delivered well, provided the most disturbing, impassioned implosion in rock. And that night, on that particular song, the band were very, very good. (Though they made little impression on Bowden rock journalist, *Record Mirror*'s Mike Nicholls, latterly of *Hello!* Magazine fame, who stood aloof and unimpressed.) And Ian Brown, a kid at the front. A kid with a mate who had brought his tiny twelve-year-old sister to the show. The latter, showing considerable front for one so young, pushed through the post-gig liggers, to ask Ian Curtis for one of his badges. Curtis, jokingly one hopes, replied that she could have it, ". . . for a blow job." Understandably, Ian Brown was appalled, and the trio hurried from the venue. Brown wasn't impressed with the gig either, though in Joy Division's defence, he *did* only have Marc Bolan TV shows to compare it to . . .

His next live gig proved to be Slaughter And The Dogs' second live showing at Wythenshaw Forum. It was a less wild, far less violent and suspiciously more 'showbizzy' affair than any of the Dogs' shows during the punk era, but Brown enjoyed it nonetheless. The Dogs, we can presume, were closer to his psyche than the somewhat insular and, at that point, terribly hip Joy Division. Brown: "I never felt hip. That was always a big thing in Manchester . . . all those Factory bands. It was all so insular and I never even felt close to any of that. In fact that is why I was attracted to Slaughter And The Dogs, because they were just kids on this estate . . . and they never tried to be anything else."

---

[5] For the record, the author was in attendance too and regards that gig as one of the defining moments of his life.

Nevertheless, Ian Brown was hip enough to be drawn into darkest Gorton, to the infamous crumbling wreck known as The Mayflower Club – once the low-brow, druggy Stoneground, the ultimate pre-punk hippy hangout – to catch Manchester's biggest act of the punk era, The Buzzcocks. Lead by one of the most distinctive songwriters of the time, Pete Shelley, The Buzzcocks – in a radical volte face from the more familiar punk themes of riot and revolt – actually dared to sing love songs, albeit off-kilter punk-pop love songs about frustration and disappointment. Brown warmed to the band, although the hint of pretension in their esoteric musical approach made them less of a prospect for hero-worship than the full-on blast of The Clash.

By mid-1979, Manchester's restricted music scene had thrived and died several times since the birth of punk, giving rise to all manner of diverse fads and cliques, from the Bowie clones at Pips nightclub to AC/DC-adoring metalheads; from the trendy young new industrialists clad in suits stolen from their fathers' wardrobes, to latent soulies and parochial punks. And so it was until the inspired commandeering of the funky West Indian Russell Club, in Hulme, by the Factory gang who, exploiting the prevailing air of menace and gloom – the club lay deep in the shadows of the infamous Hulme Crescents housing estate, Valium City to BBC2 documentary makers – created the perfect, shadowy showcase for the whole mess of experimental post-punk bands.

2

WE ARE THE MODS

It was the days of the punk come-down. The afterworld, where pretentious post-grads would attempt to install a sense of modernistic style into a thin synth-powered noise backed by a drum machine, a tape loop and a selection of holiday snaps. Or, equally disturbingly, where bands who had barely mastered the three chord thrash would attempt – sometimes with genuinely inspired and edgy results, viz A Certain Ratio and The Pop Group – to climb into areas of funk generally reserved for the tasteful dexterity of black bass players from Harlem or Chicago. The paradox of asexual white ex-students pushing a rash simplistic polemic across a backbeat based on the act of pure sex, was simultaneously the most entertaining and the saddest aspect of 1979.

The fact that punk was the catalyst that caused a million kids to grab guitars and climb on to a stage has been universally celebrated as a positive move. But those of us who cowered in front of endless thrashing dullards blessed with all the innovative foresight of pub cabaret and no musical deftness whatsoever sometimes tend to disagree. Especially as these same groups would gain acres of coverage in the music press, a music press that had started to genuinely baffle Brown. "I reacted against all that," he says. "I mean, we were still out there with The Clash. That was fun. I didn't like it when all these bands started taking themselves really seriously. As if they were creating these monumental works of art. The thing is, they had notions of being great artists or something and yet, so clearly, didn't have the talent or the sense of real commitment. The music press was at fault because it encouraged them too much made them feel like stars before they were ready, often with disastrous results. I was young, but I could see all that. I wasn't particularly interested in becoming part of it."

The fickle nature of the music press might have rankled with Ian Brown even then, but the act of making music itself was fast becoming a priority. John's guitar playing, and sundry in-house gatherings involving mates, had evolved into a group of sorts. A band of outcasts, who clung to the social edges of South Trafford College – the latter a box-like further education

16

college which, in those days, doubled as a deadening Formica-covered hangout for those who hadn't jumped from school into low-key employment. The college system, refreshingly lax after the rigours of Altrincham Grammar (at which Squire and Brown had each acquired a modest fistful of 'O' Levels), allowed huddles of kids to gather in the refectory, or skive off to the cafés of Sale or Altrincham. Almost without effort, a band, called The Patrol, formed in 1980, their moniker instantly stating their allegiance to the local scooter gang-scene, towards which Ian and John had both been steadily gravitating.

Ian, in particular, yearned for a Kerouacian open road, for something beyond the strangulatory grip of a job, a marriage and a mortgage. He was still prone to wandering off on his own through Manchester and occasionally even further afield, sometimes to Blackpool. Strange to note that, although John Squire was the quieter of the two by far, and surely the one who could lay greater claim to cultivating an existential detachment, it was Brown who would spend more time drifting from the pack. He acquired a bass guitar but lacked any serious enthusiasm for the instrument, his rudimentary playing skills already languishing some way behind Squire's increasing confidence and ability on guitar. But with Simon Wolstencroft, later of The Smiths, The Fall, Colourfield and The Ark, on drums and Andy Couzens on vocals, The Patrol were a full band. Another mate, Pete Garner, who showed negligible musical aptitude, took on the role of 'hanging about', looking slovenly.

Couzens' entry to the band was one worthy of Sid Vicious himself. Ian had become aware of this young skinhead hanging around college, though he had never made a strong impression. But Brown's curiosity was well and truly aroused one afternoon in South Trafford's featureless refectory when Couzens decided to end an argument he was having with a boy considerably larger than himself by beating the living daylights out of him and hurtling him over one of the tables, where he lay supine and defeated. The incident gained Couzens considerable local kudos; Brown was impressed and with a conscious nod back to tales of McLaren and The Sex Pistols, strode purposefully over to Couzens and asked him if he wanted to be in a band.

After receiving the affirmative reply, Brown asked, "Can you sing?" Couzens didn't know the answer to this but, his enthusiasm undimmed, that night duly trooped down to rehearsals at Simon's parents' house. For Couzens, it was immediately terrifying: four lads he didn't know all pumping away on their instruments. Edging into position, his nervousness overwhelmed him to the extent that he had to turn his back on the rest of the band – which they found wildly impressive – before starting to screech into the microphone. The resultant cacophony was unbearable, but nobody there seemed to mind. The Patrol had been born and Couzens, himself a Clash fanatic, wholly devoted to the notion of 'being in a gang', slotted neatly into place.

They punched and plucked away, to little effect, rehearsing in a scout hut in Sale. Though Brown would later dismiss the band as of secondary interest ("just something to do for a while, it meant little to me"), The Patrol, like most, if not all embryonic bands, spent too long, deep into the bitter fuelled haze of 'band meetings', planning ahead, dividing up royalties that would never arise, collectively dissecting the music press and looking longingly from afar at the Manchester music scene which was evolving rapidly without them.

The Patrol's sound was, as one might expect, highly derivative. Their song titles − 'Jail Of The Assassins', '25 Rifles' − are very much symptomatic of the vaguely political stance adopted by many bands born in the aftermath of punk. Musically, The Patrol were a noisy splicing of rather badly executed soul and The Clash. The latter were loved to death by John and Simon, who travelled the country to catch the band − and the harder edged punk of The Angelic Upstarts, The Meteors and, rather surprisingly, The Stranglers, Ian's faves. The Stranglers, despite being adopted as 'mates' by sycophantic local punks, The Drones, were never really accepted in Manchester, their slide from pubby prog rock to ageing punks always deemed too dubious to be true; one reason why Ian, ever the individualist, was drawn to them. They also stayed in Manchester a lot and, coincidentally perhaps, had a habit of partying in Sale.

It wasn't The Stranglers but, strangely enough, The Clash, who provided The Patrol with their first sniff of rock'n'roll glamour. Ian and Pete Garner were aware that the punk icons were recording in Manchester so, taking a chance, they made their way through Manchester's elegant Granby Row, to the infamous Pluto Recording Studios, and waited. Sure enough, The Clash duly turned up for a recording session, which was to result in their dub-influenced classic 'Bankrobber'. The awestruck duo did some fast talking and, incredibly, were allowed to enter the studio as fringe members of The Clash's entourage. It was to be a day that would be etched into Manchester rock mythology.

The Clash were never a band who suffered from a sense of their own self-importance, and often allowed fans to sit in on their sessions ("It keeps us alive," Strummer once perceptively noted, during the recording of 'Capital Radio'). They were more than happy to allow the young musicians to simply 'hang out'. Brown and Garner were transfixed, just a pair of doe-eyed fans, crowded in the studio corner. Topper Headen chatted to them like old mates and Jones, despite his obvious rock'n'roll-isms, made time to talk also. Curiously enough, it was only Joe Strummer who remained aloof, acting the archetypal withdrawn artist, crouching, cross-legged beneath the studio's grandfather clock, clicking his fingers to the beat of the track. Brown was less than impressed: "He was a hero, of sorts . . . more to John and Si than me, but it was a bit of a let down. I thought he was a bit of a dick, to be honest." Incredibly given the depth of his devotion, John Squire was elsewhere that day, and so missed out on meeting the man he had immortalised in a mural.

The Patrol's own career continued on a hesitant trajectory. They did succeed in gaining a peppering of local dates in youth clubs, though the gigs were tiny and all too frequently a faction in the audience seemed bent on some juvenile violence. It didn't help, perhaps, that The Patrol performed with two hopelessly obscure Stretford punk bands, Corrosive Youth and Suburban Chaos, whose names spoke volumes about the music they played. But at least they were playing; early dates included Stretford's Lostock, at the Sale Annex and – this must have been a classic – Hale Methodist Church.[6]

The Patrol's one brief stab at fame came when they chanced upon the crumbly Mayflower Venue in Gorton where the highly agitated promoter had a hall full of discontented local punks and no band, Adam And The Ants having broken down on the motorway. Wanting to avoid a riot, he needed to put a band, any band, on that stage as swiftly as possible. The Patrol remained blissfully unaware that the last time Adam And The Ants had played The Mayflower, just fifty people had turned up and the whole event had degenerated into an ultra-violent scrap between the sparse audience and Adam And The Ants' roadies, and that there was a contingent in this audience who might well be bent on a spot of revenge. All things considered, it is to their credit that The Patrol actually went down well with the crowd and the gig passed off peacefully.

In Brown's mind, The Patrol were perpetually crumbling away from any kind of career path, or musical direction. Despite Squire and Garner's enthusiastic practising, the band still lacked heart, Brown as much as anyone. His muse was absent, and he felt himself drifting away from the music 'scene'. The band's final date, and this author remembers it well, was a dire local band pile-up at South Trafford College, depressing music performed artlessly to a room full of beer-numbed girl-chasing braggarts who spent much of the gig arguing about football while all around lay a sea of plastic beer cups. There was no spark, no remote hint of a scene, no positive vibe. Stockport band Alien Tint slashed through a Ramones-like version of 'Fireball XL5', unencumbered by charisma or style. Ditto The

---

[6] Hale is the super-plush green edge of Altrincham, full of giant detached houses and homely country pubs.

Patrol, who came across that night as an archetypal sub-Garry Bushell outfit, though at least they had the good taste to finish their set, and their existence, with a cover of The Sweet's 'Blockbuster', although 'Ballroom Blitz' would have been more appropriate. The gig was notable for one other detail, though – their closing number saw Ian Brown take over on vocals for the first time, Pete Garner deputising on bass.

Although Squire and Garner still hoped the band might continue after the gig, Brown knew the truth. Allergic to musical stagnancy as he would be to any form of inertia, he quit, sold his bass guitar for £100, and purchased a genuine love machine: a scooter. And not just any old scooter. A Lambretta J 125.

* * *

The late Seventies' scooter movement in north-west England was both patchy and reactionary. It was, of course, a revival, a desperate stretch back to a time of violence, naïveté and freedom. The period between '68 and '73 had been Lambretta boom time, covering the period of skinhead to Northern Soul. Giant packs of scooter boys surged out every Sunday from the big Lancashire towns – Rochdale, Bolton, Wigan, Oldham and Swinton – avoiding the faster, dirtier motorbiking 'greasers' and clashing with each other in Blackpool and Southport. These were days of Crombie coats and two-tone 'tonic' trousers, of brogues (Royals) and Barathea blazers, of smartness, neatness, in clothes as in music. The whole shebang was soundtracked by snappy two-and-a-half minute blasts of Motown, Ska and ninety-mile-an-hour Northern Soul. And the most in-demand accessory? The mighty Lambretta. White LI 150s, sporty SX 150s or, king of them all, the Lambretta GP 200, golden yellow and gleaming, two black stripes along the side panels and, most important this, the name of the owner's favoured US city painted on the side; Detroit, Denver and, for sophisticates, Des Moines. It was the great post-mod scooter age, eventually killed off not by punk's raw blast, but by the all-conquering soundtrack of disco: Ford Capris blasting out Barry White and his treacley smooth Love Unlimited. Disco changed the larger world outside the punk explosion, transforming the clothes, the vehicles, and the attitude of a generation.

As such, the scooter revival of the late Seventies was something of an oddity, and difficult to pin down. It was, indeed, a cult and one that wasn't even centred on the mod revival. The scooter owners were more concerned with the machine – the mechanics, the practicalities – than the look. This time around, scooter fanatics favoured bulky bomber jackets, khaki trousers and Doc Martens. Although Northern Soul was still dominant, scooter boys' listening habits spread across a disparate mass of cult skin and punk bands, from Ian Brown's beloved Angelic Upstarts to the dread Bushell-hyped Cockney Rejects and the entire nasty Oi collective. Only in the late lamented *Sounds* music paper could this non-pretentious, profoundly working-class upsurge be glimpsed. The scooter scene was just one tiny aspect of it, but it served usefully to counteract the growing intellectualism of the post-punk 'industrial' bands . . . and the *NME*. It is highly significant that Ian Brown, desperately seeking some kind of camaraderie, and burning with a traveller's urge to freedom and the open road, should find solace in a local scooter gang rather than a local rock band. The selling of that guitar was symbolic.

And he really did join the throng too. Drifting towards the north Manchester soul scene rather than the more rock-orientated scooter clubs of South Manchester and Cheshire, he joined several clubs, and spent long afternoons sitting on the driveway, fiddling with bike parts, polishing and adorning his machine with badges. His passion would see him own five scooters during this period, most famously, a pink, 'chopped' Lambretta GP 200 with extended forks, banana seat and no leg shields. It was a strikingly skeletal vehicle which Brown christened 'Sweet and Innocenti' and it boasted the legend 'Cranked Up Really High' on the side. If you caught him riding through Stockport, at first glance he would look, rather paradoxically, like a trike riding biker. (And never have the scooter boys and the bikers seemed so close to each other as at that time. So close, in fact, that it was known for them to hold joint rallies. Unheard of in the Sixties and early Seventies.) Undoubtedly, the scooter scene was a serious concern, not just a fashion statement, and Ian Brown was fully immersed in it. Another prize possession was a Vespa Rally 200, emblazoned with the line 'Angels With Dirty Faces', though it remains debatable whether the inspiration originally came from Jimmy Cagney or Jimmy Pursey.

It was the era of scooter rallies. Long, arduous treks down to Brighton, Yarmouth and the Isle Of Wight, or up to Scotland. Devotees burned along the A roads, swaying in the wind, hindered by the scooter's low centre of gravity, and gathering together for fish'n'chips and frolics, on seafronts, or burgers in designated fields. Some camped en route, while others would find cheap B&B.

It took two years for Ian to entice John into the scene, taking him down to the Manchester Arms, in Stockport, or the Black Lion in Salford for scooter meetings, prising him away from his beloved guitar. For a short while, ear-bashed by Ian and tempted by the rush to purchase scooters post-*Quadrophrenia* (the overrated film, not the overrated double album), Squire neglected his music in favour of assembling his own Lambretta, a GP 200 re-built from the frame. Scooter culture was all-enveloping and required inexhaustible dedication. Mercifully, and despite the rather savage nature of the punk thrash bands who muscled into the scene (daft King Kurt, the power rockabilly combo, The Meteors) violence wasn't a key factor in this scooter revival, apart, perhaps, from the odd ruck down at The Beehive in Eccles, where the scooter lads would clash with the locals. Ironically enough, these locals included future members of Happy Mondays, who would hang around, looking for some bother and picking out scooter lads as prime targets.

Andy Couzens was a scooter boy too. Not, perhaps, as devoted as Squire and Brown but interested enough to join them on a number of trips. "I didn't mind in the summer when it was warm and fun just to hang out," he remembers, "but those trips at the beginning and at the end of the season were real killers. Sleeping under some pier and freezing to death. That wasn't my idea of fun although Ian seemed to really love it. I remember one trip in particular. To Weston-super-Mare . . . because we couldn't go on motorways, we all had L plates and, anyway, scooters are not good on motorways, we had to use all the B roads. It took us 24 hours to get to Weston because it's just fucking miles away. And, once there, we were so knackered we just curled up on a bench for a day and then came home. It was absolutely fucking pointless. But, again, it was all part of that gang mentality. Real bonding. We went to a lot of Northern Soul nights. I wouldn't really dance much, but I'd have a go. Same with John and Ian. Then we'd emerge into the daylight the next morning and go and have a breakfast in some café and just die together. You know, feeling like shit and wondering why on earth we were doing it. But it was good in a way. It was a strange kind of camaraderie, really. I've not known anything quite like it since but that remained with us right into the Roses. I was called Ghandi, because we went to a lot of Toga parties and me, being so fucking skinny, would look like Ghandi. John or Ian put a picture of Ghandi on the front of my scooter, A Lambretta LI 150 . . . and that was it. I was Ghandi."

Football-related violence was still in the air at the turn of the decade and none of the ex-members of The Patrol were particularly shocked by the sight of a large ruck. Indeed, in Couzens, they had found a genuine, self-confessed soccer thug. He'd attend matches just for the fighting and would happily change his colours accordingly. "That's true," he laughs now. "We'd go to Maine Road and stand in the Kippax and fight on the side of City against whoever and, the next week, we might go to Old Trafford and fight on the side of the Reds. But the best fights were at Stockport County. Charging down Stockport Station approach after Bradford fans . . . real nasty bastards they were. That was always an incredibly violent clash, violence on a level you wouldn't believe. But, having said that, no one ever really got hurt. It was only later, when Stanley knives came out, that it started getting really heavy and I dropped away . . . I'd say it was always thug against thug. Very few innocent people got caught up in it. But it was only one stage further than reading Richard Allen books and thinking Joe Hawkins was cool. And everybody did that."

Andy Couzens never held full-time employment. He survived, by working with mates in the building trade, by doing odd car jobs – his passion was American cars – or by working for a while, on the caravan business owned by his uncle in the nearby Cheshire reserve of Poynton. Although Couzens would restrict himself to 'maintenance', there was something about the business which appealed to Brown. Indeed, Brown badgered Couzens for a chance to attend an interview with his uncle with a view to him becoming a salesman. Surprisingly perhaps, indeed incredibly, Brown got the job and spent the next few months escorting dull middle-aged couples around the caravan yard, explaining the functional necessities of the Calor Gaz mechanisms, water barrels and toilet systems, storage space and tow bars. To the untrained eyes, such a dip into the beige culture of the caravanners might not seem particularly rock'n'roll. To Brown however, the idea of stalking the showroom, dressed in a suit costing three weeks' wages and simply exuding youthful affluence, was the ultimate affirmation of the mod ethic. This was practically a *Quadrophenia* lifestyle.

It wasn't to last, though. Such romantic notions tend to fade when the reality is day after day of dreary Poynton, and another day chatting to couples bent over stretching their budget to acquire an artless white slug to park next to their Wilmslow semi. Before long, the gimmick wore thin, Ian left and, for a good twelve months, vanished from the lives of Couzens and Squire. Couzens. "I didn't see him for ages . . . he had a few strange ideas around that time. It was a time when you were either an extreme socialist or a racist, people were forced out onto the two extremes . . . at least a lot of the young rock type people were. A lot can be made of Ian at that time because of his interest in the Oi thing.[7] It's fairly common knowledge that, for a while, Ian did dabble with the right wing thing . . . the NF and all that. But I don't think it ever went any deeper than just a case of picking one side, more often than not people went along to rallies and things just for an excuse for a fight. I'm not saying Ian was a fighter, but he got caught up in it. The politics of the whole thing was pushed very much to the back. I'm not sure anyone really thought too deeply into it."

[7] Oi was largely invented by *Sounds* journalist Garry Bushell to add spice to its pages. It drew inspiration from a collection of skinhead/punk bands, mainly from Bermondsey, some of whom had unfortunately gained a following forged from braindead racist idiocy.

It would be all too easy to make a deep rooted issue of this, but that would be skirting the truth.[8] The whole mod and scooter scenes, were undeniably shaded with a right-ish bluey tint. Strongly materialistic and profoundly anti-hippy, it cannot seem surprising that, in such a volatile cultural climate, things could easily swerve too far to the right, or to the left, depending on whichever strain of naïveté one felt attracted to. Both Ian Brown and John Squire (as we shall see later) succumbed, if only briefly, to a magnetic pull to the right.

[8] This period of flirting with right-wing ideology cast a long shadow. In 1998, Ian Brown enraged the *Melody Maker* readership by apparently linking homosexuality to violence, and to Nazi Germany.

3

ON THE WATERFRONT

The Eighties dawned with the bright glow of a second era of glam dressing on the horizon and the scooter scene noticeably receding. The new decade found John Squire at the famed Cosgrove Hall animation studios in Chorlton in a position that had previously been held by Joy Division's Bernard Sumner. It was perfect for him, just as it had been for Sumner who subsequently voiced occasional regret about leaving the artistically rewarding and secure nine-to-five job for the high pressure lifestyle of a pop star. By all accounts the shy and awkward Squire fitted in seamlessly with the Cosgrove Hall elite – mainly bright, Bohemian post-grads, too lazy to move to London and too artistic to fall into the computer industry or banking. Squire loved the atmosphere; he was good, too, scraping away at the heads of models and sketching movement; he ended up working on *Wind In The Willows* and Mike Harding's *Dangermouse*, gleaning a degree of aesthetic satisfaction rarely encountered in the average sedentary job.

Pete Garner, meanwhile, had taken up residence behind the counter of the Paperchase record, magazine and paraphernalia shop in Manchester city centre. Since the days of punk, when Paperchase had been the only place to stock the hipper punk fanzines, *Shy Talk* and *Ghast Up* (20p a throw) the shop had remained a quirky appendage to the city centre shopping experience. The once-bohemian Virgin shop had long since degenerated into a bland megastore. Paperchase was its antithesis – friendly, dusty and always filled with left field sounds, it was young, mad and daft. Garner thoroughly enjoyed the atmosphere, the laid-back life-style of constant music and chatting to the punters. One Saturday, these included his old mate John Squire.

Squire's tales of Cosgrove Hall intrigued Garner and soon they began plotting a story, to be completed in animation form by John, using up his considerable stock of studio 'down-time'. Although the idea soon fizzled away, the pub meetings brought the pair together again. These meetings would provide the catalyst for a new musical adventure: a new gang, and a new group. Both were smarter and more skilled than before, especially Squire whose improved playing astonished Garner. All those nights spent listening over and over to his personal guitar heroes agonising over tricky chords, had started to pay off.[9] John Squire had become a genuine musician.

The new venture swiftly became a tangible reality, falling together with surprising ease and, before long, a band was forming and starting to put in rehearsal time. Andy Couzens rejoined the fold and, from the Oldham edge of Manchester, drummer Chris Goodwin. And a new face from north Manchester entered the picture: bassist Gary 'Mani' Mounfield.

★ ★ ★

Gary Michael Mounfield, born November 16, 1962, in Crumpsall, had experienced the nastier side of the Altrincham lads, including Ian Brown, back in 1978. In a pique of bravado, Brown and twenty of his young, dumb chums had set forth for the heart of mighty Moston, a mercilessly tough north Manchester area bordering the equally infamous Middleton (and the Langley estate), to seek out a particularly notorious skinhead who had been bullying many of the area's younger kids. The fact that the skinhead sported a swastika tattooed on his head, only intensified their fervour. After all, they had been devouring the fervently anti-racist music press. The street grapevine carried the hype: this would be the ruck to end all rucks.

Except, of course, that it wasn't. The skinhead in question was, indeed, 'dealt with', but it ultimately took little more than a swift flurry of fists. As the scrapping went on, Brown noticed a figure on the periphery of the action – it was Mani, sitting on a nearby wall, wanting no part of the trouble. Although ostensibly from rival camps Brown and Mounfield spoke briefly, and a connection was made.

But it remained a distant connection. Mani continued to flit around the north Manchester scene; like Ian Brown, he was seized by the twin tornadoes of punk and Northern Soul. Punk offered Mani some much-needed stimulation – based in Oldham which was, until the emergence of Clint Boon and The Inspiral Carpets, ferociously insular, Mani found himself hopelessly adrift from the excitement of more central Manchester. But he ran the full gamut of youth movements, from punk to Perry Boy (Casuals to the rest of the country), picking up bass guitarist skills along the way, via his allegiance with local punksters The Clingons (featuring Clint Boon and *Muze Magazine* designer John Hamilton) and later, T'Challa Grid. Indeed, Mani's first sight of the inner cogs of the Manchester

---

[9] As well as the aforementioned Mick Jones, Squire favoured Yardbirds-era Eric Clapton, and The Smiths' Johnny Marr – the first genuine guitar hero of the post-punk era.

scene came through his association with Boon who, as highly vociferous manager of T'Challa Grid, would drag Mani into town, flitting from journalist to journalist, going to unbelievable lengths to capture press attention. (How unbelievable? Like building and designing clocks to go in journalists' offices, and providing individually painted artwork for each T'Challa Grid demo tape.)

It's worth pointing out that it was Clint Boon's enthusiasm, that helped to drag the Oldham scene out of the dour shadow of the Pennines. At a time when it seemed that nothing other than the unfathomable Barclay James Harvest would ever come from the town, Boon never lost faith. He kick-started his own musical project, largely based around dabblings in his self-built low-fi studio, called it T'Mill [10] and drafted in Mani on bass and Grid drummer Chris Goodwin. T'Mill was a curiously reactionary affair, which dipped back to the underground albums of the late Sixties, complete with thick flowing organ and flowery lyricism. Inevitably a concept album was recorded and although, to date, it hasn't seen the light of day, a cassette did do the local rounds at the time, encased in a typical Boon-ish cover. Said tape thus has a claim to fame as the first time that Mani, subsequently regarded as one of the most accomplished bassists of his generation, was heard. Truth be told, the tape is of more historical interest than entertainment value; if nothing else, it provided the grounding for The Inspiral Carpets, whose oft-maligned but actually rather impressive career as purveyors of tuneful, organ-driven pop, undoubtedly began with T'Mill. For years Boon's Peter Tork pudding bowl haircut would be openly mocked by short back and shaven arties or wedged Perrys at Manchester gigs. In retrospect, however, this little backwater recording, fired by Boon's clever though hugely untrendy, psychedelic fixation contained the germ of two hit bands. And when you add the fact that a certain Noel Gallagher became an Inspirals roadie a little later on, Clint Boon becomes a significant figure in the story of the two most influential bands of the Eighties and Nineties.

Shortly thereafter, Mani, Chris Goodwin and a Moston-based vocalist known as 'Kaiser' (Dave Kaitey) were tempted into an embryonic young Sale-based band, called The Waterfront, who had evolved from the reunited John Squire, Pete Garner and Andy Couzens. The band, a rather rocky affair, heavily influenced by the Velvet Underground-isms of the then highly credible Orange Juice, proved too conventional for the esoteric Goodwin, who skipped out after just three rehearsals to reunite with Boon and T'Challa Grid. Undaunted, the rest gamely soldiered on, though Kaiser's somewhat ferocious stage demeanour was giving cause for concern:

---

[10] Later altered to the less colloquial 'The Mill'.

a skinhead with attitude, Kaiser was prone to 'nut' the microphone from time to time. For a while, this hard image complemented the material the band were producing, for soccer violence and general youthful thuggery was never too far from the subject matter of their songs. Early numbers recorded in a Chadderton four-track studio included 'Normandy (On A Beach In)' which extolled the virtues of having a good old soccer ruck. The lyric was actually written by Kaiser, following his adventures scrapping with Euro-thugs at a soccer tournament in France. In this respect at least, he was ahead of his time. Perhaps the band were reading too much Garry Bushell; they were certainly more *Sounds* than *NME*, more street than art college. Their sound was pinned down by two things, both stemming from John Squire: his songwriting and his playing ability. The level of his musicianship was now at such a high level that his domination of the rehearsals began to give cause for concern; he flooded the songs with guitar trickery that stopped only just short of self-indulgence. When he heard the Chadderton demo, Ian Brown was highly impressed and, sensing the beginnings of something way beyond the potential of The Patrol, he agreed to step in and, if only in rehearsal, tentatively share the vocals with Kaiser.

His decision was partly prompted by a classic piece of rock'n'roll folklore. Brown held a party for his girlfriend's 21st birthday at his flat in Charles Berry Crescent, Hulme. Who should turn up but one of Northern Soul's true heroes, Geno Washington, one-time leader of The Ram Jam Band, who had played a gig that night at Manchester University! Geno Washington, the hero of Dexy's Midnight Runners' first number one (and Dexy's were very rated by the fledgling Roses), in Ian Brown's Hulme flat! Geno was after some spliff, and asked the young Mancunian how to get to the Reno club. After Brown told him, Geno offered him some unexpected pearls of wisdom. "He told me that I was a star and I should be in a band," Brown told *Vox* magazine in 1995. "It was just a few days after John had asked me if I would sing, and I knew that Geno was being honest. When he said it, I thought: I'll go with that. I've got to. I just had to."

If nothing else, the Waterfront experience deepened the bonding between the future Roses. Rehearsals were loose affairs. The band would get together on Sunday evenings in the cellar at Andy Couzens' parents' house in Macclesfield. Their set was an eclectic mixture of Oi angst, mainly courtesy of Kaiser, Johnny Thunders, Slaughter And The Dogs, a New York Dolls backbeat thrash and, care of Squire, a curious swing towards melody. Andy Couzens: "It kept us out of Manchester for a start, and Manchester was really horrible at that time. Kind of nasty. Everyone staring at you and getting irritable. I don't know if that was a general thing, or whether it was something to do with us but every time we went into town we would end up in some kind of fight. It was always inevitable, really. And the city centre was all poky little clubs . . . horrible. Oh, we'd go to The Hacienda, but that was about it."

The bonds were strengthened by long post-rehearsal gatherings around the television where, in a bleery beer and dope ambience, they devoured a series of cult road movies on BBC2's *Moviedrome*. Two films made a particular impact: *Two Lane Black Top* and *Vanishing Point*. (The latter would inspire a 1997 Primal Scream album of the same name, featuring Mani on bass. The circle comes around . . .) A run of Woody Allen films, augmented by Mani's perfect Woody Allen impressions, completed the scenario: the band were becoming a gang.

Despite all the positive signs, Waterfront were an unstable prospect and before long Ian quit, deciding abruptly that the rock star life was either unattainable or not for him. Perversely choosing the polar opposite of the freewheeling musician lifestyle, Brown became a civil servant for a brief spell, by all accounts applying himself to his duties with studious determination. But somewhere, a little ambition remained. A dull ache, niggling away, urging them to begin again. Brown knew full well that he wasn't born to organise people's Giros – he didn't feel quite right trooping down to Sale at lunch times, mixing with fellow workers. For a self-confessed 'gobby git', he soon grew strangely aloof, gazing into space, dreaming of Kerouacian wandering, scooter thrills and rock'n'roll.

★   ★   ★

1984 was an odd year in Manchester. Within twelve months the city would be thrilling to a splendidly diverse array of new talent, but at the start of the year the big three – The Smiths, The Fall and New Order – remained wholly dominant. Manchester was heavy with 'Afflecks Palace chic' – vintage overcoats, American bowling cardigans, greasy Doc Martens shoes, white T-shirts – purchased at the Afflecks Palace emporium on downbeat Oldham Street. Afflecks was the spiritual home of The Smiths' devotee: dusty, floorboarded and offering clothing well within the student budget. All this and a café serving lentil burgers and samosas.

But as the new year dawned, bright, over-the-top New Romantics still sparkled on *Top Of The Pops* and BBC2's *The Oxford Road Show*. Frankie Goes To Hollywood were in the ascendant: their Manchester mentor, music journalist and ZTT executive Paul Morley, gleefully sloganeered 'Frankie Says . . .' on large T-shirts and watched them become one of the most popular fashion statements of the decade; the band dominated the pop scene. When not on the lookout for the next Smiths, any A&R men who bothered to come to Manchester were often treated to showcase gigs by New Romantic funksters – Porch Party from Stockport, Absent

Friends, Object Action or Awesome Precinct – bands who seemed to have spent more time at the hairdressers than in rehearsal. Manchester's venues were uninspiring – the grubby Venue, reminiscent of a late Seventies' punk cellar; Cloud 9 and Manhattan Sound, elektro-discos commandeered by hopeful local rock promoters on Tuesdays; The Gallery on Peter Street; Deville's; all were frequented by a regular pub rock underbelly that included The Cheaters, Tarzanz Milkmen and Immaculate Fools. At the top of the pile were the Factory acts, big in the music press, small in reality. James were the hottest tip, riding on Factory's lively new slogan, 'fuck funk, folk's in'; staunch politicos Easterhouse were a great rock hope for a while, before internal band squabbles robbed them of a promising career. (A later Manchester in-joke would run: What would you have if you took the politics out of Easterhouse? Answer: Oasis.)

This was the scenario into which The Stone Roses were born: arguably the tiniest rock scene that the city had seen since 1976. As a sign of the times, local listings mag *City Life* sported a folk section that was larger than its rock page. In a sense, the imbalance created by The Smiths' domination of the Manchester music scene provided a chunk of inspiration. Although Ian Brown had known Smiths' bassist Andy Rourke as a young boy, and was certainly proud to have had early contact with some kind of pop star, The Smiths inspired a curious loathing within his loose gang who would soon start reassembling for rehearsals. Squire might have admired Marr's talent, but there was an undercurrent of unrest about The Smiths, a natural, working-class reaction against Morrissey's increasingly precious persona and deep intellectualism, both of which were regarded by many as pure affectation. The comparatively low-brow and loyal following for The Chameleons in the north of Manchester was fuelled by this particular attitude. Pete Garner sums it up: "I can't remember hating a band more than The Smiths . . . people kept saying how they represented Manchester. They didn't represent Manchester at all. They didn't represent me, or any of my mates. I felt this very strongly at the time. We needed a band who represented us. The ordinary lads." Nevertheless, The Smiths were everywhere: omnipresent in every young music fan's record collection, their records on every decent radio show, Morrissey's lyrical wit and Marr's sparkling guitar lines the perfect soundtrack for the disaffected youth of the early Eighties.

Andy Couzens, numbed by boredom and still keeping faith in the spark that had initially fired The Waterfront, went to visit Ian and managed to persuade him that, perhaps, just perhaps, they might get something going again. Couzens: "I still couldn't free myself from being a bit of a fighter. It was something that was still in me at the time . . . I would still get into scrapes and, well, there was one in particular that was looming really heavy. I really thought I was going to get sent down for a while . . . And it was during this period of uncertainty that it dawned on me. It was only my involvement in bands that had kept me out of trouble. This is why I decided to try and resurrect something from The Waterfront thing, because we had come so close to getting something going. It just seemed like it was the only positive thing I'd been involved in. I know it seems a bit of a cliché . . . form a band to stay out of the nick, but that was part of it." Echoes here of Joe Strummer's torrid vocals, chuffing out, "Every job they offer you is to keep you out the dock." And it's not impossible to imagine a very different destiny for the members of the Happy Mondays, the Roses' fellow Manchester pop icons, had Factory Records not offered them a record contract.

For all Couzens' enthusiasm, Ian Brown remained unconvinced that rock'n'roll could provide a viable future. "I don't know. I had given up on it, in one sense," he admitted later. His eventual decision to give it another go had as much to do with the lack of alternatives as any belief in the music. "There wasn't anything else happening . . . Manchester was so dull at that point and it didn't take long for me and Andy to start getting excited again. A lot depended on how John would react. He was the only one who really knew what he was doing, in musical terms. But he was so obviously searching for a band, or for something, that he instantly agreed to have another go. We just started practising." At least one enduring myth regarding the band's subsequent name changes can be laid to rest: "We were never called English Rose . . . I don't know where that came from. Probably some press report, somewhere, but that was never our name. And The Stone Roses name didn't come from the novel. Not as far as I know. It was just a name that John came up with . . . meaning 'opposites'. Stone Roses . . . like Led Zeppelin in a way. Heavy and light. It sounded a good name, well balanced. I always liked it."

Squire brought Garner back into the frame and, together, they dragged back the old Patrol sticksman, Simon Wolstencroft, who had achieved some local fame back in 1981 when he joined hard-edged funk band Freak Party. Wolstencroft thought that at last he was onto a real winner, especially as the other two members of the group, Johnny Marr and Andy Rourke, seemed equally committed to the Brit funk cause. However, after rehearsing for a full year without managing to find a suitable singer Wolstencroft departed and the band mutated into The Smiths. Wolstencroft then attempted to further his funk credentials by auditioning for ABC; he failed to get the gig, but has a claim to fame as performing on the first-ever Smiths demo, which featured 'The Hand That Rocks The Cradle' and 'Suffer Little Children', as well as on several early bootlegs.

Over the next year there were lengthy discussions in front rooms and pubs as each band member got to know the others again; and it seems somewhat ironic in retrospect that this twelve-month period of bonding, should form the nucleus of a band who would eventually include only Brown and Squire. Nevertheless, The Stone Roses as a real band can be directly traced back to that tight-knit five-piece. The band rehearsed in Spirit Studios, Chorlton, solidly, for five-hour stretches, every day. Squire's playing was as impressive as ever, and this time it really did seem as though the band might have a future. The only glaring weakness in the line-up was Brown's frail, wavering voice. Such was the camaraderie between them all, however, that rather than look for a replacement, the rest of the band urged Ian to try singing lessons. And he did, in some trepidation. He ventured down to a house in the shadows of Victoria Station, at 6 pm on weekdays, where vocal tutor Mrs Rhodes, would greet him sternly, fling open her windows, kick-start her 80-year-old pianist, and steer Brown through renditions of 'Strawberry Fields' and 'After The Goldrush'. Brown managed to survive three weeks of this necessary ignominy before returning to Spirit; admittedly, his vocal technique had not noticeably improved (accusations of weak vocals were to plague him even through the Roses' glory years) but, at least, he now knew how to exercise and develop his voice.

This line-up was not to last, however. Six months in Simon Wolstencroft decided to up sticks. It wasn't a personal, or a musical issue: he just wanted the chance to earn some money from his drumming, and quickly. He'd continued auditioning throughout his Roses spell – quite openly, nobody blamed him – and finally joined fellow Mancunian high-achiever Craig Gannon (who would also spend time with The Smiths and Terry Hall's Colourfield). This may have been good news for Wolstencroft, but it was a disaster for The Stone Roses, who were now forced to continue to rehearse without a drummer. That said, their set was building, albeit very slowly, and fully formed songs had started to poke through the blanket of noise. Five songs, including an early version of 'Misery Dictionary', all built from the same base. Undoubtedly, they needed thumping into shape. They needed a drummer.

A note pinned optimistically on the noticeboard at Manchester's A1 music shop, produced few promising results. One guy, from Bradford's The Skeletal Family, resplendent in Adam And The Ants Indian punk apparel, set up his drums and pounded through a series of tribal beats before, shaking his head, standing up behind the kit and announcing, "I just can't hear a tune, lads . . . sorry." After which, he dismantled his drum kit and departed. "He was a complete dickhead," says Couzens, "and we just looked at each other and shrugged. We knew this wasn't going to be easy. Drummers are a strange breed." More auditions followed, mostly taking place among the discarded chip wrappers and scurrying rats of Beehive Mill, a dilapidated warehouse shell.

The band's first contact with Alan John Wren (born April 10, 1964, in Manchester), known as 'Reni', came from a phone call to Andy Couzens. At the time, the drummer went by a Frenchified variant of his more famous nickname (René) and this, delivered in a suitably over-the-top French accent, was how he introduced himself on the phone to Couzens. The latter was nonplussed by the affectation and he wasn't particularly optimistic when he dutifully set forth for the heart of Belle Vue to pick up the owner of the pretentious name, and his drum kit, and take him to the audition.

Reni made a strong visual impression immediately. Resplendent in long black coat and moon boots, he instantly showered the fledgling Roses with his bombastic personality. Thankfully, his larger-than-life persona was complemented by his drumming, which powered the songs in a manic, Moon-like kind of way. A forceful character, he immediately impressed the others by offering ideas about the arrangements of each song. This was new territory for The Stone Roses: even John Squire had yet to acquire such a level of musical sophistication. Reni was a self-confessed heavy metal fanatic and had spent time in Manchester's aloof HM fringe. His professed favourite song was Van Halen's 'Jump' – just about forgivable for a drummer, suicidal for a guitarist. Reni hit the stuttering Roses like a hurricane, clearing away the musical debris, and empowering the rest of the band with a studious determination to develop their own skills to a comparable level. Couzens: "We all knew, straight away, that Reni would be the catalyst. He just lifted us on to a higher plain. He's an extraordinary drummer but also an immensely complex personality. That's a problem, in a sense. There are 15 Renis . . . you are never quite sure which one you are dealing with! After six weeks I think we'd started to know about four of them. It gave us something to think about but, if he'd been an average drummer, no way would he have lasted. But you can't sack a musician of that quality, can you?"

Reni himself was initially unimpressed by the band's musical abilities, but their belief in themselves – an endearing trait of the Roses – struck him immediately. "I thought that they were a horrible racket, but I was struck by their commitment," he recalled later. "The whole group were such an oddball collection of long hairs, scruffs and smoothies that I just had to join."

The Stone Roses' début gig was at the Moonlight in Hampstead, in late 1984, and saw Reni playing alongside a genuine living legend. Ian Brown had seen an advert in *Sounds* for bands to take part in an anti-heroin benefit gig in London. He sent down a demo tape along with the usual spiel about the band having a massive following. "I lived in Hulme, where everyone was on skag except me," Brown told *Record Collector* in 1998. "So I wrote this letter saying I'm surrounded by skagheads, I wanna smash 'em. Can you give us a show? And they did." The Roses were to play alongside Mercenary Skank (a Welsh Goth band), High Noon and a 'special guest star'. On October 23, after intensive rehearsals, the band made the trip south. Their first-ever performance outside a rehearsal studio got off to an encouraging start – their cover of the Nazz's psychedelic classic 'Open My Eyes' received an unexpectedly enthusiastic response from those who heard the band run through it at their soundcheck. Then the special guest headliner turned up, looking for a backing band: it was Pete Townshend, fresh from playing to 50,000 people in Shea Stadium with The Who! Mercenary Skank were happy to oblige on guitars, but he still needed a drummer. The Roses were pumped up for the gig on sheer adrenaline (and – save for Reni – speed) and delivered a blistering set. "We came off stage," Brown remembered, "and Townshend was, like, you look really good up there and your drummer's great. Then he said, as an end-of-the-night thing, I wanna play a couple of tunes. Do you want to do it? Reni's like, yeah! We'd do soundchecks and Reni had people with their mouths open." Although, allegedly, he didn't know the drum parts to the songs, Reni excelled himself, thrashing away on 'Substitute' and 'Pictures Of Lily' to great effect, and mightily impressing Townshend who, after all, knew a thing or two about great drummers . . .

The gig had been organised by Mercenary Skank's manager, Caroline Reed. After the Roses' soundcheck, she rushed over to offer her services to the Mancunians; they accepted, as you do, though nothing material ever came of the arrangement. The band returned to Manchester high on the impact of their set, but still managerless.

4

GINGER RISING

Howard Jones came from the dour five-town pottery sprawl of Stoke-On-Trent. An art student with a natural bohemian leaning, he decamped for the brighter lights of Bristol at the age of 20 where, at least, an interesting and innovative arts scene was fermenting. Local girl Julie Burchill still maintains that the Seventies Bristol which fascinated Jones had little more to offer the world than The Wurzels. But that is to discount the early stirrings of Rip, Rig And Panic and a mass of esoteric groups, artists and workshops, that would form the base for the much-celebrated, innovative Bristol scene of the Nineties which was to produce artists such as Massive Attack, Portishead, Tricky and Roni Size's Reprazent.

By 1974, Jones had started to make a name for himself as a promoter blessed with an eye for off-kilter underground acts. He put on shows that he now describes as 'sound and visual experiences'. "I had the ability to really get things moving," he states, "and Bristol was fantastic for that. Just the right size to get some kind of scene going. It's funny that the city still produces non-mainstream acts . . . and that's how it was back then." The period was, of course, the era of progressive rock, and no student worth his patchwork loons would entertain notions of following commercial acts. Albums alone were regarded as worthy of serious attention – singles remained the almost exclusive preserve of pop acts. "I put a lot of shows on . . . it was a very creative place," remembers Jones, before continuing more mysteriously, "I got involved with a lot of . . . er . . . let's just call them 'characters'." Whatever it was that these 'characters' did, it was enough for several of them, including Jones, to be asked firmly to leave the city.[11]

While still in Bristol, Jones became involved with a few Mancunians who invited him to stay in Chorlton-cum-Hardy. To his delight, he found

---

[11] Jones won't elaborate on exactly why he and his cohorts were unceremoniously run out of town. Instead, he offered only the following qualifying statement: "It was nothing sinister. They were more anarchists than gangsters."

it to be an area like Bristol, where creative leanings were openly championed, and he remains there to this day. By 1976, the rather uninspired Manchester music scene had started to wake up to the incoming heady rush of punk. Jones, who wasn't at the Sex Pistols' Lesser Free Trade Hall gigs but did make it to their even more chaotic appearances at The Electric Circus, found himself in the right city at exactly the right time. Chorlton's local punk venue was a rectangular edifice which adjoined a vast, imposing Gothic pub, The Oaks, situated on Barlow Moor Road. Twice a week – Tuesdays and Thursdays – local promoters and self-confessed mouthy wide boy 'gits', Vini Faal and Rob Gretton, both involved with Slaughter And The Dogs, would put on highly unlikely gigs among the plastic palm trees of this modest room. Hence Slaughter And The Dogs, Siousxie And The Banshees, The Heartbreakers, The Buzzcocks, The Slits and The Vibrators all found themselves performing in a dusty south Manchester pub, to a volatile mixture of local punks, Teds, football crazies, assorted Chorlton nutters and remnants from The Oaks infamous 'disco' period. By the time that Jones found himself waking up one morning to find his bed occupied by The Slits – it was strictly a 'sleeping' arrangement – he realised that he was beginning to get irreversibly involved with the local music illuminati.[12]

With an eye to filling the hole left by Manchester's premier punk venue, The Electric Circus, which had been closed after failing to secure a food licence, Jones began promoting gigs in the cellar disco and sometime infamous folk venue Rafters, a club which would subsequently play a highly catalytic role in the evolution of music in the city. Slaughter And The Dogs, Magazine, Rich Kids, XTC and Elvis Costello all played there, as punk metamorphosed into New Wave. Through Rafters, Jones became firmly networked into a music scene that admittedly, by today's standards, seems laughably minuscule. Two years later, when an ex-Rafters DJ, Joy Division manager Rob Gretton, was searching for a venue to try out his shaky post-Ian Curtis unit New Order, Jones offered the band a gig at UMIST (University Of Manchester Institute of Science and Technology). In the dressing room following New Order's tentative appearance, Gretton, impressed with Jones' seamless organisational skills, began talking to him about Factory's rather loose plans to create a new nightclub in Manchester. Notoriously clueless when it came to business, Factory were attracted to the tight, no-nonsense attitude of Jones; he might, they reasoned, balance their anarchic aesthetic.

---

[12] It may be of little significance to this story, but the previous evening, The Slits had presented Jones with a stolen chicken. Together they had attempted to cook it using Jones' inadequate kitchen equipment, which resulted in the whole gang going down with food poisoning.

Thus it was that Jones spent the next eighteen months scouring Manchester for the perfect site, finally acting on a Gretton hunch that, "That marina place on Whitworth Street might be worth a look." From the second that Howard Jones wandered into that dusty shell, he knew he had found the site for their club. Working with designer Ben Kelly for a further nine months, Jones oversaw the construction of the most famous nightclub in the country, despite an ongoing mess of mismanagement and gross over-spending in which the whole idea rested on a business projection created out of gargantuan optimism and blind hope. Against the odds, The Hacienda managed to open and, with Jones ensconced as general manager, spent the next two years attempting to defy the heavy gravity of atrocious economic reasoning. Nevertheless, blessed with the most innovative booking agent in the country – Mike Pickering – The Hacienda's troubled early years were peppered with some of the most memorable gigs in Manchester's history. For Jones himself, the chance to watch some of the finest acts of the early Eighties at close quarters, from arrival to soundcheck, from killing time in the early evening to the post-gig dressing room trauma or celebration, proved refreshingly educational. Although his job was to stay in the background, deep within the machinery of club management, he simply couldn't resist the magnetic allure of the live performances and all the fascinating peripheral traumas.

Perhaps inevitably, given the man's need for creative stimulation and risk, the day-to-day business of running The Hacienda, coupled with the tedium of paper shuffling and occasionally bitter office politics, began to bore Jones. He wanted to be out there! Involved! That, after all, was the reason he had wanted to become involved with the music business in the first place. After his second Christmas, finding himself increasingly marginalised into managerial dullness at the expense of innovative young upstarts like the inspired Paul Cons – the first person to realise the immense potential of The Hacienda as a nightclub, rather than as a rock venue – Jones decided that he'd had enough. He was thirty-two and office bound. He was not, he realised, cut out for the role of club manager; he wanted to be involved with rock'n'roll again. He wanted to be involved with a band; a great band. Jones decided to leave The Hacienda to see just what was out there.

* * *

Back in Chorlton, out of work and understandably anxious to find some direction, Jones put the word around that he was looking to manage. He had connections, credibility, nous and a little money. Almost immediately he was contacted by two name bands, including Carmel; though tempted, he rejected their offers, foreseeing that involvement with them would push him straight back into the office. Jones wanted a 'hands on' role; he wanted to evolve with a band, as part of a band. He hadn't forgotten the spirit of creative partnership that he'd experienced in Bristol.

He put the word about and even admitted to himself that his search might prove to be a tad naïve. The practice rooms of Manchester were not filled with great bands; they were filled with grotesque Smiths copyists, dourly slashing their way through sets full of tedium and dirge. Jones was aware of this but it didn't stop him from asking a friend who worked at Spirit Studios on Barlow Moor Road, Steve Atherton (aka Steve Adge), to keep an eye out for any passing bands who might be in need of his innovative managerial services. Within days, Atherton called him back, with news of a young band, currently thumping away in one of the rehearsal rooms. "They need a manager and I think they might really like you," stated Atherton, before adding, "They are unusual. There's something about them. Come and see."

So it was that The Stone Roses, guitars, amps and hangers-on, duly huddled into a tiny room with Howard Jones and, refusing to turn the sound down, slammed their way through a set which sounded like World War One held in a phone box. They studiously ignored the figure of Jones, hovering nervously near the door, attempting to separate melody from sheer barrage of sound. And then, after twelve five-minute blasts, they stopped and, saying nothing, fell into a curious mass gawp, perhaps expecting Jones to fall into the expected pre-managerial gush, perhaps anticipating some kind of witticism, or even biting criticism. Although he didn't know how to express it, Jones was rendered genuinely speechless. "I knew straight away that there was an incredible vibe about them. It wasn't really the music which, frankly, I couldn't really hear, but it was this aura of confidence. They seemed like the complete item. There was no doubt about this at all and they had a collective confidence which I found amusing because, before entering that room, I had felt like the big shot, the big time ex-Hacienda manager who was going down with the nobodies. I was a totally arrogant git really. I thought I knew it all. I thought I'd done it. I mean, I had hung out with Boy George and Martin Fry. I'd seen, tasted success and who the fuck were this lot? And yet, despite that arrogance, I still felt as though I was the one being auditioned rather than the other way around and that, to be honest, attracted me to them. I couldn't believe how they could be so fucking confident. Later on. Andy Couzens told me that he thought I was a complete tosser at the time, but I didn't feel that at all. I thought that they knew where I was coming from.

"I suppose I could have easily walked away there and then, thinking that they were all arrogant and unmanageable. They did seem like a whole lot of trouble. But, then again, I realised that if we pooled all our resources, their confidence, my contacts, in a positive way then things might begin to happen."

Andy Couzens takes up the story: "Yeah . . . he's right about one thing. I did think he was a tosser. In fact I thought he was an annoying loud-mouth red head. We all did, at first. But these are not necessarily bad things for a manager. He tried a few things on. Like asking us to turn the volume down at rehearsals. We gave him short shrift with that. In no uncertain terms we told him that it had fuck all to do with him. I mean we really were having none of it . . . I think he thought, and perhaps he still thinks, that he got close to us. Became one of the gang. No fucking chance, mate. He was miles away. Never came close. From the very start we decided to use him. That's just how it was. It wasn't nasty. It was, I suppose, cynical. We had decided that we would do anything to get on."

Ian Brown: "We did use him. Took him to the cleaners, really. I'm not too proud of that, looking back, but a lot of it was his fault. Howard can look after himself."

The most worldly Rose at that juncture, if not later, was undoubtedly Reni. When Jones calls him, "the most brilliant drummer I had ever seen or have ever seen since" he doesn't mean in the egocentric manner of prog rock drummers, whose bands would halt their set for twenty minutes to allow the sticksman to flex his muscles and his ego, but as a confident, talented musician who powered the rest of the band along. Jones: "When Reni got behind a kit, the kit became an extension of him . . . in the same way that Hendrix's guitar would be. He is one of the few people who could sit behind anybody's kit and just start playing by feel. Fact is, they couldn't afford a kit good enough for him." For his part, Jones, allergic to any hint of Goth, requested that Garner might trim his locks a tad; he might also have been well advised to have banned the wearing of Paisley or, in John Squire's case, bandannas. The band who would later famously vie with the Happy Mondays to find the coolest gear around determinedly dressed down at the time, favouring black leatherette trousers, Cuban heeled boots and scruffed denim jackets. Manchester audiences, despite The Smiths, despite The Chameleons also, still felt generally troubled by the sight of such rock clichés.

Jones wangled some cheap demo time for the band from his mate, Tim Oliver, at Spirit Studios. The results were rough but promising, with hints of a melody rising from a muddy backbeat. Listening to these tapes now, the faults – too much reliance on the music which was around them at the time, too much respect for their lesser talented peers – seem clear. The songs, 'Going Down', 'The Hardest Thing', 'Heart On The Staves' and 'Shoot You Down' amongst them, seemed shackled by an all-too tentative musicianship. Curious to note how a city which prides itself on its continual sense of innovation frequently creates a style and sound which becomes so dominant (The Smiths, Oasis, the Roses themselves) that it stifles the originality of most young songwriters. Wary of moving too far outside the prevailing idea of what's hip, many inevitably resort to diluted versions of that dominating sound rather than holding out on the strength of their own originality.

But the Roses' demos were encouraging enough for Jones to approach Martin Hannett, after the pair had been reintroduced to each other by photographer Dennis Morris during the launch of his book of Sex Pistols photographs, with a view to him producing the band. It was a courageous approach. Jones had initially met Hannett only days before the completion of The Hacienda. On that day the legendary producer, having fallen out with Factory after the label had decided to spend their money on the nightclub rather than providing Hannett with a Fairlight computer and a new studio, stormed into the club waving a writ. It was a shaky moment. For Jones, two years of work seemingly hung in the balance of threatened legal action. Panicking, Jones returned to Factory directors Rob Gretton and Alan Erasmus who told him not to worry. "It's only Martin," they explained, "you'll soon understand . . . Martin doesn't live in the real world. Don't worry about it."

Despite this bizarre introduction, Jones liked Hannett and believed that the credibility carried by the producer, still regularly championed for his extraordinary work with Joy Division, would rub off to good effect on The Stone Roses. Hannett had more ambitious plans. Still nursing his anti-Factory battle wounds, he suggested to Jones that they, "Start our own Factory. Our own label . . . let's become Factory Records Two."

A difficult proposition. Though the label was plagued with financial problems there was still a sense of artistic worth attached to the packaging of Factory records which raised it above that of their indie competitors. Indeed, most major labels would question the wisdom of spending £5,000 on the design of a Stockholm Monsters single sleeve. The problem was that any new Manchester label would have to compete with the aesthetic triumph of Factory's product. If Hannett wished to seriously challenge Factory, he would have to find some way around that problem. On the other hand, and with some justification, he regarded his own skills to have been an essential part of the initial Factory package. As Jones also nursed a slight grievance towards Factory, following his brisk exit from The Hacienda, the idea of starting up in competition held a certain appeal. And so, with Spirit's Tim Oliver also on board, a new record company, The Thin Line, was formed. Arrogance, optimism, a great sounding band in the Roses, a mighty if erratic producer and a splattering of naïveté all combined to kick-start the label. And Hannett, practically 'in house' producer at Stockport's Strawberry Studios, was owed a considerable amount of down-time from the studio management. As such, The Stone Roses would join a growing list of Manchester bands who took their first steps into recording at a top class studio, via Martin Hannett's relationship with Strawberry (Happy Mondays would follow, Simply Red had done the same thing twelve months previously).

The Roses themselves, however, were not without their reservations. Couzens: "We were all a bit pissed off with that Thin Line stuff. In fact it annoyed the hell out of us. We'd have long meetings about this. OK, so Howard was the manager but, all of a sudden, he was also our label boss, and suddenly there was some kind of publishing company. It was all like a big stitch up. We never wanted any of that. He went from being a manager looking for a deal to being our boss three times over and we were really pissed off about it. We just thought he was being really greedy and had started taking a lot of things for granted. I mean, we still didn't really know him or what he did."

Couzens' memories are, perhaps unsurprisingly, somewhat contradicted by those of Howard Jones. For Jones, the deal meant the band could start recording material and getting some publicity without having to spend months trying to attract established labels. "We all agreed that, rather than keep badgering record companies who weren't really interested, it would be far better to go this route, to produce our own record and take it from there. It was just the best thing at the time. And I talked about that a lot with the band. There was no question of reluctance on their behalf. They were up for it, totally. Thin Line, Martin, everything and, let's be honest, they couldn't get arrested at the time, could they?"

Jones' influence on the band's direction remains a matter of some controversy. Admittedly, he took them up a level and made them work on a professionalism to match their undoubted talent and self-confidence. However, Couzens, whom Jones would later manage as a member of The High, while conceding that, "He's not a bad person", still has strong feelings about Jones' approach. "He was bullshitting us throughout our time with him. He played these power games. He would try the old divide and rule tactic, he'd work on one portion of the band and set them up against the other. He was so divisive and it meant that practically everything we did with Howard was just no fun at all. There was always in-fighting, like all bands, I know, but this was really intense stuff and mostly it was Howard's fault."

Jones disputes this. "I was trying to get the band working as a cohesive unit. They were very together in some ways but, in others, they needed guidance," he argues.

The situation was, perhaps, typified by one particular evening during which Jones went into overdrive: he decided that the band should sack Reni. Jones' reasons might have stemmed from the drummer's bombastic personality, which may have appeared to threaten his managerial dignity; Reni, frankly, took the piss a lot. Moreover, the sheer force of Reni's drumming did, at times, tend to dominate the rehearsals, and this may have been an influence on Jones' attitude to him. When quizzed about this, Jones initially refuted the claim: "Reni was certainly the most accomplished musician in the Roses at the time. He'd been playing all his life so it was just all so perfectly natural, fluid drumming. I didn't have a problem with it. In fact I thought he powered the band along perfectly." However, it's clear that something about the effusive drummer rankled with Jones: "I had to spend a lot of time thinking about the Reni problem. And he was a problem. It was a band dynamic thing. He was very disruptive. I was worried about their unity. They needed that or they might become fragmented, like so many bands. You must understand that The Stone Roses may have seemed very tight, but they were also always on the edge of splitting. I thought Reni might have pushed them over the edge."

Whatever the real motivation, Jones spent hours punching this view across to Garner, Couzens, Brown and Squire. Slowly but surely, the band began to see his point and at the end of one talk session duly clambered into a car to travel across to Belle Vue and deliver the news. And it was only as they were approaching Reni's home in Gorton Street that they came to their senses. Reni was one of them: he stayed.

The other Roses still remember the incident with some passion. Brown: "That was just an example of the madness at the time. Sack Reni? Reni was the one main reason why The Stone Roses were so special. Any idiot could tell that. The reason we became so popular, the reason we were loved, was because we always had a great beat. We had Reni. There's no bands around today who have a beat like that. To sack Reni would have been the dumbest thing ever."

Andy Couzens sees it in simple terms. "Howard definitely didn't like Reni at that point. There's no two ways about that. You've got to understand that he reduced this band to a series of slanging matches. You couldn't hold a conversation with Howard, it was just shouting all the time. Some people may say that that's just part of the magic of a band. You know, the tension, but I thought it was negative . . ." Couzens' point is further illustrated by his memory of an incident that occurred long after The Stone Roses disbanded. "In 1997," he recalls, "me, Ian, Reni and Pete Garner all went round to Howard's to have a meeting about band royalties from that time. I thought it would be fine. We'd all got on pretty well since I had left the band and I saw Reni all the time anyway. So it was all going to be very civilised. But, as soon as Howard came into the chemistry, we all started slagging each other off again. After all these years, he was still setting us up against each other. He didn't even have anything to gain this time."

It was Couzens himself who stumped up the £1,200 to finance the recording of what would be their first single. The song 'Misery Dictionary' was dropped as first choice for the A-side: the band felt, with justification, that it might instantly tie them to the Joy Division/Smiths school, which made Manchester out as a raincoated hell of doom and gloom. Instead, they opted for the brighter, brasher title, 'So Young'. Ian's lyrics stemmed from his time spent in the Hulme flat blocks, watching young neighbours waste their days languishing in bed until tea time. To Ian, ingrained with a strong work ethic, this empty scenario seemed tragic. Worse than that, that kind of life was becoming accepted as the norm in Hulme, which included, increasingly, the negative influence of heroin, a drug which Ian despised. Brown's move to Hulme had coincided with a mid-Eighties rise in local musical activity. In the main, the area gave rise to harsh gritty politico funksters like Big Flame or uncompromising industrial noise makers like Tools You Can Trust. Bands who had evolved directly from the sharp end of studenthood and gained intelligent coverage in the pages of the highly literate *Debris* fanzine. None of which particularly suited Brown although the loose, alcohol-fuelled camaraderie of the Hulme Crescents' endless party scene wasn't without its advantages.

Brown found the ease with which local youngsters drifted into hopeless inertia on the estates depressing. "It was as if these kids . . . really bright kids too, were falling right into the Hulme stereotype," he recalls, "and it was just so pointless. It certainly wasn't romantic, it was grubby and cheap. 'So Young' was, in effect, a rallying call, telling people to get out of their beds . . . All that talent draining away. I hate that more than anything. So it was an angry song but a positive song."

A good way to introduce your band to the world, though Brown remained dissatisfied with the single. In conversation with *Record Collector* in 1998, he recalled going for a drive with the band at the time and playing the song on the car's stereo: "Reni's nose exploded, blood everywhere – there was so much treble on the record, it hurt! We should have gone with that version but we said, no . . . His nose just went with the frequency!" Though it wasn't the sound that would make them famous, at least the band had managed to make a convincing statement on record; convincing enough, at least, for the single to get to number one in the local record shop charts. "It just sounds like what it is," Brown reminisced 14 years later, "four lads trying to get out of Manchester."

★ ★ ★

Since grasping the baton of 'alternative DJ on commercial station' from his predecessor Mark Radcliffe, Tony 'The Greek' Michaelides, record promoter, plugger and Neil Young fanatic, had settled into a 7–10 pm Sunday evening slot where his *Last Radio Programme* would marry the best of local music with the incoming rush of American guitar bands. In retrospect, the music press would regard 1985 as a lull in the Manchester scene. Not so. Anyone wishing to research the background of the late Eighties Madchester 'explosion' could do worse than listen to a couple of tapes of that show where, behind Tony's intelligent, enthusiastic patter, a giant grumbling mess of bands desperate to force their way out of the shadow of The Smiths can be clearly heard. Fact is, with a few exceptions, the London music press couldn't be bothered with mid-Eighties Manchester and it is still referred to as a period of 'pre-scene'.

At the time, one local radio station (Piccadilly) served the entire town, lambasting its listeners with incessant 'hairdresser DJ' patter by day; anything 'alternative' – such as R.E.M., The Smiths or New Order – was sneaked out in the evening. In such days a whole scene would seem to be squeezed into one show and, come Sunday evening, The Smiths fans of Rusholme, The Chameleons hordes of Dukinfield, would tune in to Tony The Greek, many of them hoping that Tony would slip their own home-made demo in-between 'The Boy With The Thorn In His Side' and 'SubCulture'.

Howard Jones had known Tony for several years. Indeed, as Tony, wearing his promoter's hat, often furnished Jones with discs at The Hacienda, Jones granted Michaelides permanent guest-list status at the club. Knowing the strong local impact of *The Last Radio Programme*, Jones was quick to contact Michaelides and rant on about a fantastic band that he was managing. Michaelides liked Jones but he knew the sound of local band manager patter when it gushed down his receiver. What's more, it had only been a couple of months before that Jones had paraded his intentions of going into management around town. Truly great bands are not discovered with such ease; they come along once or twice in a lifetime. Nevertheless, Michaelides did manage to summon up a veneer of enthusiasm as he wandered into the Piccadilly Radio reception area one Sunday afternoon, to be confronted with the figure of Pete Garner, very much the most forceful member of the Roses, and therefore, Jones' right-hand man, eagerly clutching the promised demo tape.

The Last Radio Programme was a loose affair which benefited greatly from the casual manner in which it was spliced together. And on Sunday nights, when all the rant and fire of daytime radio offices was done, Tony would drift in, accompanied, more often than not, by his unofficial helpers – eager teenagers Paula Greenwood and Ro Newton.[13] Together, with the aid of a few local drifters, they would cobble together a heady cocktail of local gossip, informed band info and music. Their enthusiasm can be measured, perhaps, by their willingness to actually listen to the stack of demo tapes, mostly dreadful, that awaited them each week. And that Sunday, as The Stone Roses tape was dutifully slapped in place, it took just three seconds for all three of them to stop ferreting amongst the desks, and listen carefully, very carefully, to the sound of 'Misery Dictionary', blasting through the empty office.[14]

"We had expected a certain type of demo. There was definitely too much of a Manchester sound going on, but there was something about this tape that completely floored me," admits Michaelides. "It just came rushing out. We all stopped and sort of said, 'What the . . .!' There was something about that guitar . . . that manic singer . . . those drums! It wasn't particularly unorthodox, far from it . . . but it still sounded so unusual, so special I suppose. We must have been impressed because I took it straight into the studio that night and played it. Funnily enough, we received a flood of calls. Now it could easily have been just the band's mates. I'm not being cynical, I wouldn't have blamed them for that. You could play a tape of The Dogshits from Dukinfield and get a few callers who are mates. I don't know, but they did sound genuine. And Pete Garner rang at the end of the night to thank me. I knew, at that point, that we'd have to seize upon this, somehow. This was really special. We needed to be the first to highlight the fact that this was a major new band."

Michaelides and Jones met three times during the following week and an idea began to form. A unique aspect of *The Last Radio Programme* had been kick-started when ex-Buzzcock Pete Shelley had unexpectedly wandered into the studio one day brandishing a 12-string guitar and had thrilled the listeners with an impromptu four-song live set of 'What Do I Get?', 'Ever Fallen In Love', 'Sixteen Again' and 'Homosapien'. Not to be outdone, the following week saw his ex-Buzzcock partner Steve Diggle

[13] Paula would later become a successful label owner of Playtime Records, early home of the Inspiral Carpets. Ro became one of the first hip, young mouthy females on Radio One in addition to presenting the *Old Grey Whistle Test* and introducing Liz Kershaw to the world of broadcasting.

[14] 'Heart On The Staves', 'I Wanna Be Adored' and 'Tell Me' were the other songs on the tape.

tramp down to the studio and blast through an acoustic selection of his songs. Over time, as other artists, including Richard Thompson and Virginia Astley, contributed unplugged sessions of their own, the Tony The Greek live acoustic session became something of an institution. Michaelides asked Jones about the possibility of Squire and Brown coming in although, sensibly, they soon realised that Brown, a showman rather than a singer in the traditional sense, would thereby have his vocal weaknesses rather cruelly exposed. To accommodate this, Jones hit upon the novel idea of taking this live session a stage further – taking the whole band into the studio and letting them play live. It was risky, to say the least, but Michaelides insisted that, if it could be done, it would have to be completely live. Broken strings, bum notes, swear words, the lot.

Back at Piccadilly, Michaelides asked his engineer, Gerry, about the possibilities of this. To his astonishment, the reply was positive. If the band came in during the afternoon, complete with Reni's full drum kit, and soundchecked in the unused studio, it would indeed be possible. It would be patchy. It would be all over the place. But it could be fun. The band, sensing the glamour of on-air anarchy, agreed immediately. Much more fun, surely, than allowing Tony to subject them to the usual dull, local band interview; even then, The Stone Roses knew what they did best . . . and charming DJs and journalists with elegant rhetoric, would never be regarded as their strong point.

And so, that Sunday afternoon, the five-piece Roses marched through the grey shell of the cavernous Piccadilly Plaza, to Piccadilly Radio. They were determined to do a professional job, to make a splash, to announce their arrival. Local radio it might have been but, for The Stone Roses, it was their first chance to reach an audience. And they were determined not to blow it. Not surprisingly perhaps, the soundproofed doors of Studio One were not strong enough to hold in the full force of a Stone Roses soundcheck. Indeed, listeners to Mike Shaft's elegant Sunday afternoon soul show, could actually hear, behind the sweet vocals of Luther Vandross, the dull thumping of Reni's drum kit. Shaft was understandably irritated by this unruly intrusion. Storming into the studio, he stopped abruptly in amazement when confronted by a rock band in full rehearsal. "But Tony, it's going out over the air," he pleaded, adding, "if the programme controller hears that . . ." Mercifully, he didn't. The soundcheck was duly squeezed into the two hours, 5-7 pm, when Piccadilly would succumb to blanket broadcasting and The Network Chart.

Michaelides' memories of The Stone Roses' first airing on the radio remain fond: "In many respects, radio professionals might call it bad radio. I thought it was wonderful. Certainly the most significant thing I ever did during 12 years of broadcasting. The band played four songs and it was everything that live music should be. They made mistakes and there were bits where they would continue playing at the end and just jam along, Reni would be crashing away as I was back announcing . . . all that stuff. When I play it today, I just sound like the man you shouldn't ever put on the radio. I was just gushing with boyish enthusiasm but it was genuine enthusiasm.

"They were in the next studio, so I couldn't see them. I was trying to ask them questions and just hoping that I was turning the right mike up at the right time. There was no eye contact so the whole thing was really 'gappy'. But they still sounded great, the girls in the studio were going wild and, again, the calls rushed in. It could have been the same mates ringing in. I don't know. But I sensed it was genuine. There was a terrific buzz in the studio and I'm sure it transmitted. It was a little strange because, if you think about it, they were just another local band. Nobody knew who the hell they were and yet it was so obvious that they had something. And that session has been repeated so many times in later years on Piccadilly . . . by people like Terry Christian and Pete Mitchell. I remember driving home that night and thinking, at last, I've actually achieved something significant. It might not sound like much to people in London but it meant a great deal in Manchester. It was a first footing for the band."

* * *

Two weeks after the session, Michaelides received a phone call from the London's Camden Lock rock venue, Dingwalls. A deal, of sorts, was in the offing: would Michaelides like to assemble a Manchester showcase gig featuring five local bands, sell tickets over the air and take the whole caboodle down to Dingwalls for a showcase night on February 8? It was a simple and highly effective idea which helped Dingwalls stretch beyond the scope of rather dull bands who clogged the London small venue circuit. (Usually replacing them, admittedly, with equally tedious outfits from Leeds or, quite possibly, Manchester.) Instantly Tony agreed, knowing full well that his headlining band would be The Stone Roses. After consulting Howard Jones and the band, the deal was closed and Michaelides spent the next three Sundays pushing the tickets on the Piccadilly Radio airwaves. Ro and Paula helped, of course, mailing tickets and sorting through the mountain of demo tapes in order to select a quartet of hopeful local acts.

There was a lottery element to the selection. One of the five eventual choices was Arthur Kadmon's Glee Company, a jazz/swing/pop off-shoot from the weird and legendary Ludus. The Glee Company had produced some of the finest demos that had ever graced Manchester to date, although their live act was frequently less impressive. Lively popsters Laugh were another band of hopefuls – they would later form the nucleus of indie might-have-beens, Interstella. Below these came two names plucked, almost at random, from the tape bin. Fictitious Names and Communal Drop, two bands eternally locked on the north Manchester rock venue circuit. And with the Roses, that made five. Each band would be taking their own following, and a lively and competitive night was assured. Jones spent the week before the gig earbashing every approachable A&R man in London, all of whom promised dutiful attendance. As every other band on the bill did exactly the same thing, probably to the very same A&R men, it was assumed that Dingwalls would succumb to a swelling guest list.

It therefore came as a considerable shock to The Stone Roses, if not to Jones who knew that a following in Manchester meant nothing at all to the London elite, when none of the A&R men bothered to turn up that night. Apart, that is, from Elektra's lively head of A&R, Simon Potts and even he only attended because Michaelides, a mate from way back, was staying at his house that night. Michaelides: "It was slightly awkward because I didn't want to push the Roses too hard to Simon. He heard all that banter day in day out, so I decided to lay off. He had good ears though. It was Simon who took me to see Simply Red when I hadn't even heard of them. I remember that night, standing at the bar with him, watching the Roses. Ian Brown was fantastic. He didn't seem to care that the audience was flimsy. He just wanted to show off . . . walking right up to people and singing into their faces.

"Simon turned to me and said, 'Tony, this lot are wild.' I know he was impressed but not impressed enough to sign them. The thing is, there was no need for him to sign them at that point. He probably made a mental note to keep tabs on them. There was a sense that it was a little early. That they would improve with experience. It was a good night but, in terms of gaining record company interest, a bit depressing. I remember thinking how impossible it seemed for the acts on the bill to actually get signed."

* * *

Preston's cityscape sits, almost impressively, to the west of the M6, to the north of deepest Lancashire and to the east of gruesome Blackpool. Too far away to be regarded as a satellite of Manchester or Liverpool, too small to offer a serious cultural challenge and yet large enough for a scene of sorts to flourish.

Preston remains profoundly provincial. As such it has maintained a strange musical importance. During the early Seventies, the city remained a furiously independent outpost of Northern Soul and, later, as

Manchester and Liverpool remained inherently affected by the grip of studenthood, a school of unpretentious rock bands began to play to audiences of speed-fuelled, expensively garbed football crowds – the Perry Boys – who demanded something more challenging than a weekly trip to the local hook 'em, fuck 'em, chuck 'em disco.

In 1985, New Order, who had found the Perry Boy element of their gigs beginning to swell for some time, came to Preston and stood astonished on stage as the Preston crowd fell into full-scale riot mode right in front of them. "I don't know who these people are," Barney confessed after that gig, "they don't look like our normal audience. They are completely different to the crowds we may attract in London . . . or even in Manchester. Something weird is happening in Preston."

Something weird was happening in Manchester, too. The joke was that, already, most houses in North Manchester contained at least one Chameleons album while no one in the more student-dominated south side had ever even heard of the band. The Chameleons were working class, rock- and song-orientated and offered an accessible alternative to The Smiths. For a good eighteen months, despite being largely unknown to the music press, they remained the biggest draw in Manchester, filling the Free Trade Hall on one occasion. And yet this writer recalls receiving a frantic phone call from Factory boss Tony Wilson, who demanded to know, "Who the fuck are The Chameleons? And are they any good? Nobody at Factory has ever heard anything by them."

To Howard Jones' astonishment, and, no doubt to the smug shrugs from the band, The Stone Roses, by performing in a series of innovative 'warehouse parties' – hastily arranged gigs in railway arches which were precursors to late Eighties raves – had already started to make inroads into this curious new audience. "It stunned me, before I knew what was happening I was managing a band who, by simple word of mouth, could attract a thousand people, a thousand mental nutters, too. I didn't even have to work at it . . . it just happened. The band didn't think there was anything odd about this. I think they just thought they were the best so the people would naturally turn up. I thought that was really stupid of them and it did tend to wind me up a bit. They had no idea that people would actually work very hard to promote a show. They just thought, 'We are the Roses . . . people will come'. And, incredibly, they did. They were very lucky in this respect. There are many extremely talented bands who never manage to get across to anybody . . . it was funny. All people could talk about in the music press was The Smiths, New Order and The Fall, but we knew something else was happening. So we put them on at Preston Clouds. We used no pre-publicity, no posters . . .

nothing. But we knew that, if nothing else, half of Manchester would take the trip up there to see us . . . and so they did."

Clouds was a traditional disco: a large, chrome'n'mirrored monstrosity, pre-*Hit Man And Her* which, generally, was home to white-socked, slip-on-shoed mechanics and electricians out on the razz. Confusingly, Friday nights was set aside for 'indie night', which attracted a trickle of students from Preston Poly, a few straggly Goths from Lancaster, and the aforementioned Perry boy tribes. A volatile cocktail of club goers, to say the least. Add 500 travelling boozed-up Mancunians on speed to this blend . . . and stand well back. Jones had attempted to secure the services of the very fine Oz PA Hire but the club, seeking to keep costs at a realistic level, pieced together a house system, a cobbled hotch-potch of local PAs that left much to be desired. Understandably, the band seemed sullen and disappointed during the soundcheck, their frustration hardly helped by the knowledge that all the national music papers would attend – *NME*, *Melody Maker* and *Sounds* all sending their local stringers, while, it seemed, every fanzine in the north would also be in evidence. The whole event had started to attain showcase proportions.

Jones: "I tried really hard to gee the band up. I said, look, the PA's crap but if you can prove that you can play really well despite a bad PA, then you'll end up as winners." The Roses were reluctant but, as the house began to fill up, and as the Preston and Manchester contingents began to bubble dangerously in front of the stage, they realised they had little choice but to go on.

Within a raucous five minutes, the PA crackled to a fizz twice, fights began to break out at the front of the stage, surging from left to right and then, swirling backwards, causing those towards the rear to retreat with potentially dangerous consequences. Howard Jones was standing next to the mixing desk, numbed, as the fracas escalated; at one point, he instinctively leaned forward, grabbing two young female reporters, Ro Newton working for *Melody Maker* and Paula Greenwood from Manc glossy *Muze Magazine* (yes, ex-Piccadilly Radio), lifted them clear of the retreating crowd and dumping them unceremoniously in the aisle. By song two, at least eighteen separate fights were bouncing around the hall; the music was no longer the main attraction.

Six songs in, with the band beginning to get into their stride, the club management decided enough was enough . . . and the gig was abruptly pulled, leaving Ian Brown standing stage front, screaming "STOP FIGHTING . . . STOP FIGHTING YOU FUCKING MORONS." The fucking morons refused to comply, of course, and the band, their immediate circle of friends and a bemused gaggle of journalists, decamped to the backstage area, where their breathless chatter was interrupted only by occasional crashing noises from out in the disco. On and on it raged, with a team of bouncers swiftly called in from across the city centre to help deal with the fracas.

The atmosphere in the dressing room was, to say the least, strained. In one corner an *NME* interview (not published) was taking place with the interviewer clearly hoping to ask his questions and get the hell out of there before the marauding hordes crashed through that backstage door. And at one point it appeared that that was indeed about to happen. The door flew open and in fell one guy, full of beer and venom, slagging off everyone in sight, making a general nuisance of himself. He was actually a friend of the band but, at this point, he was a pissed, idiotic friend they didn't need. Especially not in a room full of impressionable journalists.

Jones attempted to placate the newcomer: "Look mate . . . there's an interview taking place. Can you calm it down a bit?"

It was to no avail. On and on he ranted, changing his tack only when it was necessary to have him escorted from the room. "Oh, fucking typical that is," he screamed, "and I thought we were supposed to be mates. You are all the fucking same you fuckers . . ." His departure was followed by a stony silence, and apologetic shrugs. The friend's name? Gary Mounfield . . .

"His attitude was bad that day," recalls Jones, "and he knew it. A week or so later he came round and apologised. He was cool and the band weren't bothered. It was all heat of the moment stuff. But I was worried. We were getting a really bad reputation and the problem was that it was deserved. I knew that we would have trouble playing anywhere in Britain, after that. Those same people would turn up and inevitably it would end up in a fight. We didn't want that. This wasn't The Pistols in America. The band wanted to play their new songs, to get them across to the audience. None of us were fighters. I mean, we weren't wimps or anything, but we were never into that mentality. We found it embarrassing. I knew that, if the band wanted to play live, to tighten things up and try out their songs in front of a new audience, we'd have to go somewhere else . . . away from Manchester . . . away from England."

★ ★ ★

It began with Ian Brown. On one of his periodical wandering stints Brown hitchhiked through Europe, bragging to anyone he could collar about the successful rock band he was in. One of these people, Andreas Linkaard, took Ian at face value and, flexing his connections with the Swedish media and rock scene, told Ian to keep in touch, promising that he could set a series of Swedish gigs in motion. All the band would have to do was turn up on Swedish soil. It seemed a loose promise, and had

Howard Jones not mentioned the need to get out of England, the connection would almost certainly have been lost. As it was, Brown produced Linkaard's number at a band meeting and, passing it across to Jones, remarked that the band could be rewarded with a string of top-notch shows. Furthermore, Brown maintained, it would be cool, so cool, to be massive in Sweden.

Tentatively, Jones called Linkaard. To his astonishment he was immediately promised two gigs, somewhere to stay and the money for a return ferry trip for the band. It all seemed alarmingly simple, especially as Couzens, an obsessive American car freak, just happened to be in possession of a Chevy truck. Not the ultimate in comfort but spacious, blessed with enough room, just, for the band, Jones, a drum kit, two guitars, two combos and a small stack of equipment. At a band meeting, Jones instructed them all to go away and find £50. When the gigs and open-ended ferry tickets were confirmed, they simply piled in and set off.

The day of the ferry sailing happened to coincide with Reni's 21st birthday, a terrific excuse, as if one was needed, to immediately drink their way through most of the spending money at the ferry bar.[15] Stumbling onto the quayside, in Sweden, was enough to immediately stun them out of their respective hangovers. It was cold – bitterly, unbearably cold. Colder than they could ever have imagined, causing any exposed skin to take on a blue hue, causing finger joints to fuse and lips to crack painfully. At this point, the sheer insanity of the trip began to dawn on them: here they were, broke, hungover, frozen solid, with no idea of where they would stay, or play. They had only a vague meeting place in Stockholm to aim for and, to their horror, they soon realised that Stockholm was a 15-hour drive away. Even the normally unflappable Jones began to realise that, perhaps, this hadn't been one of his brighter ideas. Nevertheless, huddling into a Chevy that didn't look capable of surviving such an arduous drive, the Roses set forth, peering forlornly through the windows at the inhospitable Swedish terrain.

"The meeting was set for 8 pm the following day, at the railway station in Stockholm," explains Jones, "and it was a million-to-one chance that he'd even be there, really. But he was. Trouble was, after about five minutes with him we realised that the whole thing was a complete shambles. Yes, he kind of had us a couple of gigs but even they were pretty dubious. The band all turned to me and said, 'Come on Howard, you can do it. Get some gigs together.' We camped down in the guy's flat on one of the islands in Stockholm, with me on the phone to everyone, using my Hacienda background as an introduction. It worked. The

---

[15] An eerie little precursor of a pre-fame Oasis jaunt, several years later.

promoters had all heard of The Hacienda. I told them that The Stone Roses were the big Hacienda band of the moment. They fell for it and we managed to string a few gigs together. That took two days, during which the guy had decided that he had had enough, and moved out of the flat, leaving us on our own."

The unsteady relationship between Jones and the band worsened, if anything, in Sweden. The fact that he had blagged the only bed in the flat didn't settle too well with the band, and Manchester rock mythology would soon be blessed with the tale of how the band took all but two of the supporting struts from his bed, causing him to crash to the floor as he settled down. Perhaps as a childish prank it might have seemed amusing on the first occasion, but the band orchestrated this trick for 15 days on the trot, after which, unable to take it any more Jones departed and stayed elsewhere. To be fair to Jones, starvation played a part in his decision to move out: it seemed he was the last in The Stone Roses' food chain. A sordid situation, to be honest, with Reni hiding bacon under his pillow, Ian and Andy grabbing the food first and John and Pete sifting through the scraps, leaving Howard with, well, nothing at all.

"We were real bastards to him," states Couzens. "I mean, he deserved it really, 'cos he was still being really nasty out there, but perhaps we went too far. We'd kick him out of the van and leave him to walk back. In the middle of Sweden at something like 5° under. It really wasn't on but he just took it all in his stride. We'd call him The Rhino because he was so thick-skinned, or Cochise the Big Thick Red Indian. He didn't seem to care. The worse we got, the more he liked it. Perhaps he was a masochist . . ."

The gigs stretched into three weeks. At the same time, Martin Hannett was screaming from England for the band to get back on Manchester turf before the release of their single. But for the meantime English activities were sidelined as The Stone Roses stormed through the gigs, delighted to discover that the rock-starved Swedes instantly fell for them. Jones: "We were amazed because we started getting the same reaction as over in England. Not the violence, just a load of kids really getting off on it, just tasting the sheer enjoyment. It really perked the band up. For the first time they knew that they were getting a response from an audience who weren't just mates, or even people who had read about them. Just a pure, untainted reaction. It was remarkable in those clubs."

Remarkable too, it seems, on the streets of Stockholm where the band, waltzing through the market, would be approached by adoring young Swedes – yes, mind-bogglingly stunning blondes among them – all of whom seem to take great pleasure in mouthing the words, "*I Wanna Be A Door*"! A door of perception, presumably. Whatever, a small cult following in Sweden seemed preferable to marauding thugs in Preston. Not that things were going too smoothly with regard to life's essentials. As ever, food and money were scarce but by way of compensation, the band had taken to swilling down a local brew normally sampled only by tramps and winos. It had the benefit of being warming, strangely filling and removed all traces of shyness.

In Stockholm, The Stone Roses became expert blaggers. One night on the town saw them hovering outside the Royal Palace – a kind of Swedish Stringfellows – and pushing Howard Jones to the front, where his managerial bullshitting slipped into overdrive. "Hey, we're a band called The Stone Roses. You must have heard of us? Yeah . . . we're the biggest band in England at the moment." It worked. The all-powerful girl on the door fell for the line in no time: "Yeah, of course. Hey Stone Roses . . . yeah man, 'course I've heard all about you, brilliant . . . er . . . where are you?" Jones pointed to the end of the queue where John Squire, for once overcoming his natural reticence, was urinating in full view of everyone.

The girl's eyes widened.

"Hey . . . you guys for real or what?"

Apparently Squire's act had sealed it. Only genuine superstars would urinate in public, in a queue for a plush nightclub. Once in, the band ran from bar to bar, feverishly gobbling up the peanut trays and blagging free drinks at a rate of knots. They couldn't afford egg and chips and yet here they were, swilling down £5 Margaritas like Rod Stewart on a stag night, with an effortless brio born of boundless confidence. And there was Howard Jones, nursing a beer, allowing the man he believed to be some stoned local film director to rant on and on about some flick he'd managed to push onto the European circuit. Jones yawned when he heard the title, *Brazil*, not realising that he'd just spent an evening in the company of Terry Gilliam – and Jones, a Python fanatic – and that Gilliam, equally unlikely this, was actually aware of the band called The Stone Roses. Funny how quickly reputations can tend to spread, even in, or perhaps especially in Sweden. The next day the band were blagging again, this time at the Hard Rock Café, where Gilliam's film was launched. Curiously, without trying, The Stone Roses were hanging out at exactly the right places, influencing exactly the right kind of people. Some things, as they say, are just meant to be.

But they still had to eat. Superstar ligging doesn't push such pangs away and desperate measures were called for. Cynically befriending a bemused part-time supermarket worker, they persuaded him to unlock the supermarket doors in the middle of the night. Once opened, the band grabbed a trolley each and stormed down the aisles, falling into a hilarious, though highly criminal, supermarket sweep, before grasping their illicit gains and retreating swiftly to the van. They ate well for the next seven days, although the fifteen cartons of chewing gum, 25 cartons of cigarettes and 40 packets of bacon – nicked by Reni – clearly had their gastronomic limitations.

"There's only so much fucking bacon you can eat," says Reni.

Naturally, they also gatecrashed parties or accepted party invitations with impolite haste, turning up, pushing through the dancing yuppies to the kitchen where they would proceed to get all the pans out, peel the veg and start making themselves food, more often than not in front of an audience of Stockholm trendies, all asking, "Who are these people?"

* * *

There is no doubt that Sweden emboldened The Stone Roses. If they were arrogant before they left, they were endowed with a confidence born of hard, rewarding gigging on their return. Rather like The Beatles' pre-fame sojourn to Hamburg, the Roses' jaunt had tightened them up considerably, both musically and personally. It was impossible for them not to feel flushed by their taste of success so far, and they fell back into their circle of friends simply brimming with on-the-road anecdotes. It felt like being in a real band at last. Not at all like the legions of duffers who couldn't get gigs beyond the deadening sub-Hacienda gig circuit.

Then again, while the Roses had been storming Sweden, something had changed in Manchester: the anti-rock mood that existed at The Hacienda, and was still in evidence at that club as it began its Pickering-fuelled journey into dance culture, had been countered by a new and unexpected reactionary trend. In Longsight, deep in student-land, the old Oceans 11 venue, following spells as a disco, show bar and 'mature cabaret joint' – the great Odyssey had recently performed there to a crowd chowing down on steak'n'mushroom and Lambrusco – had been hastily transformed and given a new name, The International. This transformation, intentional or not, seemed to mirror the mood of a city still swelled by ex-students, by twenty- and thirty-somethings, many of whom forsook the burgeoning dance culture in favour of a less bpm-oriented music: the ubiquitous indie scene, but also blues, folk, and world music.

And here, haunting the murky foyer of The International, we meet, for the first time, one of the pivotal figures of The Stone Roses story. Whatever happened next, for better or worse, nobody can deny that the whole tale was driven by the moving and shaking of one man, Gareth Evans, whose influence would shade and colour and twist this story into something quite extraordinary. While it's impossible to say what would have become of The Stone Roses had they never met Gareth Evans, it would have surely all been very different and, almost certainly, not nearly as exciting.

It was a portentous moment in mid-1985, when Evans, a bizarre animated vision bouncing back and forth, from door to bar, bar to door, ushered two young lads through the ambuscade of bouncers, proffering a good deal of, "Look after these lads . . . let them in. Important band . . . important band." The lads in question were Brown and Squire. It is doubtful that Gareth Evans had the faintest idea who the band really were, and he'd probably succumbed to a verbal onslaught from Howard Jones regarding 'the greatest band in Britain', but nevertheless, the two lads cast bemused, intrigued expressions in his direction, kind of liking his 'full on' routine, his sales patter. Maybe they made a mental note, there and then? Nobody remembers. However, within six months they would ask Gareth Evans to become their manager.

5

HURRICANE GARETH

Gareth Evans was twelve years old when he first gazed upon the still soot-blackened buildings of Manchester city centre. It was, literally, the start of the Sixties although the incoming rush of colour, of vibrancy, of flourishing local culture that one might associate with the beginning of that most intoxicating of decades, wasn't immediately apparent. This was an awesome, towering place, a city full of shadows and a populace with the grim reality of survival etched into their faces. For the first twelve years of his life, Evans' family had lived a quiet rural life in Cwm, a small farming town in Clwyd, where Gareth's brother John developed a taste for Welsh nationalism. No such patriotic passions for the half-English Gareth Evans, who remained in Manchester after his mother, unable to adjust to city life returned to the Welsh farm. She left Gareth to live with family and willingly soak in the sights, the sounds, the atmosphere of Sixties Manchester, a dynamic era in one of the most dynamic cities in Britain.

"I was just waiting for my life to begin. And I knew it would begin in Manchester," he says now. Evans, an idiosyncratic and strangely charming character, openly admits that part of his daily act is to add embellishments to his tales, to add drama if you like. That said, his adventures in and around the underworld of Manchester from the Sixties to the Nineties, are worthy of a hundred feature films; and all are vitally linked to this story.

The Manchester that welcomed him at the age of twelve was something of a paradox. Its geographical aloofness from the attractions of London – this was, after all, pre-motorway Britain – had caused a Manchester nightclub scene to develop in the late Fifties which exploded beyond the scope of anything seen before or since. Often referred to as the nightclub capital of Europe, Manchester's nightlife venues went through several sea changes in the decade. The lavish peppering of dark cellar bars which evolved in the Fifties gradually disappeared as the Sixties wore on, and as the folk and Merseybeat scenes faded from view, Manchester became Britain's second city of rootsy R&B. By 1967, Gareth Evans' character itself had gone through a few sea changes too. There were no longer any traces of wide-eyed rural innocence. Halfway through his teens, Evans had become a full-on mod. Although scooterless himself – "real mods didn't have scooters," he blithely informed me – he was always welcomed on to any 'ranking' pillion, garbed, as he was, in full-length suede coat, mohair suits and all manner of top notch apparel. "We used to nick a lot of that gear," he now admits, apparently unaware that such ventures into petty juvenile crime actually add romance to his story. Banned from some of the best clubs in Manchester, he would regularly accompany the massive scooter gangs of Manchester and Liverpool, on wild and often rather violent forays to the south coast, to Newquay, to Hastings to Brighton.[16]

Although the mod/rocker conflicts would, literally, scar him for life – which he proves, by standing up in a gentle garden centre coffee bar, in June 1998, and lifting his shirt to reveal an intriguing array of healed punctures and slits in his torso – he managed to avoid the worst extremes of such trendy violence. "I was one of those who always relied on his mouth," he states, adding, "I was a very lucky guy. I discovered that you can talk your way out of any situation. When I first went down to the Flamingo Club in London in my leather coat, a guy instantly came up to me and told me that he wanted my coat and my watch. I refused and immediately started a conversation with him. We became good friends . . . I wasn't tough, I wasn't a hard guy and if you couldn't battle your way out you had to use the verbals." In retrospect, Evans' experiences as a young mod clearly stood him in good stead for later experiences in the music business: "One guy, in London, used to carry a shotgun around on his Vespa. He did three Post Offices to my knowledge, and all before his sixteenth birthday! Being a mod prepared me in a way because it knocked away any traces of naïveté." Which was probably just as well, as Evans was about to tumble into the dubious world of Manchester nightclubs.

His first job, as booker/runner of The Jig Saw Club in Cromford Court, came by chance when the owner, David Sedge, "left for Persia" leaving his club keys with his Jewish partner. He, in turn, handed them over to this neatly dressed mod, instructing him to, "open the club for a night". The next day Evans briskly handed over £100 profits to the startled partner. "Normally I only get £50" he was told; thereafter, to his astonishment, Evans found himself in charge of one of the liveliest clubs on the R&B circuit. His first coup was to hire the Oxford-born blues enthusiast, Roger Eagle, as DJ. (Eagle would work with Evans again almost two decades later, at The International Club, after kick-starting the whole Liverpool punk scene and discovering Mick Hucknall.) Then, as now, the heart of any successful club

---

[16] One close compatriot in Evans' gang was the actor Warren Clarke, another celebrated ex-mod.

depended on the prowess of the DJ. Although The Jig Saw Club had a distinctly seedy side to it, it was to provide Evans with his first intoxicating brushes with celebrity, and the stories from his tenure there flow thick and fast. One thinks of Evans persuading Martha Reeves to venture down and perform in The Jig Saw's dark cellar, after she had initially refused. She fled after singing just five numbers when, turning to look towards the side of the stage, she saw a huge rat. (These Americans, no staying power . . .) It's not difficult to imagine Evans laying on the charm, taking The Yardbirds to dinner, or allowing Keith Moon to drive Evans' car (a Ford Zephyr) through the city centre.[17] Then again, there was the time that P. J. Proby, took hold of a gun during a performance of 'Get On Your Pony And Ride', and fired it in front of an audience which included the local Vice Squad, resulting in a near-riot.

"It's frustrating," admits Evans. "I must have taken so many future legends out for something to eat. I just wish I knew who they were. I'm sure I took Clapton for a Bolognese. I was only informed recently that Elton John was in Bluesology. I knew those guys really well. I wish I had known that earlier, I would have definitely used it."

However, to run a nightclub, in Manchester, in the mid-Sixties, was to be forever flirting with a young criminal element, for whom the mod scene provided perfect cover. These characters would be smart, sharp and ferociously ambitious, raging through the night on blues or purple hearts, doing the business by day. It's hard to deny a certain romance in the lifestyle: drifting out of the club at the end of a long night, wandering into Galleon Casino to hang out and scrounge a free breakfast, all the time making acquaintances and profoundly unholy alliances that would survive three decades. Evans: "There really was honour amongst thieves back then. I mean, people would look after each other. They would always repay favours. They would always remember − what was that phrase − there would always be 'someone waiting at the prison gates'. That was the code that I was taught and nobody even considered going against it. People, whether they were rogues or not, it wasn't in their nature to coldly betray their workmates. And that is what would eventually shock me about the Manchester music scene in the Eighties. About The Stone Roses as people. About Simply Red as people. There was no sense of honour at all. It was stone cold and calculating. I found that very shocking because of the background I came from. I knew some real dodgy people, but even they had a warmth about them. I looked at John Squire during the time of The Seahorses and I realised that I always knew that John had

---

[17] He regretted it immediately − the drummer careered the wrong way up Market Street, causing chaos.

his own plan up his sleeve. Very cold and calculating. He won't ever admit it, perhaps not even to himself, but he owes an awful lot to the other Roses, especially Reni. Musically speaking, that is."

Gareth Evans' circle of friends at the time included a great many people who would later skip Manchester for Marbella – as indeed did he for a while – sitting on their large wads, playing real life chess from afar, as it were. Evans was never a central player in the Manchester gang scene, neither was he ever a gangster, but the boundaries do tend to blur and his connections strengthened considerably as the decade wore on. "I met a lot of people, saw a lot of things without actually taking part," he admits and, although he is often prone to the embellishment, I, for one, believe him when he tells me his greatest tale of all.

"I don't know why . . . but I was actually there, on Manchester's Piccadilly Station, when the Kray Twins were (famously) escorted out of Manchester and dumped on the London-bound train. I had no idea, really, what was going on. I certainly didn't understand the significance of it but it was all explained to me later. If the Krays had got in, Manchester would never have been the same again. Think about that. The ramifications would still be in evidence. There probably wouldn't have been a Factory or a Hacienda. Everything would have been controlled. As it was, London tried to get in and failed. They were beaten back and, again, it was a kind of comradeship that helped save Manchester from that particular invasion. I don't think the police had much to do with it. I didn't partake. I didn't know what was happening. But I saw it all and the people I was with would help me through the years. Being there. Seeing that. Being around. It all served to give me a lot of respect. I was like one of the lads. People would look after me. They still do and I'm grateful."

Gareth the mod may never have been a 'face' (a top ranking mod, to whom The Who – as The High Numbers – paid tribute in their earliest single, 'I'm The Face'), but he was certainly more than a 'ticket' (less lofty 'soldier' mods). He was a scenester, moving constantly between Manchester and London. And it was in London that, with almost corny perfection, he found himself sitting in as a mod model for Vidal Sassoon at his Bond Street salon. "That was true too," he laughs. "I just fell into that Sassoon thing on my way back from finishing the surfing season at Newquay. I was staying in Swiss Cottage but it was weird in those days. You tended to land and immediately became part of a 'scene'. It was possible to just drift around in a way that couldn't be done these days. It would be too expensive, I guess.

"I suddenly found myself in the company of people like Sassoon and Mary Quant. They didn't know who I was, I'm not trying to say that I was close friends or anything but Sassoon liked me and took me on. I think he liked my chat, really . . . my cheek. He taught me just one trick. How to cut'n'blow. It took six months and I then moved back to Manchester. All I could do was cut'n'blow wave. I knew nothing about perms, or colour or anything like that but, stone me, cut'n'blow waving suddenly became the big thing. I worked for James And Peter in Manchester. Blow waving all day long. I had no qualifications or anything like that, but I was known as the best blow waver. I don't even know why I did it. I didn't earn much money but it was just great fun. I got to meet and chat with a lot of people. I realised that that was the way the wheels became oiled . . . by chatting. I never expected the hairdressing to lead to great things."

But it did. By the dawn of the Seventies, Gareth Evans had joint control over 30 hairdressing shops – named 'Gareth and Colin Crimpers' – in Bolton, Stretford, Burton-on-Trent, Dusseldorf (I'm not making this up), and two in Stockport. Glam had arrived and demand for the cut'n'blow was at its peak.[18] By this time, Evans was flying. Always an ideas man, he began to diversify his business interests. He kick-started a company called 'Salon Masterplan', which specialised in fitting out new unisex hairdressing salons. He went heavily into sports retailing, before eventually selling out and turning his attention to . . . gold bullion.

Helped by his girlfriend, Page Taylor, Gareth started a company called Gold Inc. He would regularly travel down to London on the train, to Hatton Garden, returning with a suitcase stuffed with cash. This regular and rather risky journey eventually saw Evans flirting with disaster: the Regional Crime Squad, on hearing that Evans was about to be 'hit', issued a warning through British Rail instructing Evans to, "not get off the train until you get to Piccadilly". "Yeah," he admits now, "I have had a few dodgy moments. If the Regional Crime Squad hadn't been on their toes, who knows what would have happened to me then. But I did realise that, perhaps, I was getting a little bit too close to serious action. I didn't want to be looking over my shoulder all the time. I was, and am, a single parent with a 'Downs' child – Mark – who I adore and he was becoming my priority. I decided to go back into the nightclub scene. I knew about Oceans 11 and I also knew that it was a great size for a rock venue."

Hence, in 1985, Evans and his partner Mathew Cummings bought Oceans 11 from a consortium of local 'businessmen' which included the renowned Manchester clubland figure and soul singer, Dougie James. The switch towards a hipper musical policy was cemented by the appointment of the legendary Roger Eagle. Eagle's credentials were impeccable. He arrived in Manchester from Oxford in the early Sixties and, aside from his work for

---

[18] I speak from personal experience. As a fifteen-year-old Bowie freak, my blood-red locks needed to be regularly blow-waved into the Ziggy norm. And where did I go? Gareth and Colin Crimpers, Tiviot Dale, Stockport, naturally. It was Bowie heaven.

Evans, had reigned supreme as DJ of the Twisted Wheel Club, the very heart of Manchester's fabulous R&B scene. Immersing himself in Manchester work through to the mid-Seventies, he had subsequently decamped to Liverpool where he ran Eric's Club and Eric's Records, and soon found himself overseeing the early exploits of The Teardrop Explodes, Echo And The Bunnymen, Wah Heat and Big In Japan. He befriended young DJ and singer, Mick Hucknall, and shunted Hucknall's Frantic Elevators records into a world that wasn't willing to listen. By the time he returned to Longsight, Manchester, with Hucknall's Simply Red about to explode to adult pop heaven, Roger Eagle was held in high esteem.

He was 43 and happy to be placed in charge of a club he regarded as . . . "Warm, inviting and absolutely perfect for live music. The best live venue I've ever been in, let alone worked in." And immediately, Eagle's International was successfully presenting sets by such disparate acts as Echo And The Bunnymen, Thomas Mapfumo, The Chieftains, Prefab Sprout, Louden Wainwright III and, triumphantly, the ascendant Simply Red. The broad roster of artists packing them in at the venue suggested that many felt it was time to enjoy music for its own sake, regardless of fashion or inky music weeklies. Indeed, The International was the first post-*NME* music venue. It was a living precursor to the oncoming CD age, to *Q* and *Mojo*. Manchester? A reactionary town? Perhaps not, but, in instigating The International, Evans and Eagle provided the perfect antithesis to the stark modernity of The Hacienda.

Clearly, some kind of alternative to Factory domination was building in Manchester; but it had yet to catch on. That was probably because most people were stuck in foggy studentville of the Hulme Crescents, skipping into town to catch the ragged art rock of local lads Big Flame, or getting down and political with angry young Marxist sloggers Easterhouse. The Factory bands still had the highest profile: A Certain Ratio, Kalima, Stockholm Monsters, Jazz Defektors, Happy Mondays all milling around The Boardwalk, a small, scrubbed out venue on Little Peter Street. Not so The Stone Roses who remained distinctly outside looking in. And nobody noticed their absence when, in August 1985, Brian Turner organised a free festival in Platt Fields Park, adjoining the Manchester festival site where, on a stunning golden afternoon, the cream of Manchester – Simply Red, James, Easterhouse, Marc Riley And The Creepers, Kalima and The Jazz Defektors – all performed. Nobody noticed, that is, except the band themselves.

Ian Brown: "I noticed all right. I felt that we were a million miles away from Manchester and it did hurt. I'd be lying if I told you that it didn't. I knew also that something was at last happening in the city that didn't revolve around The Smiths. That was positive. That was good. I knew we were better than any of this lot, so it was just a matter of time, really."

6

GARAGE FLOWERS

Warehouse Parties: the first sighting of rave.

"What," screamed a headline in local Manchester music glossy, *Muze Magazine*, "is a Warehouse Party?" It was a good question and one which couldn't be fully answered for a good many years. The idea behind the concept came in part from Steve Adge, who was contemplating a solution for The Stone Roses' complaints about the limited gigging circuit on which they were being forced to work. The band wanted more local gigs, better local gigs and gigs that meant bypassing the depressing bottom-rung venue circuit. They had played, for instance, at The Gallery on Little Peter Street, an uninspiring box of a venue, permanently suffering from organisational chaos, rickety PA systems manned by apathetic hippies and a general lack of atmosphere. Despite having its moments of fame – a live broadcast of *The Tube* came from here; Marillion, R.E.M. and The Alarm all famously packed the place – it was unwelcoming enough to see The Stone Roses supporting Lavolta Lakota without attracting more than a handful of their usual raucous local fan base. Sitting in the upstairs dressing room that night, Ian Brown could be heard complaining, to journalist Paula Greenwood and Steve Adge, that ". . . there's just no point in playing gigs like these. It just feels as if we are going backwards . . . I mean, we are no better than Laugh or A Conspiracy . . . or any of them others."

Adge's notion – to hire one of the thousand deserted warehouses or railway arches in the city centre and hold a private gig of his own, featuring a solid, respected DJ (and, later in the evening, The Stone Roses) – has often been championed as the true source of the rave scene which would intimidate rural communities across Britain half a decade later. There is some credence to this, especially as his first night would feature the band who would become the accepted link between rave and rock but, in truth, similar events had taken place in Manchester before. Factory Records, for instance, had held disastrous Christmas parties deep within the rat-infested Gothic piles of Oldham Street – where A Certain Ratio once played in front of a full scale brawl. There are other precedents:

Northern Soul nights had been held, in cavernous warehouse shells of Blackburn and Preston in the mid-Seventies; and Adge himself has also indicated that his idea was partly inspired by similar events in London. Whatever the genesis of the idea, Adge and his partner Mark, from Blackmail Records, contacted British Rail and hired a railway arch on Fairfield Street. Advance notice of the event, though not of the venue, came via word of mouth and countless tiny posters, peppered across the city centre. It was to be called The Flower Show and only those in the know, or in touch with Spirit Studios, would be fully aware of just what was going down. Perhaps here, in the increasing barrage of phone calls to Spirit enquiring about a secret event at an improvised site, the true seed of the rave scene was planted.

Auss Parsons, Manchester based DJ, journalist and scenester, remembers it fondly. "I didn't know what was happening. I didn't know where it was going to be. I had to sort of suss it out as I was to write a review of the gig later. But it was kind of romantic, in a way. And those who attended represented a wide cross-section of musical tastes."

The Stone Roses soundchecked in the early evening: they weren't particularly happy with the results, especially as the sound bounced around the empty semi-cylindrical shell like a pinball, reverberating back and forth to an eventual mushy effect, Brown's vocals echoing like a gang of cub scouts in a pot hole. Moreover, this kind of gig was uncharted territory, and could easily backfire. "It was worrying," Brown later admitted, "because we didn't know if anyone was really going to turn up or not."

The worries proved unfounded, however, and by midnight, amid black shadows and yellow street light glow, the unlovely, silent area of Fairfield Street was suddenly alive with the scurrying of Warehouse clubbers, all trying to find the mysterious venue by following the distant rumble of Chicago house. In theory, there was no alcohol allowed; in practice, it was prevalent. Indeed, the intrigued members of the constabulary, who could easily have simply halted proceedings, there and then, actually stood outside taking secret swigs of free (and in this case, illicit) beer. It was that kind of night. Sensibly, the police didn't see any reason to push three hundred people back out onto the streets, and the party raved on. The only problem – and it was a major problem – was the complete lack of toilet facilities. It was 1.30 pm by the time that The Stone Roses gathered on-stage, delivering a set that was still hampered by the appalling sound, but the assembled punters didn't seem too worried. Steve and Mark lost £200 on the night but seemed content nevertheless. As the party eventually fizzled to a 5 am dawn comedown, the entrepreneurial duo were already talking about their next event, which would feature the Factory talents of A Certain Ratio and The Jazz Defektors. That first gig had announced a new concept of a gig – a secret, deliciously underground gathering of like-minded music fans after a good time rather than a scrap. And The Stone Roses were in there at the start, driven even then by their concept of themselves as a special band worthy of a special kind of gig.

★   ★   ★

Martin Hannett was a Manchester legend. Unpredictable, at times apparently insane, he nevertheless staked his claim to rock'n'roll fame by producing one of the most influential bands ever to emerge from the city – Joy Division.

From his work/night-time home at Strawberry Studios, Stockport, across the road to the Wellington pub, up the road to Strawberry's sister studio, Yellow Two – this was the triangle which defined Martin Hannett's world as a producer.[19] Hannett had a style all of his own, dispensing with the tiresome duties one might normally associate with record production, like sitting behind the mixing desk and actually listening to the music – tasks which he swiftly delegated to the brilliant engineer Chris Nagle. Instead, Hannett would take long naps in the equipment room, studiously reading the *Beano*, emerging only to bark some incomprehensible command every couple of hours or so . . . or he would sit in the Wellington pub, as if lost in an impenetrable dream. More often than not at 5.50 am, he would burst into life, demanding super-human feats of musicianship from jaded, half-dead pop bands, who by now were thoroughly confused by the entire process. Mostly, it must be said, Hannett's work was wholly ineffective, allowing a session to fizzle to nothing more than a mess of bickering, an unpaid bill, a murky demo tape and a set of masters that would be locked away by studio manager Peter Tattersall. Occasionally though, Hannett would connect perfectly and produce work of sublime, inspirational genius. Without Hannett, Joy Division might never have risen from a sub-Banshees drone. In fact, The Stone Roses chose Hannett not because of his work with Joy Division, but in spite of it. They preferred the spiky attack of his more naïve, punkish liaison with his good friends, Slaughter And The Dogs; in particular their glam punk classic, 'Cranked Up Really High', all slash and bluster, all teenage screaming and dreaming.

It was August 3, 1985, before The Stone Roses finally assembled at Strawberry, undaunted by their previous experience with Hannett and happy, it would seem, to take his legacy of studio madness on board. But

[19] Sadly, both studios are now defunct. The Wellington pub is still active, although no longer graced by the sight of sullen popsters, deep in mid-recording gloom.

using Hannett's down time wasn't an ideal situation – under Tattersall's watchful eye, the sessions never broke free from their initial hurried feel. Hannett's engineer Nagle, although an essential buffer to Hannett's barbed anarchy, seems to have remained unmoved by the band's material. Whatever the obstacles, the band managed at last to get some of the songs they were performing live down on tape. The bulk were collected on the bootleg CD *Garage Flower*, released in 1996, the tracklisting of which ran as follows: 'Getting Plenty', 'Here It Comes', 'Trust A Fox', 'Tradjic Roundabout', 'All I Want', 'Heart On The Staves', 'I Wanna Be Adored', 'This Is The One', 'Fall', 'So Young', 'Tell Me', 'Haddock', 'Just A Little Bit' and 'Mission Impossible'. They capture the band just as they were about to settle into a stable, definable musical collective; indeed, though they lacked the celebrated gloss and tightness of their later work, these fourteen tracks were refreshingly spiky, a testament to a band with attitude.

The recording process wasn't straightforward: mostly the sessions drifted deep into the night, as the band attempted, often in vain, to add a final polish to the songs. Although the Roses spent three weeks with Hannett, they realised after just a couple of days that they were spreading themselves too thinly. All they had, in effect, were three fully completed songs and, inexperienced and unable to write in the studio, they spent most of their time stretching their ideas beyond their natural limit. You can hear this quite clearly on *Garage Flower*, where the guitar breaks, in particular, attempt to carry the songs onto a higher level, without quite making it. Too often, the instruments battle for prominence and cancel each other out, or distract from the flow of the melody. The true problem lay, not in the band's naïve studio technique, which could have been streamlined by Hannett had he been fully on the case, or by Nagle had he been interested, but in their clumsy approach towards songwriting. Up to that point they had been a messy, disorganised songwriting unit, a mass of ideas, all thrown in the rehearsal pot and bashed together via endless arguments. Bits were added here and there, other bits dropped, until, from the resultant chaos, some kind of tune would eventually form. But the songwriting seemed to be taking forever. Andy Couzens: "That was true. We just weren't organised. Even when we came out of that album recording, knowing that we just didn't have enough songs, and we fell into an incredibly creative bout of rehearsal . . . even then we were a mess. I would try something on bass . . . or John would, and Reni would thump about . . . and Ian would just sit there, listening to the overall racket. It was stupid but it was the only way we knew. Only later . . . much later, would Ian and John work initially together, bringing nearly completed songs into the fray."

If nothing else, the timing of the recording was excellent, and the band were soothed by the ripples of critical praise which filtered back after the release of the 'So Young' single. Perhaps not surprisingly, London A&R interest began at last to stir, starting with interest from Scott Peiring. Peiring was a record plugger linked with Rough Trade and, much to the chagrin of The Stone Roses, was also the ersatz manager of The Smiths. Thus began a lengthy and distant relationship between the band and Rough Trade; a number of times during the months that followed, it seemed likely that the link would be transformed into a deal, though the Roses themselves were not in favour of the idea. Ian Brown: "We were never comfortable with the idea of Rough Trade. We wanted something a bit bigger, a bit better. Plus there was this link with The Smiths, which we were never particularly happy about."

* * *

After the sessions were over, the band emerged from the subterranean red glow of Strawberry Studios into the comparative brightness of The Hacienda, to support flowery psychedelic indie-poppers, Playne Jayne.

It was, I recall, one of the strangest gigs of the year. Around 150 Roses fans and friends gathered on The Hacienda's dance floor; there were flashes of Paisley and grimy denim, long-haired rockers and studded belts. In the cold, angular Hacienda – a place accustomed to the sounds of New Order, latter-day elektro and embryonic Chicago House – the vaguely Sixties' feel seemed hopelessly passé, though in a few short years pudding bowl haircuts, shuffly drum beats, Hammond organs and jingly guitars would be back with a vengeance. Hacienda regulars, such as they were, were neat little kids then, linked (or so they liked to think) with the cutting-edge clubbers of New York, where smart street style and dance chic had blown away the denim residue of rock. Yes, it was all so different down the road at The International but, once inside The Hacienda, all that seemed to be in another universe. There is no doubt that in the eyes of the A&R men present that night, The Stone Roses were a band jammed firmly in 'retro'.

Funny how history records things differently. This gig has often been cited in a number of esteemed publications and books, as one of the band's defining moments. Where Ian Brown, leapt joyously into the crowd in a sumptuous swallow dive, and bounced around on a surge of adoring and sweaty ecstasy. Viewed from the dance floor, by the converted fan, this might have seemed the case, but from the back, from elitist pigs (like me) gathering at the bar, the entire evening, the invasion, the fan-like ecstasy, the retro image . . . well, it all seemed so dubiously contrived. The Roses, it was clear, would have been fine in a different setting, in a field in Hampshire perhaps, but not in our ultra-modern dance temple. No way.

As the set finished, we turned away in relief as the sounds of hip hop shattered the rock atmosphere. Up on the balcony, slumped over the mixing desk, Martin Hannett had, at least, enjoyed himself, sending the brittle edges of John's guitar work bouncing around the club like sparks from a lathe. Undaunted by the 'muffle' of the club's atrocious acoustics, Hannett decided to record the gig for some kind of posterity. (And indeed, a tape of the show duly appeared at an infamous bootlegs stall in Afflecks Palace three days later; it was still there, in August 1998, as it happens . . .)

By the time that aptly named Plain Jayne had slurred to the end of their allotted half hour of tedium, the brief flurry on the dance floor had been forgotten and The Stone Roses drifted around the club, nervously gauging the appreciation of the 'crowd', accepting the sycophantic tributes, sponging drinks and swapping gossip. It was a strange night. A night when, it seemed, The Stone Roses couldn't have pitched themselves further from the hip heart of Manchester; a fact cemented by one Factory Records Director, Alan Erasmus, who had stood stage side throughout the entire set and, rather mockingly, remarked, "We could never sign a band like that. They were OK but they'd just cut directly against the Factory image. We wouldn't even have been happy with The Smiths, even if Rob (Gretton, New Order Manager) had convinced us that they were worth signing. Because, for us, they were too rocky but this stuff . . . it would drag us back 15 years. Horribly dated. Paisley shit . . . urgh!"

Fed up with their mediocre public profile, one evening that summer two of the Roses decided to embark on a spot of self-promotion with a spray can. Manchester's citizens awoke the next day to find the legend STONE ROSES sprayed on notable landmarks from West Didsbury, along Oxford Road to Peter's Square; it screamed from the Central Library, the Cornerhouse Arts Complex and the walls of Rusholme. Prompted by their actions, the publisher of Manchester music magazine, *Muze*, Howard Shannon, telephoned the band to see if they would own up to a bout of reckless self promotion. Their denial was deafening . . . and they maintained this line of innocence throughout the afternoon when an outraged reporter from the *Manchester Evening News* also attempted to find out the truth; the paper proceeded to produce a damning feature, while vicious condemnations came from *Muze*, listings mag *City Life*, local TV magazine programme *Granada Reports* and a whole string of local radio shows. Factory Records boss and Granada TV presenter Tony Wilson noted, "This is probably the most pathetic attempt of self publicity I've ever seen and for any band to sink so low, certainly hints at desperation. I can't believe Martin chose to work with these people."

Desperation or just misguided ambition? The latter probably, at least according to Andy Couzens. "I have to say that it was Ian and Reni. They did it but it could just as easily have been me. They were astonished by the outcry, actually, and, well, we never really thought much about it beforehand. It was a bit like the old football thing. I remember we used to follow the mod band Seventeen, who later went on to become The Alarm and they had a bit of a yobbish following . . . also, wherever they went, they spray painted their name. It was seen as a kind of punky thing to do . . . again, a bit like The Clash." Exactly like The Clash, actually. Joe Strummer had proved himself rather handy with a spray can around the environs of Chalk Farm. But the amount of media indignation aroused by the Roses' actions in Manchester was phenomenal. Unwittingly perhaps, The Stone Roses had well and truly ostracised themselves.

As hinted by Couzens, the album recording session was, in effect, the catalyst that triggered the band into serious songwriting action. In Strawberry, their shortcomings had been all too blatantly exposed. They had entered the building convinced that a classic record would emerge, but that belief fizzled away as the stark reality had set in. The burst of songwriting that followed the recording was fuelled by the band's desire to recapture that pre-Strawberry glow, to deepen their well of material, to add much needed weight . . . and to learn, next time, to do it right.

And it worked: their songwriting sessions produced 'Sally Cinnamon'. A brittle beauty of a tune, the song was a definite shift towards unashamed, brash pop, and thereby ran the risk of alienating those hard core Roses fans who preferred the band when they rocked out. This new, potentially lucrative direction had started with 'Here It Comes', another delicious slab of melody born, it has been claimed, from a particularly infectious Garner bass line. And gradually, from these intense rehearsals sessions, a new, more melodic Stone Roses began to emerge. Couzens: "Yeah . . . it was like that. The change was just kind of a natural process. I mean, the songwriting was still ridiculously slow, but things had started to slot into place. It was easier somehow. Perhaps we all reached a level of proficiency that just unleashed a new level of writing. I don't know . . . but we had solved our problem. Coming out of Strawberry we felt kind of thin, empty . . . incomplete. But now we had gained confidence again. Once again we felt as if anything was possible. It was fantastic really and it felt so great to be in the middle of that period of creativity. Things were changing."

In direct contrast with the 'softening' of the songs they were writing, the band's attitude hardened. So much in fact that, with Thin Line pushing 'So Young' as hard as they could, and with Rough Trade still mumbling about releasing the album, The Stone Roses decided to break free from Jones. They had lost faith in an album which didn't seem to be representative of them anymore – the songs from their recent burst of creativity had made most of the old stuff seem horribly laboured. What a shame, perhaps, that Hannett hadn't managed to catch the band at this revitalised stage of their career.

Jones had no legal hold on the Roses, the result of a surprisingly laid-back business attitude: "I never signed the band to a contract because I felt like I was part of what they were doing. It didn't seem necessary. I thought we would go on and on." The 'all for one and one for all' attitude implicit in this comment is somewhat undermined by Andy Couzens' version of events: "Well, Howard continued for a while after we had written 'Sally Cinnamon'. In fact he brought that other guy, Tim Oliver, more and more onto the scene as part of the team . . . But we never knew what the fuck he did. We regarded them all as leeches. Good for exploiting and then . . . sod 'em. That was how we treated it. And then we decided. Howard had to go. Simple as that."

7

YOU ARE THE ONE

An ordinary day in The International. It was 5 pm; roadies were shuffling around on stage, and Sheffield elektro funk band Chakk were sitting around a table prior to their soundcheck, tucking into a feast of Indian cuisine, supplied by one of the famous restaurants lining the streets of Rusholme, a quarter of a mile away. The only note of discontent stems from the man fluttering around the band, conspicuously attending to their every need. Gareth Evans enjoyed fussing around visiting artists. It was hands-on stuff, direct contact with the music business that he loved. At the time Chakk, ably managed by Sheffield ex-*NME* journalist Amrik Rai, had become stars of the music business trade sheets, after securing an extraordinarily large record deal. Gareth Evans knew this. Three days earlier, his attention had been captured by a *Music Week* article detailing Rai's clever courting of the major labels and, prompted by this, Evans began to think seriously about band management; hence, today, poor Amrik found himself deflecting a torrent of questions. Once Gareth managed to get the bit between his teeth, little would shake him. Evans knew he had a touch of madness but, in rock management, he reasoned, such traits are championed. Roger Eagle, having been stung on numerous occasions in Liverpool, when a city's entire music scene developed away from him, leaving him languishing in a dusty club, would have none of it. "Mug's game," he commented, dismissively.

At the start of 1986, everyone in Manchester appeared to have a hand in managing fairly hopeless bands. The chances of success, even the kind of contractual success that Rai had achieved, were distressingly slim. But Evans would have none of it. He put the word around, placing adverts in local listings magazines, printing flyers: "Band wanted!" A great way to ensure that a flood of crackly old cassette tapes would arrive in the club's post box. (Mostly to be stashed away, unheard, and re-used, later, for Gareth's own demo needs.) But only one band actually wandered into that club foyer, demanding an audience with Evans. They complained noisily about their Howard Jones experiences, and made it clear that they wanted someone with a touch of style and power to take control.

Andy Couzens: "We had never met anyone like Gareth before. Ian and John immediately clicked with him. I thought he was a prat but, perhaps, a useful prat." Gareth Evans was clearly as wilfully eccentric as any rock star. He livened up their interview at one point by dropping his trousers, to illustrate a little sideline that he was currently pushing – novelty underpants. The band stared at him in disbelief. Pulling up his trousers he allowed a wad of money to drop to the floor (deliberately, they were sure). Feigning embarrassment, Evans stuffed it back into his pocket and promised the band a package full of untold pleasures: permanent free entry into The International, free alcohol and endless free rehearsal time in the club. To the young band, such inducements seemed like gold.

John Squire: "It was all so easy. It solved a lot of problems at once. People immediately thought we were mad, but we got in there and started rehearsing. Plus we were treated like 'real people' for once. It never struck us that this was a bad move."

Paula Greenwood was a *Muze* journalist who befriended, separately, both The Stone Roses and Gareth Evans; she remembers their coming together as being greeted with scepticism at the time. "When Gareth and the Roses linked together everyone was totally shocked. I doubt if a single person in Manchester thought it would be a successful partnership. People were very wary of Gareth, and The Stone Roses had been around a while without really getting anywhere. It was such an unlikely combination. I think that people just thought the Roses had become desperate and were clutching at anything. And to some extent that was true. Gareth was all over them and they seemed to like it. I saw them sign the management deal. It was just something Gareth's lawyer had cobbled together but they just signed it and wanted to get on with things."

After the contract was signed, a regular sight in Anson Road would be The Stone Roses, wandering towards The International with their instruments. They embarked on a series of intensive rehearsals, their sparse live set undergoing a gradual overhaul, matched by a considerable improvement in the band's musicianship. Slowly but surely, the set began to swell. Melodies were coming through, Squire's guitar repertoire was expanding to a level where he could compete with the exemplary Reni, Couzens and Garner thickening the sound to a real rock growl. But the band still yearned for studio experience; they needed demos and in this respect they encountered the classic problem for local bands. Studio time, even in the grubby eight-tracks of Prestwich and Stockport, is not cheap and does not instantly transform dullard bands into blasts of inspiration.

As far as the world was concerned, and certainly as far as the studio owners of Manchester were concerned, The Stone Roses were just another bunch of hopeless misfits perched in a dream state, halfway between school and trainee managerships at Dixons. Evans took the band from studio to studio where, inevitably, their sessions would break down, amid squabbles about money and the mix. It was, to say the least, a frustrating and depressing experience for all concerned.

But Evans persevered. He made another call, this time to Mick Brophy who owned a small, self-built eight-track in Bredbury, Stockport called, entertainingly enough, The Yacht Club. Brophy was bright as a button, and had sunk into the Manchester music scene in 1976, after completing his Honours Degree in History. He had spent a number of years as the singer of the very fine R&B band The Cheaters, almost reaching the charts with their powerful version of Norman Greenbaum's 'Spirit In The Sky'. More significantly, perhaps, he had a wire-perfect knowledge of recording studios and, indeed, had been ripped off by more local band managers than he could care to recall. The Yacht Club was a curious little studio, dedicated to recording a band virtually live. The idea was to record cleanly, cheaply and without undue interference from pretentious muso studio engineers. Brophy's premise was to give a band three days: one to record, one to overdub and one to mix. At the end of that, without undue hassle or expensive elongated studio time, the band would be presented with a clean demo that pretty well represented that particular stage in their development as musicians or as songwriters. Brophy provided a no bullshit approach and a non-negotiable offer: £140, full stop.

Except this time. Gareth sweet-talked Brophy so effectively that he managed to push him into agreeing to record the Roses for half this amount. The band would go into The Yacht Club for a mid-week session, something which Brophy had never agreed to before, for the reduced rate of £70, to record four songs.

For his part, though, Brophy was nervous and prepared for disaster. "I knew little about The Stone Roses, really, but I had heard the warnings. I knew that Gareth had been taking them round all kinds of studios. I was naturally suspicious I honestly think he called me because we were the last studio in the Yellow Pages, or whatever. But I was determined, from the outset, that there would be no fucking around here. They would be in the studio, record the songs and get out. I had had enough of bands who had high artistic pretensions but no money. They all expect you to work for the sheer thrill of it. They think they are superstars and little of what I had heard convinced me that the Roses would be any different. I knew they were arrogant and I was tired of working with arrogant musicians. I expected trouble. I feared the worst."

The studio, crammed into a rented house at the rear of a wood shed where coffins were made, wasn't the most welcoming or glamorous of recording facilities. The local environment boasted a row of incon-spicuous shops – inconspicuous apart from the legendary Record Finders, the best stocked little record shop in Manchester. The Roses were driven down, as always, in Evans' jeep. Wandering in and taking stock of the surroundings and seeing, first hand, the lo-fi ambience of The Yacht Club, they might have been forgiven for wondering how they had fallen so far since the heady days with Hannett in the mighty Strawberry. But this would be to underestimate Brophy's skills and, for that matter, the studio's capabilities. For it can be reasonably claimed that, in this little Bredbury backroom, The Stone Roses made their first recording of any real note. It never made it onto record – it was just a demo, after all – but it was the first time that their talent and their potential was successfully captured on tape; the first time they would be satisfied with the recording process.

Brophy was pleasantly surprised by the band's attitude. They arrived in a state of solemn determination and, unusually for an unknown quantity, they had thoroughly done their pre-studio homework, having worked out the songs, the parts they were going to play, the links and the solos. "They knew exactly what they were doing. It was just so incredibly professional, I couldn't believe it," says Brophy. "It was such a pleasure to realise that they were not going to be a bunch of clueless yobs, as expected." Reni, for one, was simply extraordinary. Playing the session one armed – he'd broken the other one and was forced to wear a sling – his expertise completely cut through any air of studio tension.

The atmosphere in that studio, as they sat down and explained to Brophy exactly what they required, seemed so exciting that Brophy secretly decided that, when the session ran out of time, as it inevitably would, he'd just carry on recording them. This was becoming fascinating. Brophy started to warm to them as individuals: Brown and Garner in particular creased him up – sitting together, planning their attack and leaning back, to leave imprints from their slicked-back greased hair on the studio window . . . grease art! (It remained there for the next two years. Brophy was going to ask them to sign it.) They played live, with the bass pumping directly into the mix, and initially ran through their selected four songs, 'The Hardest Thing' (later amended to 'The Hardest Thing In The World'), 'Here Again', 'Sally Cinnamon' and 'This Is The One'. Brophy was truly dumbstruck. "I'm not just saying this with the benefit of hindsight," he says today, "but that was the only time, in twenty years or so of recording new artists, that I have ever instantly known that I was working with a hit band. When I heard 'Sally Cinnamon', I knew, right from the very first chord, that this band would be massive. There was absolutely no doubt about it. They knew it, too. For once, here was a band with a justified arrogance."

What Brophy noticed was the effortless ease in which the whole band slipped into the songs . . . and the way the songs flowed out of them. He also recognised that, although they undoubtedly had already tasted the usual band distractions, no recreational substances did the rounds during the serious business of recording. And in 'Sally Cinnamon', thought Brophy, they had a clear-cut winner.

The hinge of that song required a sharp crunch of smashing glass, to add tension to the melodic lilt that might take the edge out of the song. Even this impressed Brophy. For, rather than adopting the yobbish norm, "Hey, we need a sound of smashing glass, let's chuck a brick through that studio window," they brought along a pane of glass, complete with a tray, a brick and a brush to neatly sweep away and traces of debris.

"They were just so fucking polite," enthuses Brophy, playing that recording in mid-1998, separating out the instruments, slicing away Squire's guitar, pulling Reni's pounding drums back into the mix. But no matter what Brophy (now settled in his new West Didsbury studio) could do, no matter how he chops and thumps the sound around, the songs – in particular 'Sally Cinnamon' and 'This Is The One' – still sound fantastic.

There was a downside to this recording session though. And it came by the name of Cressa, an old mate from the scooter days. He was the celebrated Stone Roses taste guru, vibe master and effects doctor, soon to become John Squire's on-stage guitar technician and the Roses' answer to the manic Mondays man, Bez. (Indeed, Cressa had roadied for the Mondays previous to his stint with the Roses.) Cressa was hanging heavily with the band, smoking, toking and dancing on-stage at their gigs. It was unsettling for the engineer, if not the band. This wasn't a deliberate ploy, though the band agreed that the presence of Cressa might just add that touch of tension. Well, if that was their intention, it worked. "You always get one who thinks he's a fucking record producer. And in this case he wasn't even a member of the band," Brophy seethes today, over a decade later. At one point during the session, Cressa's arm snaked in from the background, and his hand reached across the mixing desk to tweak one particular effects knob.

"And just what the fuck do you think you are achieving there?" Brophy enquired.

"Oh, I was just turning up the thing on the flanger," Cressa replied, innocently.

"Well, you can twiddle that one all day, it's not fucking plugged in," replied Brophy.

The session burned on, through the estimated time, and a bit more time too, before the band finally had their four songs demoed (although 'This Is The One' retains an unfinished feel). The band were overjoyed at finally getting what they wanted out of the recording process, and were happy to allow Gareth Evans to take the results off on his A&R rounds. Brophy's enthusiasm had done its part in lifting the band: it surfaced again one night in The International Club when Brophy, turning up to try to prize his money out of Evans, came across the band and sincerely informed them, "You lot are definitely gonna make it. You are the best I've ever heard, the very best."

Naturally they replied with a wall of blank stares.

Ironically, the very day that Brophy had ventured down to inform the band of their assured superstar status, was the day that the band itself splintered beneath that old chestnut, the first 'publishing' argument. It can be avoided only if a band leader − a Mark E. Smith perhaps − imposes some kind of despotism on the other band members from day one. If that is not to be the case, and it so very rarely is, then one sees a band that begins in a state of democratic camaraderie (and with The Stone Roses, that gang-like tightness was the very point of the band in the first place) which begins to be eroded as soon as the most powerful songwriters in the group start to dominate the band's output.

In this case the split began to develop in Ian Brown's bedroom, out of the creative surge following the disappointing Strawberry sessions. Brown and Squire, working off each other, worked their way through myriad ideas for melodies and lyrics, bouncing from one song to another, and creating, as far as they were concerned, finished items ready to deliver to the rest of the band. Of course, every rhythm section in every rock band on the planet will have suffered a similar indignation to this. When adding *that* bass line, or shifting the song's dynamics with *that* drum pattern, they believe themselves to be making significant and creative additions to the original song. Although publishing contracts do expand to cover such situations, the true problem often surfaces before any contractual develop-ments, in the writing process which results in the songs themselves. To sort out the potential rancour requires intelligent, reasoned compromise. But that state can be impossible to reach when four or five egos are battling against each other.

Such was the case with The Stone Roses. Ian and John informed the rest of the band that, as principal songwriters, their names alone would be listed under the song titles; only mechanical royalties would seep through to the other band members. Although one can understand, and even agree with their point of view, the songwriting process in a band is rarely as simple as that. Indeed, Garner was adamant that his bass-playing contributions to certain songs – 'Sally Cinnamon' and 'This Is The One' in particular – were more than merely pedestrian.

There was another factor to be considered in the argument: the enigmatic Gareth Evans. Although Andy Couzens still states that Gareth never managed to dig his way into the heart of the band, rather like Howard Jones, there is evidence that he deliberately chipped away at any sign of band weakness. Why? Evans: "Some things needed sorting out. That was my job. I had started to love that band. To really love them and they loved me in return. They did, you know . . . Ian in particular . . . loved me! And I knew that I had to work very carefully to sort the band dynamics out or they would have just collapsed." Evans perceptively noted that the power lay with the Brown and Squire partnership, and duly started to feed their joint egos at an early stage, offering them lifts here and there while sidelining the rest of the band. Bizarrely, he would buy the duo gifts – CDs, guitar strings, microphones – and would take them to one of his hairdressing shops where they would be pampered, free of charge and, out of all proportion to their actual success thus far, made to feel like rock stars. Evans' motivation in all this remains uncertain. He had little or no musical knowledge himself. How did he know that the songwriting and rehearsal contributions of Garner, Reni and Couzens were of any less significance? "I knew where the power lay but it wasn't as calculating as all that. All I was trying to do was accentuate the strengths of the band."

Whatever the motivation, to the other three, this prioritising of Brown and Squire was little short of heartbreaking. Couzens has his own theories about the situation: "A lot of it was John. Seizing power, y'know. John is a very selfish person. He always was and he still is. A lot of this split wasn't just the publishing aspects. It was more than that. It was the fact that suddenly we didn't seem to be featuring in John's dream. If that makes sense. Gareth was pathetic in so many respects. Everyone could see what he was doing. He had absolutely no subtlety whatsoever and that was what hurt the most, I think. The fact that he was treating Ian and John like little superstars in the most embarrassing and obvious way. Buying them meals and haircuts and all that. And that they actually started accepting it all and believing in it. I couldn't believe that they could go for that and not be bothered about how it was damaging the band. That's what really hurt. Not what Evans was doing but the way they meekly accepted it. That felt like a huge betrayal and for something so dumb."

Gareth Evans didn't like Couzens. Not one bit. Almost from day one he criticised him – happy to let Couzens provide the band's transport, Evans was the first to criticise if that transport broke down, as it occasionally did. And there was much more. Gareth would occasionally rage at Couzens like a man possessed, quite irrationally. A favourite approach would be to accuse Couzens of being, 'nouveau riche':

"You're posh you are . . . not one of the lads at all. You are a Poynton git . . . Nouveau riche you are, not one of us. You don't even eat the same kind of food as us."

Evans apparently saw nothing out of order with such an accusation. One has to point out that Couzens was a skinhead, not a wine bar-haunting Thatcherite. (Unlike Evans, it has to be said, who could often be seen, green-wellied and ruddy-featured, striding through the muddy lanes of Knutsford, keen to break into the insular Cheshire set.) During the weeks preceding the split over publishing, Evans intensified his attacks on Couzens, frequently going face to face with the guitarist and, from the distance of an inch or so, screaming the most absurd insults at the top of his voice. Couzens was relieved that, for a while at least, Squire and Brown also regarded these outbursts as indicative of a peculiar madness on Evans' part.

Then came an offer. In mid-scream, Evans, obviously convinced by now that Couzens' presence as The Stone Roses' rhythm guitarist was standing firmly in the way of the band's future, offered Couzens £10,000 if he would leave the band that week. Stunned rather than hurt, Couzens reported this offer to the rest of the band, all of whom fell about laughing; they joked that Couzens should accept the money and, after sharing it between them all, should leave the band and rejoin the very next day.

But the attacks continued. Not content with charging Couzens with being 'nouveau riche', Evans then came up with the notion that the hapless guitarist was (I'm not making this up) an undercover drugs operative. Couzens: "It was the most ludicrous situation of my life. In fact, it was just plain daft. So daft that I didn't take it seriously for a while. I knew Gareth didn't like me. I think it all stemmed from the fact that I wasn't impressed with his stupid money. He would do things like drop a wad of tenners in front of us. He was always doing that and we all knew it was just the bar take or something. It meant fuck all but he kept doing it. And he kept having pretend conversations on the phone with his banker . . . I just laughed at it and I think that angered him. But the weird thing was that Ian and John started to go for it after a while. They kind of liked this flashiness."

How two intelligent men like Brown and Squire fell under the shallow spell of Gareth Evans, remains one of the biggest mysteries in the story of The Stone Roses. But under his spell they were. He'd still drop wads of money in front of them; he'd receive phone calls from business associates and pretend they were from pop stars; he'd constantly push his own celebrity connections. But Gareth Evans, whatever his absurdities, always retained a certain charm. He has a knack of edging his way into people's affections. Down at The International, he'd gush and swan about, flapping around supposed VIPs, ushering them past the bouncers (over whom he had no official control), and buying them drinks at the bar. He was, and he was smart enough to know this, a walking, talking rock manager cliché. And, strangely, people seemed to love him for it: some members of New Order, for example, happy to escape the austerity of The Hacienda, warmed to Evans' overwhelming bonhomie, not to mention the free beer that came with it, and in due course invited him on sailing trips on the Solent. Amazingly, the band's gang-like tightness seemed to have emerged only a little bloodied, following the squabble over publishing. Couzens and Reni both left the band for a while, but eventually returned. That said, whether Couzens would remain or not was certainly hanging in the balance. Evans, knowing this, readied himself for a final assault.

Using his connections with Manchester scrap metal merchant Donnelly – father of the Donnelly Brothers, owners of the brilliantly streetwise Gio Goi clothing company – Evans arranged for the band to play at Dublin's legendary McGonagel's Bar (subsequently, The System). It was at McGonagel's that the embryonic U2 once demanded a £37 performance fee at a time when the standard support band payment was £25; where Phil Lynott once cleverly staged an Alternative Eurovision Song Contest; where most of the movers and shakers of Eire's remarkable rock hierarchy had spent long hours amid a swirl of feedback and heavy gossip. For up and coming bands from Manchester and Liverpool keen to flex their Irish heritage, a gig at McGonagel's was essential. The romance of a trip across the Irish Sea was undeniable.

The reality, however, proved rather more prosaic. McGonagel's was a standard, dark, rock cellar bar, where, even by day, stale tobacco clung to the corners like cobwebs, and the floor was a tacky reminder of a thousand spilled pints. The Stone Roses couldn't have known it as they walked through the door, but they were about to embark on – after Preston Clouds – the second truly legendary gig of their existence. In later years, too many Manchester Roses fans would tell of the time they found themselves entrapped in the darkened hell hole of McGonagel's, with all-out war raging all around them.

Before the gig, the band were ebullient. Nobody told them, as they ran through their soundcheck, that they had been booked to play on one of McGonagel's uncompromising Heavy Metal nights, where the crowd would be warmed up by a pre-gig DJ spinning back-to-back slabs of Motorhead, Lizzy and UFO. Where the crowd, far from being an eager, open-minded rock audience, were lured from the biker fringes of HM. The Roses were lined up to face a solid, uncompromising mass of leather and studs, grease-covered Levi's and motorbike boots, black T-shirts and denim cut-offs, sporting motorclub death's-heads. Not a crowd to be soothed by the lilting melodies of 'Sally Cinnamon'. Displaying a sense of timing that verged on the comedic, John Squire chose this gig to clothe the band in a curious array of sunny surfer bowling shirts à la The Beach Boys, which he had made himself. Hence, The Stone Roses wandered on to the stage and into an atmosphere of simmering tension, dressed more appropriately for a Malibu barbecue in the early Sixties.

They were barracked from the start, though initially the violence was purely verbal. The smouldering atmosphere was finally ignited by John Squire who, for sheer devilment, launched into an impromptu run through of 'Smoke On The Water' between songs, about halfway through the Roses' set. Although clearly an exercise in piss-taking, Squire displayed his genuine knowledge of Deep Purple by copying the live version of Ritchie Blackmore's famous riff, as found on *Made In Japan*. A genuine Purple fanatic should have been intrigued at the very least. Instead, the crowd exploded before the band's eyes, with glasses crashing onto the stage, sending shards across the backs of the band members who abruptly decided to retreat to the safety of the backstage area. Holed up in their dressing room, the band engaged in a bitter argument with the promoter – who should have been shot for orchestrating such a mismatch – while outside, chaos raged.

The next day saw the band assembling back at the docks for the eight-hour sail back to Liverpool. This arrangement, however, was of little comfort to Couzens, who had work to do in Stockport on that day. Using all his spare cash, he duly booked himself a flight back to Manchester. It was no big deal, no intended snub. It was, however, the moment that Gareth Evans had been waiting for. When all concerned were back on English soil, a meeting was called in a café in Manchester's Piccadilly. Present were Gareth Evans, the band and Andy's mate, Stephen Lee, a lawyer who had been helping the Roses out. (Evans didn't like *that* arrangement either.) Evans launched into a bitter attack on Couzens: "How come you get to swan home on a plane? It's typical. You think you're a cut above . . ." The scene was becoming ugly, with Evans barely able to control himself, and Reni and Pete Garner desperately trying to calm things down.

The argument continued back at Evans' office, where more outrageous slurs were thrown in Couzens face. Couzens soaked it up for a full half-an-hour before turning to face Brown and Squire who, throughout the outbursts, had remained ominously silent.

"Do you two agree with this?" demanded Couzens.

The pair sat silent as china dogs, all vacant stares and flushed faces.

Couzens couldn't believe his eyes.

"So that's it then?"

It was his final attempt.

"I knew then that something special had gone. Completely gone," he states. "Until that moment I really had believed that we were together in it all and that Gareth was an outsider . . . but it was ruined for me. There was no point. Even success would have been unbearable in that situation because I knew I'd lost Ian and John, and that was that." Couzens stood up and walked away, leaving behind him The Stone Roses and a chance of rock stardom. Evans must have been inwardly smiling. He'd won a difficult battle. They were his band now.

Gareth Evans offers an alternative view: "That's not quite right. I'm a very loyal person and if a band has a weak link I believe it is to the band's good that they persevere with that weak link. That becomes part of the soul of the band. I do not like this idea that a dominant member of a band continues to shed all his musicians as soon as it suits, like Simply Red or whoever. I don't like that. I believe in loyalty, in camaraderie. That's the whole point and if Andy Couzens had shown loyalty, he would have remained in the band. But you do not fly back on your own. You don't travel first class. That was always my thing. You all travel together, with the people. I think it was the old Marxist coming out in me. When Andy flew back from Dublin he broke the code, as far as I could see and I could also see this disloyalty leading to bigger problems along the road. I wasn't deliberately attempting to get him out of the band before that. But I was, perhaps, testing his loyalty."

Couzens re-emerged in purveyors of brittle pop, The High, under the management of Howard Jones. Things were going well for the band until, cruelly, they innocently fell foul of a chart rigging scam famously exposed in *The Cook Report*. He subsequently joined the band India, who failed to trouble the charts. Andy Couzens hasn't enjoyed his spell of post-Roses freedom. Although he remained in distant contact with the band, and claims not to have felt too envious as they shot to fame, it can't have been easy for him, especially as Gareth Evans' name would inevitably feature heavily in many of the music press features. It could be put down to paranoia, but, for several weeks following his departure, strange things began to happen around Couzens. He became convinced that he was being followed. A number of times, he would spin around and see a figure diving into the shadows and, more than once, convinced himself that the face in the shadows belonged to Gareth Evans.

Although the band continued rather tentatively as a four piece, Gareth Evans, at least, seemed ecstatic. A pity perhaps, that he didn't notice that Couzens' fleshy rhythm guitar had added weight and power to the band's live performances. At a Leeds Warehouse gig, perhaps not the most atmospheric of venues, the reduced band's sound was scattered too thinly across the material for them to turn any heads, and they left the stage numbed by a sense of anti-climax. As a result, they immersed themselves in weeks of intense rehearsal, a general tightening-up period peppered by endless meetings about a possible replacement for Couzens. In the end, what started as a potential disaster ended up more as a refinement of the Roses musical power, another piece in the jigsaw. The need for a replacement gradually receded as, awe-struck, Brown, Garner and Reni realised that the gap was being filled by the rapidly expanding virtuosity of John Squire.

In July of 1986, Manchester celebrated its ragged musical heritage with the Factory-run Festival Of The Tenth Summer, which centred on an all day event at Manchester's soulless G-Mex centre, featuring New Order, The Smiths, The Fall, Wayne Fontana & The Mindbenders, Pete Shelley and John Cale. The day passed by in a haze of nostalgia while, the preceding week, burgeoning hopefuls such as Happy Mondays and Easterhouse attempted to grab the attention of local and national media folk desperate to catch a glimpse of Manchester's musical future. It was a curious moment and it might be noted that Manchester in general seemed more than happy to allow the Smiths/New Order/Fall dominance to continue unhindered. Even The Chameleons, at this point the pride of North Manchester, failed to clamber onto that bill. As for The Stone Roses? Frankly, they seemed little more than a dull ache in the back of Manchester's head, a footnote in the making. It might be noted that, when Tony Wilson chaired an initial Festival Of The Tenth Summer meeting, a list of thirty local bands were initially drawn up. The list took in such luminaries as The Fleshpuppets and The Membranes (from Preston) but The Stone Roses were nowhere to be found. Profoundly unhip, then, they would later make noises to the effect that that was just the way they liked it, stubborn outsiders with no interest in 'joining the Manchester elite'. It was bullshit, of course, for The Stone Roses could not help but regard the recognised Manchester scene with envy. Of course they wanted in. They craved local acceptance, not just by a growing army of devoted fans, but by the very elite they professed to hate. Why else would they, on three separate occasions, attempt to get Factory Records to take them on board?

As if to highlight their marginal standing, they performed their first Manchester date since the departure of Couzens at Manchester's beautiful Ritz venue – unwisely choosing Monday's Goth night, supported by the aforementioned Fleshpuppets – to a half-filled hall, many of whom seemed to be personal friends of Couzens.

* * *

One notable characteristic of The Stone Roses' story is the band's utter refusal to give up, their determination to succeed which drove them on when other bands would have quit. Thus, during this period of uncertainty punctuated by unsatisfactory gigs, they booked themselves into rehearsal rooms in Denton for solid practice. (Solid, allowing for the fact that John Squire had a job at the time as a runner for the Mersey Television soap, *Brookside*.) By now the band had consciously decided to edge away from their solid rock base, in favour of developing their more melodic side. Squire's influence here was tangible: his chiming lead guitar chords, light and waspish, would be topped by tiny snatches of soloing, embellished by a graceful run of notes; and, a little way back, Ian Brown's vocals, while brittle, were developing an undeniable charm. Brown's voice had always been too delicate, truth be told, to carry a slab of ear-bleeding rock effectively.

The sound which they were evolving had its roots deep in Ian Brown's record collection. From snatches of Prince Far I, from *War On The Bullshit* by Osiris, from belligerent Arthur Lee's ironic lyrics and sweet melodies on Love's *Forever Changes* . . . all thrown in a mix already strengthened by the usual elements of Beatles, Floyd and Hendrix. And, although the emergent sound would hark back strongly to the West Coast sound of the late Sixties, nobody mentioned the most glaringly obvious influence of all, The Byrds. The fact is, Johnny Marr had already sliced into the heart of Byrds territory and, subsequently, The Stone Roses, allergic to any possibility of attracting any damning Smiths comparisons, decided to tread very lightly in that particular area. Squire, in truth, was never troubled by the Marr technique of creating and dominating one instantly obvious sound. In a reflection of his character, he preferred to sit back and punch in touches of brilliance, to lead from behind. He'd even add touches of The Jesus And Mary Chain; the Glasgow foursome's love of white noise chaos and pure pop, their willingness to namecheck The Shangri-Las alongside The Sex Pistols, made them one of the most inspirational and influential bands of the Eighties. The Roses' eclectic musical tastes enabled them to draw on a broad range of influences. Their love of Sly Stone's classic floor-filling tunes from the late Sixties and early Seventies saw them drawing together the hitherto polarised camps of rock and dance. Without knowing it, they were working on a similar ground to Bobby Gillespie's Primal Scream who, in 1987, were emerging from their strictly indie phase to embrace samples, funky drumbeats and remixing.

The Roses had lyrics and choruses by the bagful. But it wasn't until 1987, when Ian and John decided to create complete songs before entering rehearsals, that the music really began to come together. Unlike Oasis in later years, Squire and Brown refused to allow the music of any one band to dominate their own originality. Although Gareth Evans did stand in on a number of Stone Roses rehearsals, mostly at The International, it is difficult to believe that he noticed the complex changes occurring within their sound. True enough, he probably found his ears bending to a few more accessible tunes, but I doubt that he understood just what he had on his hands. Others dispute this, arguing that Evans nurtured a genuine musical passion for the band from a very early stage. Whatever the truth, no one can ever doubt his ferocious promotion of the Roses. In the game of local promotion, Gareth Evans knew no shame.

"I just worked incredibly hard for them," he says, proudly, "and so did Mathew [Cummings]. I don't think the band ever really knew just how much went on behind the scenes. We pulled a lot of stunts . . . it could be said that we went a bit far but I believed fully in this band. Remember that free music magazine, *Buzzin'* (a tabloid music freesheet from Stockport)? I did a deal with the editor, Adam Moss, that I would pay for a print run of 10,000 copies of the paper if he'd put the Roses on the front. I personally went around distributing that. It was everywhere. You couldn't go in a shop in Manchester without falling over them. Ian's face, everywhere. What a great piece of marketing. You see I knew they should just concentrate on Manchester. I saw all these bands, going off and playing in Inverness or Sweden for that matter. A complete waste of time. I believed if you ignored London completely, just concentrated on Manchester . . . and maybe Liverpool – blitzed them – the world would follow . . . and it did. I'm not ashamed of that *Buzzin'* thing. It cost a lot of money. People forget that as well. Me and Mathew were sinking a lot of time and expense, working twenty four hours a day, genuinely, for that band. No one else would have done that."

Putting The Stone Roses on at The International night after night seemed like the obvious thing to do. After all, Evans co-owned the club. He could afford to run around town, handing out tickets, twenty at a time, as many as two thousand for each gig, although The International only held 900. If just four hundred decided to attend, it would look, to the record companies he tempted up from London, like some kind of scene. And no one really noticed that the band were actually drawing smaller crowds than two years previously. What's more, as the numbers began to swell again, Gareth found himself the centre of a tiny touting industry. Local promoter Sandy Gort recalls Evans giving him a wedge of free tickets to sell down at Ashton-under-Lyme's The Witchwood venue for £5 a throw. And this was the point when Gort, one time co-manager of the notorious pseudo-lad band, The Macc Lads, had started to act as local agent for a wealth of up-and-coming Manchester comedy talent, including Steve Coogan, John Thompson and Caroline Aherne. Gort had set himself up in the office of Paula Greenwood, by this time busily instigating the Playtime Records label, boasting, amongst others, The Inspiral Carpets. As such she was receiving constant hassle from Evans who, after consulting various A&R men, had decided that a string of UK dates would do the band no harm at all. Greenwood passed Evans over to Gort, hailing her office partner as 'the best agent in Manchester'.

In double-quick time, Gort found himself invited to meet up with Evans, at midnight . . . in the queue for The Hacienda. Intrigued by the unhinged nature of the proposition, he swallowed the bait and found himself standing amid the string of post-pub clubbers snaking down Whitworth Street. After fifteen minutes, Evans arrived and whisked Gort out of the queue and into the club where, naturally, he was placed permanently on the much-abused guest list. (At this point it dawned on Gort that the only reason for arranging such a meeting, was so that Evans could demonstrate his queue-hopping authority.) Once inside, Evans chose the club's appalling burger bar as the venue for the meeting. One of the many unfortunate, indeed daft, aspects of this alcove was its close proximity to the dance floor and, indeed, the left-hand speaker which hurtled pounding beats directly into the eatery, making any attempts at conversation problematic to say the least. After several attempts on Evans' part, Gort realised that he was being asked to become the agent for The Stone Roses, and that Evans wanted him to set up twenty nationwide gigs for the band. It would be a difficult task, and one which would only be worthwhile if Gareth could guarantee paying Gort £200 for each gig. If he could agree to that, and provide some kind of upfront payment, then a deal of sorts could be struck.

Gort was also quick to offer advice. "I think you need a press officer," he told Evans, recalling his success with The Macc Lads. "Someone who can put pressure on the local press, before each gig . . . in Coventry, Newcastle, Southampton. All that stuff. It's hard work, but it would be worth it."

"A press officer?" mused Evans, his mind spinning into overdrive.

At this point, a young Hacienda lackey wandered past, emptying the ash trays, and half-heartedly flicking a cloth over the tables. Evans hailed him:

"Excuse me, son! Do you like The Stone Roses ?"

The reply was swift and affirmative.

"Right then, you can be their press officer."

Evans turned back to Gort and shrugged, leaving the boy stunned, and, no doubt, about to go and tell his boss just where he could stuff his hamburgers. Gort, however, wasn't too happy. Although Evans had said his lawyer would contact Gort's lawyer the next day, he privately decided not to lift a finger until the money had been sorted, and he had been furnished with photos and a press kit. Needless to say, after three or four weeks, with the young press officer simply going out of his mind – "I don't know what to do. I don't know who's paying me" – and with Evans, doubtless developing plans in a quite different direction, this new setup failed to get off the ground.

The different direction was, in fact, Wolverhampton and the head-quarters of the heavy metal record label, FM Revolver, the only company, at that point, who could be bothered returning Gareth's constant calls and didn't seem to mind the task of sifting the facts from his fiction. FM Revolver was a strange company who specialised in signing appalling glittery glam rock bands from, say, Dudley, giving them £500, locking them in a studio and sending the resultant aural chaos down, in album form, to the Japanese who, apparently, were willing to buy anything by people with long hair and shiny boots. As long as the band conformed to Japan's notion of rock cliché, then things would run smoothly. Cynicism aside, FM Revolver were to be admired for identifying an easy pickings market that had eluded most major record labels. The MD was Paul Birch, a flash character who operated out of a country house in the Midlands and a Mayfair hotel room. His assistant, Dave Roberts, was a former member of the glam rock new wave of British heavy metal band, Silverwing – a likeable gang who came out of Macclesfield and lightened their HM stance with hilarious Gary Glitter theatrics. Following this, Roberts spent time as freelance writer for *Sounds* magazine and *Kerrang!*, covering the resurgent early Eighties HM scene in a sharp and thoughtful way. Through his bulging *Sounds* contacts, he met Birch and, during a spell where it seemed essential for any freelance writer to become involved in the running of a record label, they decided to pool their resources. Successfully too until, that is, Roberts signed the aforementioned Macc Lads who bombed with spectacular results. (Japan, apparently, was not ready for a band who projected an image of them-selves as drinking, fighting and shagging monsters; they were a bunch of pussycats, really.)

All of which caused Gort to collapse in hysterics when his phone rang and Evans informed him, "We've signed a deal . . . with FM Revolver Records."

"No," replied Gort. "Don't do it Gareth. Not ever. It's a really, really bad move. Gareth, promise me you won't do it . . ."

The FM Revolver connection came about through Dave Roberts' attempts to get into The International to cover touring rock acts such as Dare and Bruce Dickinson. He immediately struck up a rapport with Evans ("I liked Dave, a lot . . . he was very intelligent, he knew it was a daft situation but went with the flow"), and from this came the first proper

Stone Roses record deal. If Dave Roberts could convince Paul Birch to put a single out, then Evans would allow Roberts into The International for free. As such, The Stone Roses signed for a reverse deal (a deal in which the band are the ones who provide something on signature, rather than the company) albeit a minor one. A permanent place on the guest list. And that was it. The sum total of the expected millions from 'Sally Cinnamon'.

Evans: "There was no money, there would never be any royalties and, to be honest, I never expected any. The idea was to get the band into the indie charts as quickly as possible. That was all. I read the contract. I knew all about contracts and I knew that a crap contract like that would be completely unenforceable. But FM Revolver, or Black as they were called in this instance, would help get us noticed. It was a bit cynical but we were truly desperate. It is probably best to think of it as a vinyl demo. I knew it would generate interest."

The only problem, and it was a considerable one, was that The Stone Roses had to go to Wolverhampton to meet Paul Birch, and Birch, it must be noted, did not cut the kind of dash that would impress a gang of hip, street stylish Mancs who were beginning to pull towards the burgeoning dance scene. Paul Birch looked like a Darlington electrician's idea of a rock god, with hair flowing down to his waist, leopard skin trousers and Aerosmith boots. John Squire, resplendent in his camo-chic and Soviet Union badge, couldn't prevent his chin from hitting the floor as he first caught sight of Birch.

Needless to say, it was a marriage made in hell. Birch had absolutely no idea where the Roses were attempting to go with their music. He wanted them to return to the 'So Young' feel, to return to the more traditional rock sound which they had originally created. But he did know a decent tune and he knew that 'Sally Cinnamon' was capable of making The Macc Lads seem relatively small fry. This was a real band with a genuine chance of making it, and his dwindling bank balance could certainly benefit from an act who could provide some serious indie chart action. Of course, FM Revolver couldn't hope to finance any kind of promotion. That, like many things, was firmly down to Evans, and his subsequent orchestration of scams and bluffs was little short of flawed genius.

The new phase began on the drive back from Wolverhampton. Evans, perhaps sensing the band's unease about Birch, pulled sharply onto the motorway hard shoulder, took out his boxes of 'So Young' and threw them into the roadside before proceeding to reverse his jeep over them. A dramatic act, if somewhat undermined by Evans' apparent disregard for the future cash this rarity might garner. The band looked on in admiration and disbelief as shards of vinyl splintered across the road. Ushering the band back into the jeep, he duly sped away, announcing, "that's the ghost of Howard Jones . . . back there. The new era begins now."

Meanwhile, the managerial politics back at The International were giving rise to increasingly weird situations. As previously mentioned, there was a certain small-time gangster atmosphere in Manchester clubland at the time which was, in retrospect and compared to the big time nastiness of today, rather quaint, almost innocent; that is, if you didn't find yourself on the wrong end of it. As a journalist working out of Manchester for twenty years, the author has found himself in the company of twilight characters on many occasions and, by and large, they have been nothing less than sweet and wholly accommodating. In my time I have been wined and dined, pumped with alcohol and promises of good car deals, football tickets, club VIP passes, champagne and truffles. Some of these people, it must be said, remain friends to this day. Fact is, The Stone Roses . . . and let's be truly honest here, The Happy Mondays, The Smiths, and the entire Factory operation, especially New Order and Joy Division, Buzzcocks, Slaughter And The Dogs and practically every successful Manchester band since the early Sixties, have had some kind of involvement with small time Manchester Mafioso. That's just the way it is. And anybody who ever owned a nightclub knows that you can't get away from it.

As for Evans, he always enjoyed a touch of clandestine excitement and The International Club was never short of that: its roots went back to the Sixties nightclub boom time, when local clubland notables like Jimmy Savile and his tag partner, Count Van Den Berg, helped push clubland onto a higher business plain. That influence was still there when Gareth Evans began his own particular wrestling match with the club's co-owners, in particular, the nightclub icon and local soul singer/cabaret revue MC, Dougie James, a legendary and rather personable Manchester character. He retained a part ownership of The International, allowing Evans, the enigmatic Cummings and the artistic Roger Eagle to guide things towards a younger, trendier market. But Dougie was in the background, as things began to take off; it has even been claimed, though never proven, that Dougie James' claim on the club also included a percentage claim on The Stone Roses. Whatever, as The Stone Roses began to gain a large following in Manchester, the internal politics of the International became curiouser and curiouser. Dougie James, for instance, after a dramatic falling out with the Evans/Cummings partnership, developed an obsession about the duo and started, literally, to follow them around. Genuinely hurt by the nature of their parting, James would book gigs for his Soul Train band in pubs near Mathew's house, simply to be able to fall into an anti-Cummings rant from the stage. If he saw Gareth wander into an estate agents' office, he would swiftly dive in, offering the unsolicited advice, "Don't do business with that man."

Sandy Gort: "I once accused Dougie of becoming too obsessed. So I asked him why and he said, "I want to screw them both until I see them on a pavement with a sign saying 'hungry and homeless'. And then . . ."

8

NOTES FROM THE UNDERGROUND

The doorbell rang at 10 pm. Unusual. We glimpsed through the window to see a dark figure below us, wavering in the breeze, standing in front of a Land Rover (a policeman?) casting agitated glances at his watch. He was reaching for the bell again. Shrugging, I tentatively walked down the hallway and opened the door.

Immediately, I recognised the figure silhouetted by the orange street light glow, though he seemed . . . more agitated than usual.

"Hi . . . it's Gareth!" he announced brightly, forcing me into a hand-shake, hurrying past me and up the stairs.

"Come in," I replied meekly, closing the door and following him up the stairs to the flat. By the time I'd reached the living room Gareth Evans, for it was he, had swiftly re-introduced himself to my girlfriend, and fallen into what can only be described as a rather disturbing swirl – his arms flapping up and down expressing, I guess, frustration or angst.

But this was a side of Gareth Evans I knew and quite liked. Cherubic and simmering with enthusiasm. A Gareth in full flow was an awesome sight. Like a giant clipper ship with billowing sails, like some kind of big cat pounding around in a cage, howling for freedom. Gareth Evans in the flesh was a real prospect: his Wranglers tucked into wellington boots and a work shirt peeking from the neck of a huge Aran sweater which, in turn, was bulging beneath the kind of waxy rain jackets that only insane fisher-men or people in Wilmslow ever seem to wear. His appearance reminded you of the Gareth with social aspirations, a man with one foot in the gentry set and another stuck firmly in the streets of Longsight; and, of course, fingers in everything.

"Are you desperate?" I asked, immediately regretting it as he swerved on to the defensive.

"We are not desperate," he countered. "We are The Stone Roses!"

It sounds impressive now, with the Roses' glittering legacy set firmly in the pop pantheon. But back in mid-1986, such an arrogantly proud statement was at odds with the band's achievement so far. The Stone

Roses were no different from a hundred other Manchester bands, all hustling for a mention in the national music press: The Bodines, The Waltones, Mirrors Over Kiev, Big Flame, A Witness, Desert Wolves, and Ram Ram Kino . . . Few journalists could be persuaded to write about them; few record company men could be persuaded to come and see them. A&R men would stumble off the train at Piccadilly Station and spend an evening propping up the bar at The Boardwalk, hanging out with local muso luminaries like Tony Michaelides, Mark Radcliffe, John Slater and Dave Haslam. But the Roses' name hardly ever came up.

"Everybody hates us and I don't know why! No London papers will listen to us. The *NME*, *Sounds*, *Melody Maker* . . . none of them want to write about the Roses. I ring them . . . *all the time*. (I didn't doubt this.) All the time, man. I tell you, they are good lads . . . they're in the jeep right now and . . ."

"What?" we interjected. "They're out there now? Bring them in . . . they can have some coffee . . ."

Actually we were halfway down a bottle of Rioja but I was damned if I was going to share that with a bunch of sulky toe rags . . . and they were, too, trooping into the room like three gormless cider quaffing teens. Brown, Squire and Garner slumped on the bean bags, gazing around the room, saying nothing but occasionally nodding in agreement as Evans continued his rant. Even so, you had to admit they looked like rock stars all right . . . indeed, since The Small Faces, few young bands ever looked so effortlessly cool, so dark and intense, so utterly self-assured. For some, especially in Manchester where long raincoats were only just being discarded and the long shadow of The Smiths still seemed all powerful, The Stone Roses might have seemed a little too 'rockist'. Perhaps it would have been better if they'd come from Birmingham or Liverpool, we often thought, where they tend to go over the top a bit in the image department . . .

And then, in that flat, that night, we played 'Sally Cinnamon' on the cheap turntable I had, and the lilting melody and the ringing guitar riff splintered through the room. Ian Brown noticed me looking at him as he mouthed the words, blushed a little and smiled and continued to sing, which I found rather touching. The band and manager were head bobbing and foot tapping which, in other circumstances, might have been a sign of unutterable naffness . . . but somehow it all seemed to make sense. This wasn't some daft affectation. This was a serious band, proud of the songs they were creating, convinced of their massive potential.

Despite Gareth Evans' frustration, something was at last happening for the band. Initially, he caused some mild irritation when he forced a pre-release 'Sally Cinnamon' onto the DJ's record deck at The International, where it shimmered like a jewel amid The Smiths, Chameleons, Lloyd Cole, Jesus And Mary Chain and (if Mick Hucknall was in attendance, as he often was) James Brown. Sensing a growing local fondness for the song, Gareth took the record around the nightclubs and venues of Manchester, *making* DJs play the thing. Working from his office, handily placed opposite The International on Anson Road, Gareth Evans would take his form of 'hands on' management onto a new level, rushing down to Afflecks Palace Emporium in a fit of inspiration, trundling past Dave's Records stall, weighed down with an armful of 'Sally Cinnamon's, dishing them out to anybody who looked vaguely hip. In an era when the average local band manager was little more than a pompous oik, using the band as a potential money spinning sideline, Gareth Evans was a revelation. He'd run through Piccadilly, scattering leaflets promoting the Roses like confetti. After hearing that FM Revolver had failed to get the record onto the racks at the Virgin Megastore, Evans burst into the shop and blasted the ears of every assistant in the place . . . and he sold The Stone Roses to them. One day later, a Market Street record shop had devoted an entire window to 'Sally Cinnamon', an explosion of black and white to arrest the passer-by. And did it sell? In Manchester, you bet it did. Tony Michaelides slipped it into his weekly Piccadilly Radio slot, *The Last Record Show*, and within weeks it became his most requested track.

Following Gareth's intrusion into my flat, I managed to grab a reasonable spread in the *Manchester Evening News* for the band – an example of the unique mixture of naïveté and persuasive power that was Gareth Evans at his best. For this *Manchester Evening News* piece, naturally, the features department demanded a band photograph – local photographer Steve Wright, an ex-assistant of socialite Salfordian smudger Kevin Cummins, now perhaps best known for his work with The Smiths, did the honours. Unfortunately, Ian Brown in particular took an instant dislike to Wright and sullenly refused to co-operate. Not that there was anything particularly strange about this. Sullenly refusing to co-operate with a photographer was practically *de rigeur* for rock bands at the time, especially in Manchester. Wright managed to get a few moody shots, duly dropped his film off and, one would think, that would be the end of the story. Evans, however, had other ideas. Deciding instantly, that the air of mystery about the Roses might be rather spoilt by a photograph, any photograph, adorning a local paper feature, he called me at 7.30 pm that night to say that he wanted the rather dull collage from the 'Sally Cinnamon' single to accompany the article, rather than any boring standard press shot. I knew, of course, that such an idea would fall upon totally deaf ears at the *MEN*, then staffed by white-haired senior journos who regarded any portrait that showed anything other than a cheesily grinning fizzog to be absurdly avant-garde.

"They won't have it," I told him. "They'll pull the feature rather than use that." I was mildly irritated, to be honest; I mean, who did this sub-Malcolm McLaren think he was anyway – we weren't exactly talking about the cover of *Rolling Stone*, were we?

Acting on instinct, Gareth Evans once again jumped into his jeep and, after pulling to an illegal halt on the pavement at Deansgate, stormed his way into the offices of the *Manchester Evening News*, swamped the security guards into submission with a barrage of verbals, and charmed his way around the features office. Needless to say, The Stone Roses feature came complete with the desired montage. It looked appalling, of course, with the dark tones seeping into each other to form the kind of murky, inky rectangle one might expect in some hastily Xeroxed fanzine, but it didn't matter. Evans had succeeded in asserting his power. He'd won. And if he could do that in Manchester, he reasoned, he could do it in London.

The Stone Roses image remained ill-defined. Even their Manchester following found it difficult to focus on any definite style about the band. Manchester was still firmly in the grip of Afflecks chic, of greasy Doc Marten shoes and third-hand raincoats. Whereas you could still pick out a Smiths fan at 100 yards, or a New Order devotee, The Stone Roses' followers remained less clearly defined. For the second time in their career, they adorned themselves with hints of paisley and, in tune with the gorgeous brittle pop of 'Sally Cinnamon', the band flirted with a vaguely psychedelic image. Their increasingly intense rehearsals were pushing them towards The Byrds, rather than The Stooges, more Arthur Lee and Love than Lou and The Velvets. (Interestingly, Brown claimed that Squire was the Byrds fan; "I've never owned a Byrds record," he told *Record Collector* early in 1998.) There was a striking subtlety to their sound now that seemed to clash rather obviously with the general guitar fuzz of the indie charts. This wasn't The Jesus And Mary Chain. Indeed, a few early Roses devotees, their heads still swirling with 'So Young' and other Roses punkisms, seemed less than happy with this new approach, which seemed to represent a 'softening' of their sound.

When a local Manchester paper accused Ian Brown of engineering a change in the band's sound to attract record company interest, his response was scornful. "That's just stupid people talking rubbish. You want to see us live. We haven't softened at all. We've just got a lot better. You can't help getting better. To be honest, if people expect The Stone Roses to stand still then they are following the wrong band. We'll always move on and, if record companies can't see the quality, then that's just tough. I know they are stupid, these people. But they'll just have to catch up with us. And they will, in the end, because they will have to be in on the action. And we will be massive."

Legend has it that Gareth Evans cleverly pulled The Stone Roses out of the A&R spotlight as 1987 progressed, helping the band retain and build on their already solid northern following by providing a smattering of gigs throughout the north. This isn't quite true. Indeed, Evans, by all accounts, made hundreds of phone calls to record companies during that summer, many of them, whether through desperation or inspiration, of a surreal nature. Indeed, the Evans call was attaining a cult status all of its own in the record industry. "Hi. It's Gareth. Big Deal. Happening. Don't tell anyone. Bye." He would spend hours on the phone, firing out fractured messages, working his way through his contacts book, and then starting again from the beginning.

If the band were growing, their audiences weren't. At the Take Two club in Sheffield, they again played to a predominantly rocker audience which always tended to wind up Brown, the ex-mod. His detached arrogance served only to incite a spate of beer hurling from some rocker girlfriends of the support act, resulting in some mild rucking. At Liverpool's Planet X, less than 25 people hogged the club's walls for the band; they were stunned to find themselves approached, mid-set, by a microphone-waving Ian Brown, announcing, "Hi, I'm the lead singer . . ." Not, perhaps, the type of scene one might associate with a band whose manager was openly claiming could attract 2,000 people, anywhere in the north.

Meanwhile, Gareth Evans had turned his attention to other matters. "I had started working on the band's image, John in particular. I recalled going to see Huey Lewis and The News and Booker T at (the) LA Forum in the mid-Eighties. There was this amazing story about Huey Lewis' bass player. He was told he had to stand in a circle for the entire gig. If he stepped out of that circle or was caught in a photograph without a cigarette in his mouth, he would be sacked. It wasn't quite like that with John, obviously, I didn't have such power. But I told him that, partly because he was a boring bastard anyway, he should stand dead still throughout gigs . . . and he did, for a long time after that. It was only with The Seahorses that he started to move on stage again."

On a hot August day in 1987, the band appeared at Liverpool's Sefton Park for the 'Larks In The Park', which featured a plethora of tawdry local acts. There were two causes for celebration that day. The first was Liverpool's great pop hope, The La's, whose Beatle-tinged harmonies and ringing guitars bassist John Power would eventually adapt to find commercial success with Cast. And, of course, there was The Stone Roses, sending exotic melodies winging over the grass and over nearby Toxteth.

Naturally, the crowd were of the laid-back, bottle-of-booze-and-plenty-to-smoke type, and they reacted warmly to the Roses; indeed, their reception succeeded in no small measure in helping the band to regain their on-stage confidence which, when not appearing at their International home base, had started to ebb away.

Ironic, then, that the gig marked Pete Garner's last appearance with the band. The decision to quit was entirely Garner's – indeed, he had announced it in June of that year but generously continued playing bass until a replacement could be found. The reason for his dissatisfaction remains unclear, though it was undoubtedly rooted in the previous year's argument over publishing. Needless to say, his decision stunned the other three who, having just settled as a four piece, now began to worry about their future.

Another irony was that Garner's departure came during another spell of furious songwriting activity, with Brown and Squire spending lengthy periods bashing through a wad of new song ideas. They even went to Italy together at one point, armed only with sleeping bags and a guitar, sleeping rough and generating a handful of tunes along the way. "We'd spend a lot of time on one song and, two days later, we would realise it would be 'Day Tripper'," Brown comments wryly. "I know that a lot of other bands . . . and one band in particular, would have been happy with that, but we never were. We threw so many songs away because they seemed too close to old stuff, especially The Beatles, who are the most powerful influence of all . . . but we knew what we were doing. We were seeking originality. It's not easy . . . it's not the easy route. But that was The Stone Roses."

Back in Evans' office, a further managerial twist had occurred. The Evans/Cummings double act had expanded to accommodate Lyndsey Reade, one-time manager of, among others, the Ten Records-signed funk outfit 52nd Street, and ex-wife of Factory Records boss Tony Wilson. The glamorous Reade, a lively and immensely likeable force on the Manchester scene since the punk years, was a fascinating addition to the Roses' managerial cocktail. Having been on the record company treadmill, and having played no small part in the successes of Factory Records, Reade brought with her an understanding of the mechanics of the record industry that had seemed beyond Evans' comprehension. Reade's involvement also served to throw into light the bizarre contractual situation which existed between Evans and the band, the terms of which were massively weighted in the management's favour. Evans and Cummings, rather than coming into the contract as a single item, had effectively argued their way into equal individual status. Hence, they both held the same shares as each of the four band members. As a six-way split, this meant that Evans and Cummings were signed to receive a whacking great 33% of all incoming monies, before Reade entered the equation.

Evans: "Lyndsey? I headhunted her . . . I wanted a lot of people to talk about the Roses. Her job was to talk and she was very good at that. She knew the music business and was very good to have around the place. Very sharp."

Reade, now a Feng Shui consultant, admits to being somewhat taken aback by the chaotic nature of Evans' management style and his idiosyncratic way of doing business. "I had no idea who many of the characters were who went into that office," she says now, "but it was certainly lively . . . We only had one phone in there, and Gareth would often be talking into it and suddenly say, 'Hang on, I've another call waiting', before putting his hand over it for a full five minutes . . . and then returning to it with something like, 'Sorry, that was the head of CBS on the other phone. Now, where were we?' "

The atmosphere in the office was frantic. With Cummings beavering away silently, Lyndsey Reade promoting the Roses' cause with a good deal more success than her boss, and Gareth Evans himself flying off at several tangents at once, the activity was relentless. Evans may have been one of the loosest cannons ever to try his hand at management, but to this day Lyndsy Reade defends his unorthodox style. "You shouldn't underestimate Gareth, you know. True, he knew nothing whatsoever about the music business, other than running a club, and he is certainly a rogue, but he also has an immense charm and a considerable power. A lot of people hated him, but a lot liked him, also. He's one of the strangest characters I've ever been involved with . . . and I've been married to Tony (Wilson)!

"It was crazy working with him. Utter madness much of the time. But there was also a sense that something would happen about him. He does deserve some credit. The band weren't idiots. They were very streetwise, but they sensed something in him as well."

The untimely exit of Pete Garner was a bitter blow for the Roses. For some time he hovered around, helping them out in rehearsals, and even helping to coach a possible replacement, Rob Hampson. But, after a week of practising with them and attending two photo shoots, Hampson left the line-up. The replacement had to be a natural Stone Rose. He would have to fit snugly into place, fall effortlessly in line with the band's mentality. He would have to come from . . . well, from within the pack of Roses followers, perhaps?

One of the bands most closely associated with The Stone Roses at this point – not least because of their Roses-inspired track 'Garage Full Of Flowers', released on a free flexi-disc with Manchester fanzine, *Debris* –

was Oldham's Inspiral Carpets. The band, formed around the characteristic Hammond organ of ex-T'Challa Grid manager Clint Boon, drew on the late-Sixties underground for their inspiration. Their shows featured a psychedelic light show, and far-out background projections, their music showcased Boon's kitsch organ sound and driving guitars set against a punky backbeat. Such was the authenticity of their special effects that at one particular International appearance, it was impossible to buy a drink without seeing a globule of turquoise lights slowly climb up your chest, making the punters feel like extras from a Warhol art flick. In theory, such a retro stance shouldn't have gained an airing in increasingly dance-orientated Manchester – this band were more Soft Machine than Sex Machine – but, thanks to their ability to write a good tune (the Inspirals built their success on a brace of strong singles), Inspiral Carpets had started to attract a following.

Boon's band were rather like the dark side of The Stone Roses. The two bands shared a taste for psychedelia, and the Inspirals were cultivating a north Manchester following that hugely overlapped the Roses' audience. Oddly, nobody in London seemed to like the Inspirals, either. As such, there was a definite camaraderie between the two camps. Clint was only too pleased to lend a hand when a dejected John Squire told him of the Roses' dilemma one night at The Boardwalk. The news of the vacancy for a bassist in the Roses initially worried Boon, for their own bassist, Scott Carey, had often confessed to being a die-hard Roses fan and might not take too much persuading to switch camps. He did think of Mani with whom he had worked in T'Mill, but their paths hadn't crossed for a few months, and he didn't put his name forward. So it was by a remarkable coincidence that, the very next morning, Boon chanced upon Mani's brother, Greg, in Piccadilly Gardens. Casually informing Greg of the Roses' problems, Mani's name came up, and abruptly the problem was solved. For Mani was so obviously the perfect choice.

After just one rehearsal Mani became a Stone Rose. He had three striking attributes. A warming, infectious, personality: Mani loves to live life to the full, and his buoyant enthusiasm immediately began to rub off on the other three. Secondly, he was well known to the band and therefore fitted into the Roses' clique like a snugly fitting glove. Finally, his bass playing had improved dramatically over the years – where once he would labour and plod, he was now leading the backbeat and adding real fluidity to the songs. (In 'Made Of Stone', his bass simply ripples across the song, quickening the pulse, lifting the song onto another level.) His début, at The International, in November 1987, saw The Stone Roses edge up a gear. Their set, which by now included 'Elephant Stone', 'Waterfall', 'She Bangs The Drums' and 'This Is The One' (with 'I Am The Resurrection' waiting on the sidelines), now suddenly seemed complete.

Things were changing in Manchester. Factory hopefuls Happy Mondays, although still lurking in the shadows of their label mates, New Order, were just beginning to emerge from the scuzzy sub-funk that had filled their bizarre début album, *Squirrel And G-Man Twenty Four Hour Party People Plastic Face Carnt Smile (White Out)*. That album, which had surfaced back in May, was produced by John Cale who courageously pumped Ryder's idiosyncratic vocals to the fore. Back then, they were merely loveable, rather insular and eccentric. But nine months of lunacy had seen them emerge as a far more serious outfit, merging their experience of Hacienda dance culture with a love of rock'n'roll. For the first time it seemed that Happy Mondays, with their dancer, Bez, a caricature of an E-head, might become a serious prospect.

And alongside them were the more tuneful Roses, working at the psychedelic fringe of dance culture, with John Squire bringing his love of Jackson Pollock imagery on to the stage. The guitars, the shirts and the amps, were now all splattered with multi-coloured strands of paint. Squire and Brown sported boyish fringes, and the band wore baggy tops. The image was finally coming together.

9

THE SILVERTONE AFFAIR

Roddy McKenna was a young, hedonistic, fireball of enthusiasm. An A&R man with good ears and a healthy dislike of the usual A&R cliques, he was drawn towards the mavericks in the music industry. Maybe it was his Glaswegian upbringing that made him distrust any sense of a 'scene', particularly in London. For, however much McKenna might gravitate towards the capital, he always seemed to be looking towards the north. To Scotland, Newcastle, Liverpool and, of course, Manchester. His relationship with Manchester was intense and had begun in the early Eighties when, working for DJ Peter Powell, he would spend two days each week in the city, talent scouting for the Powell-fronted Manchester BBC TV programme, *The Oxford Road Show*.

Powell, a Brummie and one time young gunslinger on the legendary Radio Luxembourg, had enjoyed his Radio One heyday as the link man of the *Evening Session*, where the familiar songs from the chart bands of the second glam age – Duran Duran, Spandau Ballet – were intercut with tracks from up-and-coming outfits such as The Associates, The Cocteau Twins and China Crisis. Powell would take a pride in championing young bands and although by today's Radio One standards, a show like his might seem on the tame side of tepid, in the days of Steve Wright, DLT and Gary Davies, he was practically a broadcasting revolutionary. Wary of the way DJs often dilute the strength of the music they feature when they move into television, Powell promised himself, and his producers, that *The Oxford Road Show* would be, amongst other things, a regular showcase opportunity for new young bands. As such, he plucked McKenna from the Glasgow scene – where he had spent his teens listening to bands such as The Skids, The Cuban Heels and the pre-Simple Minds outfit, Johnny and The Self Abusers – and employed him as a talent scout. It is to the credit of Powell and McKenna, amongst others, that *The Oxford Road Show* managed to shunt British television towards the beckoning revolution of Yoof TV. The latter, for all its failings, had at its heart the commendable desire to make a more vital music scene accessible to the viewing public. Although not remembered as fondly as *The Tube* – which was, in many respects, inferior – *The Oxford Road Show* was colourful, vibrant, honestly flawed and optimistic.

Basing himself in the pile of ostentatious tack known as the Britannia Hotel, McKenna would rush into the city centre on Thursdays and Fridays with a genuine sense of purpose, to see any and every worthwhile band he could. He was just twenty-one and, bolstered by the heady rush of ambition that suits such an age, fell readily into the lively maelstrom of the Manchester music scene. "It was madness in a way," he says today, a thick Scottish drawl curling warmly around his vowels. "I was doing lines of this, lines of that, smoking everything and drinking as much as possible . . . great days . . ."

Great days indeed: heading down to Princess Street to hang around the office of Playhard Records with Dave Haslam and Happy Mondays manager-to-be, the profoundly hedonistic Nathan McGough; flopping into Tony Michaelides' office, sneaking a few freebies. And, by night, setting off for Little Peter Street and The Boardwalk, soaking in sounds along with the alcohol, swapping gossip with burgeoning producer Johnny Jay, rapper MC Buzz B, checking out The Hacienda, where the big beat of Chicago house music had taken control.[20] And then, to sample the rock side of the city, McKenna would try The International. He couldn't have known it, but for anyone wishing to gain an understanding of the roots of British music from the mid-Eighties stretching through to the mid-Nineties blast of Britpop, he was in the right city at exactly the right time. It was during this spell that he met and befriended Lyndsey Reade. McKenna liked the intelligent Reade and their friendship continued after he had moved to London, immersing himself in the dance scene. There, he threw his enthusiasm into piecing together a pop/rap album, *The Beat, The Rhyme, The Noise And Be Aware* which included such names as Two Men And A Drum Machine and The Wee Papa Girl Rappers, with whom he scored his first chart success when they hit the top five with 'We Rule'.

Significantly, it was an immensely innovative circle of projects, with McKenna overseeing the gathering of many of the most respected DJs on the international circuit, Cold Cut, Bomb the Bass, Kevin Sanderson (from Detroit), Jeremy Healy, Teddy Riley and Manchester's Johnny Jay. Of course, they had all been in demand for remixing duties, but this time it was a little different. McKenna was using DJs as writers and producers, encouraging their artistic edges, pushing them further than they had

---

[20] Due mainly to Mike Pickering's constant forays across the Atlantic, where he would seek out new dance sounds to bring back home.

previously been, laying trust in their extensive knowledge, their impeccable ears, their link with the clubs.

He was working for Jive Records, part of Zomba. A curious organisation, Zomba was fronted by bland pop acts like Samantha Fox but also featured a mass of esoteric black artists like the great Hugh Masekela, and the influential Jive Afrika album and 12″ series, as well as an immensely successful roster of contemporary rap artists. McKenna felt comfortable with Zomba, who were based, along with their own studios, in Willesden, north-west London, well away from the Soho-based big boys of the music industry.

Shortly after joining Zomba, McKenna received an animated telephone call from Lyndsey Reade, who bombarded him with enthusiasm about the fantastic band she had just linked up with – The Stone Roses. McKenna's boss in Zomba's A&R department gave him the simple brief to 'go out and find the happening bands', in whatever area he wished. That said, and even allowing for Reade's persuasive charm, he was far from overwhelmed by her sales pitch. Indeed up until this point, McKenna hadn't really warmed to any of her artists. That said, he tried not to sound too dismissive, fell into automatic response and asked her to send him a demo, promising that he would listen to it. He meant it, too, although Reade's cassette would have to wait its turn as part of his bulging bag of 'idiot tapes'.

He would plonk this bag of tapes on the passenger seat of his car and slot them one after another into the cassette player as he spent endless hours driving to and from blacked out dives in Newcastle or Liverpool. Some time after his telephone chat with Reade, McKenna was driving home from Wales, feeling despondent after seeing yet another uninspiring act. Needless to say, their management had, by stark contrast to the band's limp performance, been wildly enthusiastic. One of the more depressing tasks of talent scouting is developing a reliable method of getting away from the clutches of local band managers who want to become your best buddy. Inevitably, they place their act's hopeless dreams in your hands, and the phone calls rush in the following week. That night, driving back along the M4 in a dejected state, Roddy McKenna was working through his mass of demos, ejecting most of them after a minute or two to look for the next contestant. Slap! In went The Stone Roses' tape, Ian Brown's voice filling his car space: "*I'd rather be no-one than someone . . .*" from 'Here It Comes'. It was the corny moment that all great pop stories contain. McKenna was hearing something *different*. He listened to the tape, rewound and listened again, and again, all the way back to London.

"It's unlikely really, that you ever come across anything worthwhile on an unsolicited demo tape," he says. "A very rare occurrence, but I couldn't get this song out of my mind. I kept it on repeat play and, well it wasn't really the song, it was something else. It was the attitude of the singer, of the lyrics that grabbed me. I don't know whether it was a kind of arrogance, and I had been listening to demo tapes for years and years, but from this one song I knew that there was something really special about this band. I knew that I had to go and see them and so, the very next day I contacted Lyndsey to see if they had any gigs coming up. She basically said, 'Yeah, they are on at The International in October and November' (1987). It was only then that she told me that there were a couple of other guys managing them as well. She wouldn't expand on that, in fact she went a bit mysterious, which seemed a bit odd but I wasn't too bothered."

So, on November 13, 1987, Roddy McKenna arrived back in Manchester to catch the band at The International. Until this point, he hadn't knowingly met Gareth Evans although their paths may well have crossed at The International once or twice. That said, he was somewhat stunned as he wandered into the Anson Road office, to be well and truly 'Gareth-ed'. With the omnipresent Mathew Cummings sitting in the corner – Madge Althrop to Evans' Dame Edna – and with Lyndsey busily shunting paperwork to and fro, Hurricane Gareth began to blow.

McKenna: "He was obviously running a property firm from within there. He was trying to impress me with his business prowess, telling me that he had been the 'Don' of the haircut world in the Sixties, and how he was buying golf courses, property, God knows what else. It was all pretty corny stuff and I'm sure that it would immediately put a lot of people off."

Not McKenna, though, who decided that beyond the beef and bluster of Evans' performance lay something worthwhile. The shallowness of the manager's approach was so nakedly glaring, that it somehow went beyond managerial cheesiness.

"I loved him from the outset," McKenna acknowledges, without a hint of irony. "I could understand why people couldn't cope with him but I thought he was a real character. The fact is that there are so many boring cunts in the music business that someone like Gareth seemed like a relief to me. He was refreshing . . . he was fun to be around."

Forming slowly in the back of McKenna's mind was another thought. It could be seen as a positive bonus for a great band to be guided by a genuine maverick manager. With a bona fide eccentric at the controls, truly great things could happen. "It's funny, looking back but, in a weird sense, Gareth did everything right in that first meeting because I felt that, even if I wasn't going to do business with him, it would be a real blast. And that was what it was all about, after all. We had a laugh that day and so many band managers put on this mega-serious attitude, as if to stress their professionalism. They tend to forget that A&R men are, by and large, just kids who want a bit of fun as much as anything else. And they are kids who, if they sign the band, would be working very closely with them. So they don't want any hints of really heavy situations. And I knew, straight away, that working with Gareth and the Roses would be fascinating. So he did his job exactly right. We chatted like old friends and then we went across the road to the gig."

Gareth, of course, had been building up to this showcase for several months. There was barely a wall in Manchester that didn't feature a hastily slapped up poster advertising the Roses' gig. And that fact alone meant that either Gareth Evans was perfectly at home conducting business with the somewhat dubious poster gangs of inner city Manchester, or he was courageous/stupid/naïve enough to ignore their territorial claims, or he simply couldn't give a damn. The last notion remains a strong possibility: Evans, as owner of The International Club, would naturally have rubbed against and worked in conjunction with a number of powerful, potentially heavy-handed 'business people'. Perhaps he knew that any bother could be effectively dealt with. In any case, by the evening of the gig, all of Manchester knew of the Roses' appearance.

★ ★ ★

It was packed. Bar to bar. The dance floor was a seething mass of sweat and denim and at the back, the illuminati gathered, aloof from the pack. For Gareth, and for Roddy McKenna for that matter, it was a great sight and no one really minded that a good third of this crowd had been handed free tickets, by Gareth, in Manchester city centre simply because they had 'looked the part'.

The excellent support band that night were Rochdale's The Monkey Run, fronted by bombastic Jim Stringer and featuring future *Times* football journalist and author Mark Hodkinson — then of *Rochdale Observer's* pop column — on bass. It was a big gig for them too and, mercifully, The Stone Roses treated them with an unusual amount of respect. "They were fabulous with us," recalls Hodkinson, "the only 'attitude' came from Gareth, really, I remember after we had played, I left my coat in the dressing room but, by this time, the Roses had gone in there to get ready. I went back for my coat but Gareth blocked the way. He stood there, very solemn and stated, 'Nobody . . . but nobody goes into The Stone Roses' dressing room when they are getting ready.' I thought this was hilarious."

Jim Stringer has warm memories of the night. "I couldn't sing. I had a really bad cold and my voice had gone. It was really worrying because I knew that a lot of important people or people we thought were important at the time were in the audience. I remember telling this to Ian Brown and, thinking about it, it would have been in his interests to have let me go on like that. But he lent me this special throat medicine that he'd been taking, and it worked a treat. I was quite impressed by that. A lot of bands wouldn't have wanted us to have been any good but he wasn't like that at all. He was very positive and he wanted us to do well."

McKenna was obviously impressed, partly by the potential displayed by The Stone Roses on stage, and also by the devotion of their following, a fact that, he noted, had all but escaped the attention of the music press. It wasn't a classic Roses set; indeed a few devotees remember it primarily for the band's apparent inebriation, but some of the songs, and especially 'Sally Cinnamon', had started to feel like local standards. There was a definite element of recognition in the reaction of the crowd – something that every A&R man naturally searches for. If a band can connect with the audience in such a way, then they stand a chance of creating a fan base. After the gig, McKenna grabbed his Grolsch and tripped across the road to Gareth's office, where the band sat around the table, bright and attentive, eager to get a positive reaction from a genuine A&R man. The chat was relaxed and enjoyable all round. Wary of sounding gushing or superficial, McKenna told them that he loved the show and he wanted them for Zomba. He also told them about Zomba, about boss Andrew Lauder and, carefully, very carefully, about the company's current roster. This was the tricky bit.

"It was ridiculous, really. There I was, talking to the band who I had decided were the best unsigned act I'd seen in ten years. I had absolutely no doubt that they would become a major rock band, and I had to explain that the company I was working for had Samantha Fox, Billy Ocean . . . As far as full artists were concerned, we were still known as a pop company really and, although I knew that my brief was to sign something harder, a happening rock band, I thought that they would just laugh at me. Strangely though, they didn't. It was funny because this was in the halcyon days of the indie dream and you would expect a band like The Stone Roses to sign for Rough Trade or Cherry Red, labels that were doing very well and I thought it would be natural for The Stone Roses to go off with one of those. But I think I conveyed a genuine passion, a self belief. I think they recognised that plus, it seemed, they liked me and that counted for a hell of a lot. I don't think The Stone Roses liked very many people at all."

There was also another possibility. Far from being put off by names like Fox and Ocean, the band may actually have been drawn by them. They had, after all, already decided that they were not going to be seen as an indie band at all. They wanted to make it on a grand scale, bigger than The Smiths or New Order. They wanted an upbeat, commercially minded label that could lift them beyond that grubby, small-minded word, indie. That idea, to grasp the full force of record industry hype and use it to full advantage, seems the only attitude worth adopting today, post-Burnage Brats, but back then the amateur aesthetic of Factory lingered heavily, especially in Manchester. One recalls Ian Brown, sitting in a downbeat promotions office in Manchester's Corn Exchange complex, attacking the notion of indie credibility with numbing gusto. "Factory made a lot of mistakes and seem to take pride in them," he argued. "We don't understand the logic in that. We want to do it right. We want as many fans as possible. It's stupid to think otherwise. You are either fucking good or you are not." Without doubt, the germ of Oasis began in this thinking. The arrogance that stuck around the Roses can be directly related to that desire to avoid the chummy smallness of indie. Which is one reason, and only one, why Rough Trade, who had started to show an interest in the band, were not as close to capturing them as they believed.

McKenna, buzzing with excitement, returned to London, worried only by the struggle he might face when attempting to convince Lauder: he knew only too well that his boss just wasn't tuned into this kind of act at all. And, despite bowing to McKenna's unbridled enthusiasm, bolstered by the knowledge that McKenna's ears had sought out commercial success for the label before, Lauder remained only partly convinced. As did Stephen Howard, drafted in from the publishing company to run the label. McKenna took Steven Howard to see the band at an infamous Dingwalls gig in Camden Lock. Although poorly attended, those who managed to prize themselves out of their bedsits were treated to an early sighting of Ian Brown's sulky monkey impression, all wide-eyed stare and bent-backed slouch. Now a celebrated stage stance, which has influenced the style of both Richard Ashcroft and Liam Gallagher, spending the entire set moodily avoiding the spotlight is not the traditional way to induce zipping noises from record company purses.

But then, it was a strange night. For one thing, it was the night that the dynamics of the Roses management team began to shift away from Reade and back to Evans. Although it had been Reade who had originally contacted McKenna, Gareth Evans had told her that Rough Trade were the front runners. Acting on this, Reade had brought Rough Trade's Geoff Travis to the gig, fully intent on kicking negotiations into action. Standing next to Reade – and, as it happened, under the watchful glare of an anxious McKenna – Travis allowed just one song to wash over him before turning to Reade with, "That's it . . . I'll sign them. Let's do it quickly." Lyndsey Reade: "I thought, 'My God, that was easy'. For years I'd been pushing bands towards record companies and, mostly, I'd been continually amazed by how incredibly difficult it was to get some kind of decision. But here was Travis, apparently fully committed. I was ecstatic and immediately told Gareth."

Gareth Evans, assuming the position as 'lead manager', told Reade to commence negotiations with Travis. "I want to do the first single with Rough Trade . . . then we'll see," he told her. Oddly, both McKenna and Evans, while agreeing that Travis was there, and that he made the offer, also state that McKenna locked the band and Evans in the dressing room after the gig, not allowing Travis, or any other vulturous A&R people near the room. But where was Reade? With Travis, of course. Confident that she was sealing the deal. "Well I thought that was it," she now admits. "It was only to be a singles deal but we were on our way. What I didn't know was that, while I was setting things up with Rough Trade, Gareth, without telling me, was also setting things up with Zomba. Although I was involved in the Zomba deal, I really think that little betrayal was the end for me. I couldn't believe what Gareth did."

Perhaps unsurprisingly, Gareth Evans has his own version of the night's events. "No . . . maybe I told Lyndsey that on the night but I knew that Rough Trade wasn't right. They just wanted to do a single, see what might happen and take it from there. We'd already done that with FM Revolver. I didn't want to do that again. I didn't see the point. We needed solid commitment and Rough Trade couldn't deliver." But that wasn't the end of the story; the situation continued to develop along even more bizarre lines. Consider this. Later, on the very day that The Stone Roses eventually signed for Zomba, Gareth Evans would attend a marketing meeting with Rough Trade, during which they discussed the strategy for the release of their next single.

And even *that* might not have been the end of the story. Evans adds a deliciously idiosyncratic post script to the tale. "Do you want the truth? . . . I expected somebody to rush in, to come in major for them brandishing a massive deal. I thought that would come out of the blue and . . . well, nobody did . . . Nobody phoned our office even though the band were picking up a lot of press. Isn't that peculiar? But maybe that was the best thing because . . . Zomba would eventually work very hard for the Roses . . . I would spend an awful lot of time in that office in London and I would see how hard they tried. Would EMI or someone have put in the same amount of work? Probably not."

The signing wasn't speedy. Following the Dingwalls gig, Roddy McKenna, Andrew Lauder and Stephen Howard all decided that they wanted to sign the band and, despite the strong interest from Rough Trade, McKenna remained convinced that the band, Gareth and Lyndsey would all be happy to go with Zomba. The business heads and legal people at the company were instructed to draft a proposal. Meanwhile, Rough Trade provided the finance for the band to go into Strawberry Studios and Revolution in Cheadle to work on an initial version of the song that would become the band's third single, 'Elephant Stone'. Evans decided to lean on his strong connections with New Order, which hinged on the fact that he was more than happy to ply the band with free beer at The International bar.[21] Evans convinced New Order bassist Peter Hook to step in and take control of the production duties for the forthcoming single.

It's conceivable that Zomba might have felt a little uneasy that Rough Trade were becoming so involved with the band they believed *they* would be signing. Not so according to McKenna: "I wasn't unduly concerned with the fact that Rough Trade had paid for this recording. That's a trick most record companies use to try to nurture a sense of loyalty between band and company. But I knew that we could always return those monies to Rough Trade, so we regarded the fact that the band were working in a studio as a positive thing."

The session wasn't without its problems. The Stone Roses had yet to settle confidently into a studio environment and Hooky, despite his greater experience of recording – he was part owner of Rochdale's Suite 16, a studio built in the shell of the legendary Cargo, early spiritual home of Joy Division – wasn't skilled in the fine art of moulding a gang of fragile egos together to positive artistic effect. That said, 'Elephant Stone' was a competent and solid recording, opening with a furious burst of wah-wah guitar from John and a storming assault on the drums by Reni. The single captured the power of the band without sacrificing the appeal of their lilting melodies – a combination that defined all the Roses' most distinctive releases. Interestingly the B-side – 'Full Five Fathom' – featured the Roses first experiments with backward taping; it was actually 'Elephant Stone' in reverse, with overdubbed vocals. The cover sleeve was the first to feature Squire's distinctive Jackson Pollock-esque paint splatters, which would become such a key part of the Roses' image over the next few years.

When, during the long summer of 1988, tapes and white labels of 'Elephant Stone' began to leak out, the general reaction in Manchester was favourable, though people were hardly knocked sideways. At the time, the band were in direct competition with some highly innovative Manchester acts – the Mondays, James, Fall, Biting Tongues, as well as the omnipresent New Order – and it is all too easy to imagine their music received as a reactionary blast rather than as a definite step forward.

It was Rough Trade's Geoff Travis who first mooted the possibility of pairing the band with producer John Leckie. As soon as Leckie's name was

[21] Ironically, despite the fact that New Order were part-owners of The Hacienda, free beer was simply not available to them in their own club.

mentioned, however, bells of enthusiasm began to ring in Roddy McKenna's head. McKenna, of course, was schooled in the Leckie-produced Scots bands, Simple Minds and The Skids. Furthermore, as Magazine, one of his all time fave acts, had also received the Leckie treatment, McKenna began to think that the notion of Leckie taking control over The Stone Roses was positively inspired. McKenna: "Leckie was a godfather figure in the studio but he wasn't the kind of producer who would swamp a young band with his ego. As a producer, he favoured a light touch. Plus he had a very interesting past. He had that heritage stuff that I knew the band would respect."

Leckie began his career at the legendary Abbey Road: he had worked with Pink Floyd – on *Atom Heart Mother* – and had assisted both George Martin and Phil Spector – probably the two greatest producers in pop history. Not bad for a start. Working on his own, Leckie's stylish hand was cast over the innovative recordings of Be Bop Deluxe, XTC and The Fall. Both Geoff Travis and Roddy McKenna were wise to the delicacy of putting The Stone Roses in a studio situation. McKenna: "I knew that he would be able to pass on his educational and musicality skills to the band in a reserved, tactful manner. It would be tricky because, maybe, the band's natural arrogance caused them to think they didn't need any teaching. But they did. I also knew that the breakdown of the band, in a musical sense, was really strange because they were one of the first bands, if not *the* first, who were mixing the dance thing with guitar rock. That was what really excited me about them but, with the wrong producer, that 'specialness', that uniqueness might well have been lost. I knew Leckie would recognise that crossover."

The musical dynamics of The Stone Roses were complex and diverse. Ian Brown and Mani were strongly drawn towards reggae and dub, preferably from Augustus Pablo to Sly and Robbie – the latter also mooted as possible producers. The two also favoured hip hop and underground house music. John Squire, by contrast, still showed the influence of his Mancunian trenchcoat rock past, preferring to lock himself in a room with a guitar and a bit of reefer than to skip through Manchester on a Friday night, checking out the small but impressive circle of club DJs. Like Squire, Reni wasn't drawn naturally towards dance music and his record collection still showed a heavy rock bias.

But there was, in McKenna's eye, still a problem. Would Leckie be able to handle this musical juxtaposition? Equally, would the band's music make reference to younger artists that Leckie hadn't heard of? With this in mind, McKenna approached Paul Schroeder, a hip young engineer with whom he had previously worked. Schroeder was aware of the modern trends in rock and dance, highly skilled and, quite possibly, the perfect link between the new world of The Stone Roses and John Leckie's stronger links with the glories of pop's past. That, thought McKenna, was the dream ticket. All he had to do now was get the names on the contract.

He was dispatched to Manchester, indeed, back to the Britannia Hotel where he met up with Gareth Evans, Lyndsey, Mathew and Gareth's lawyer. In truth, McKenna's involvement at this crucial stage involved little more than serving as a guiding messenger, running between Gareth and his lawyer and Zomba's Mark Farmer. And it was here, in the Britannia's ostentatious hotel foyer, brimming with fake oak panels, looming mirrors etched in squirls, and wild plaster friezes, that the first curious twist in The Stone Roses' epic contractual saga began.

In accordance with standard practice, Gareth was asked by Zomba to have his contract 'looked at' by a specialist music business lawyer. "We were specific about that," states McKenna, "because it was in our interests too. It's simple standard procedure: when you run a draft contract off, it contains a lot of points that are in there naturally to be negotiated out. So, in the process of presenting a contract, you always recommend that it is looked at by a competent music lawyer because you need the contract to be valid. Now Gareth was either incredibly stupid or incredibly smart. I have no idea which, but his lawyer was a property lawyer with no music experience. So the contract that went through was heavy with points that shouldn't have been in. I just found it rather odd that Lyndsey didn't say anything. She had knowledge of the negotiation of record deals. She was Gareth's 'in' with the music business. She must have advised him."

Lyndsey Reade: "Again I must stress that Gareth Evans can be a remarkably forceful personality. I did a lot of talking with Gareth, naturally, around that time and, I'm afraid, those people who say he just blundered into that deal, knowing nothing of the music business and not knowing what he was doing, are wrong. He knew he didn't know much about the music business, but he did know all about contracts. He also knew, definitely, that it might well eventually twist in his favour if he didn't use a music business lawyer . . . He was looking at a broader picture, even then I believe he had an eye on the future. He was looking beyond Zomba in much the same way that he had been looking beyond FM Revolver. I remember being quite amazed by how clever he was at that point. I'll say it again, he is a rogue, everyone knows that, he can be a ridiculously loose cannon. But don't underestimate Gareth Evans. That is a mistake a lot of people made."

And what of the loose cannon himself? "I want to put to bed the myth that I purposely did not use a music lawyer," says Evans. After a lengthy pause, he continued, " I have a lot of vision and a far-reaching mind. I understand how important press is. I knew the contract that Zomba were offering us was a 'restraint of trade'. I knew that . . . they would have to give us another one or we would get out of that one. I knew we had to sign that contract because we were committed . . . I had read a lot. I knew all standard music business contracts. Zomba didn't know what was going on. I knew we could get out of that contract, as proved. And all that press . . . that press around the contractual situation brought us a lot of notoriety. That was always in the vision. That's what it was all about.

"Did I deliberately go to a bad lawyer? No. It just happened. Well, not a bad lawyer. What's the definition of a bad lawyer? Maybe if we had had a top music lawyer then, if we had gone to Harbottle & Lewis or Russells then there would have been a lot of messing about and we couldn't have got on with it, with the album etc. And we had to get on with it. It was timed to happen at that exact point. If we were to spend a year arguing over contracts, and that is what would have happened, we might never have happened . . .

"I knew that contract was no good. That's why I let them sign it. I told that to the band. When we signed that contract I shook hands with Roddy McKenna and Steve Howard and said to them, 'Once we get in the charts will you give us a new contract?' And they said, 'Yes'. That's what our case, in court, was all about. The fact that they said they would give us a new contract and that that contract was a restraint of trade."

The one stumbling block over the contract was that the Roses contingent wanted an advance which, although minuscule in the general scheme of things, was more than the maximum amount detailed by Zomba's A&R department. After more haggling McKenna advised Mark to agree to an advance of £27,500 to close the deal . . . which he did.

The points that had been agreed in the Britannia Hotel were the standard 'Heads Of Agreement' points. Advances, royalty rates, time span, options. What would happen next is that the contract would, following the basic agreement, swell to include all the minutiae, the hugely important marketing obligations. Things that would seem beyond the knowledge of the average musician but, to a manager or a record company man, schooled in breaking an artist territory by territory, absolutely essential. All would be added with the expectation that Gareth's lawyer would slice away any points he and Gareth were unhappy about, until both band and label shared reasonable ground. This was perfectly standard business practice; legal barter. But Gareth's lawyer, not being privy to music business contractual complexities, couldn't possibly have known this. Nothing was argued away at all. No barter. The contract was signed and returned.

Thus the actual contract that Zomba were getting back was still chock full of points that should have been deleted after the first draft. As it stood, the contract hadn't changed at all and the conditions were immensely favourable to the company. That clinched the deal, and made Zomba willing to cough up the extra money for the Roses' advance.

Steven Howells still wasn't keen. It was more than he'd originally anticipated the company spending. However, Clive Calder stepped in and announced, "We are paying more but we have a favourable contract. Roddy is very, very keen. If Roddy is so convinced, and as we have such a good deal, we should sign the band."

"In effect," states McKenna, "my boss was overstepped by Clive. Without his help, the deal wouldn't have been done. It would have died there and then."

At the point of signing, the label which became Silvertone didn't actually exist. Roddy McKenna was A&R Manager for the Zomba subsidiary, Jive Records. His immediate boss was Stephen Howells who, though not particularly interested in The Stone Roses, remained loyally supportive of McKenna, trusting the Glaswegian's ears. It was McKenna who originally came up with the idea of instigating a new, guitar-based label, initially to float The Stone Roses. In tandem with this, there had been moves to bring the distinguished A&R man Andrew Lauder on board to form a new label. Although often credited as the man who signed The Stone Roses, Lauder actually came to the company after the band had put pen to paper. Indeed, it was McKenna who pushed for the Roses to move under Silvertone's wing. Hence, in a series of snappy manoeuvres, the Lauder-fronted label, Silvertone, was born, with The Stone Roses the only act on its roster. Lauder was happy enough, he liked the band, both for their artistic potential and their maverick stance, but nobody could say that he was ecstatic or, indeed, that he could foresee the fabulous success that Silvertone and The Stone Roses would soon embrace.

Lauder is a rare breed. An A&R man of distinction, of elegance even, and his successes, which stretch over two decades, are testament to his eye for quality, if not longevity. He began, quite fittingly, at the edges of the Sixties' underground scene, promoting the profoundly idiosyncratic talents of The Bonzo Dog Doo Dah Band and Idle Race for Liberty Records and, after skipping up the fast track to label manager, still deserves great credit for signing the raw and mighty Credence Clearwater Revival (for a year or two in the early Seventies, amongst the biggest bands in the world). Lauder then opted to bolster the label's credibility by signing three essential underground acts, Hawkwind, Tony McPhee's Groundhogs and Welsh avant-garde band, Man. An eclectic and exciting roster, to say the least. He helped transform one of the Seventies' pivotal acts, Dr Feelgood, from impassioned pub rockers to a mighty live *tour de force* with a number one album. Most importantly for Manchester, he was the man blessed with the vision to see that Buzzcocks had a quality that could be enhanced by the legendary wavers in Pete Shelley's voice, rather than undermined by them. From there he headed the mighty Radar Label, forever, it seemed at the time, balanced on the eccentric fringe of the mainstream, from Elvis Costello to The Pop Group. McKenna was fortunate to have a boss blessed with such esoteric vision although, strangely, one wonders if his uncharacteristic reluctance to back The Stone Roses to the hilt was because the band were slightly too conventional for him.

As for the marriage between band and label, it was a relatively smooth start. "We were all happy bunnies . . . cool as fuck," claims McKenna bluntly. "Things settled down nicely and relations between band and label, although distant, were perfect." Furthermore, the band's reticence over the 'Elephant Stone' recordings was tempered by Leckie's deft remix, which produced a sound of greater clarity, more in line with the direction hinted by the striking 'Sally Cinnamon'.

Meanwhile, in Manchester, Gareth Evans was going into overdrive. Sharp, surreal phone calls punched into the lives of most of Manchester's music media, Gareth's disembodied voice containing all the detached affectation of a Brit Awards acceptance speech:

"Hi. Gareth. Roses . . . on the way, man. Bye." Click.

"Hi . . . be down at Cornerhouse. 2.30 pm. Big deal, man. Bye."

"It's Gareth. Gareth. Today's the day. Onward. Bye."

Less than a mile from The International, nestling squarely on the edge of Plymouth Grove, sat another Gareth Evans-owned club, the inspiringly named International Two. Despite sharing a similar history – both underwent the transformation from infamous mid-Sixties discos to Irish-dominated show bars – and despite crumbling to identical levels of dilapidation,[22] the general ambience of the two clubs was always strikingly different. International (One), with its slim frontage, squeezed into an ornate row of shops, always welcomed the casual gig goer and, once inside, seemed to be perfectly proportioned. A bar to the left beckoned those who preferred to stand apart from the crowd. It was here that music scene 'notables' would huddle in guarded camaraderie, posing, imbibing, harassing Gareth and, no doubt, chatting about ancient Ray Charles recordings with resident musicologist Roger Eagle, forever slumped by the bar, nibbling Lancashire cheese, resplendent in his distinctive Hawaiian shirt. On any given night, one might find Mick Hucknall, New Order, James, occasional Smiths and a trickle of milling wannabees. On good nights – R.E.M., Waterboys, Bunnymen, Art Blakey, Bangles, Stone Roses, Chameleons – the crowd would thicken, the atmosphere

---

[22] Gregory Isaacs once remarked that International Two reminded him of Trenchtown, Jamaica.

intensify as you moved stagewards. For some reason, International One, despite being placed slap bang in the centre of unstable Longsight, always felt comfortable. But it simply wasn't large enough for the bigger acts who emerged onto the circuit in the mid-Eighties. Gareth, allergic to the sight of punters being turned away, would feed the bigger acts into the larger International Two.

International Two was a fat box, dark and foreboding from the outside, cold, cavernous and full of tension on the inside. Whatever it was that made International One so curiously perfect, was conspicuously lacking here. Not that it didn't house some mighty gigs – it did, and it could be said that they even benefited from the added tension. But, no matter how many luminaries gathered by the bar, it never felt like the heart of a scene. It never felt comfortable. This stark contrast between the two clubs was glaringly highlighted by The Stone Roses, whose jam-packed gigs at International One had simmered with a sweaty backslapping bonhomie that might seem more appropriate to a late Eighties rave. The same crowd, swelled a little and stuffed into International Two for The Stone Roses' landmark gig of 1988, an 'Anti-Clause 28' bash organised by DJ Dave Haslam. The performance itself was an oddity, with the band in blistering form behind a sullen, Lydon-esque Brown, whose dispassionate glaring and shrugs of mock boredom served only to heighten the tension, a tension which, during 'I Wanna Be Adored', cracked as fighting spilled across the front of the arena. Despite all this, Brown retains fond memories of the night: "It was the night I realised how powerful we could get," he remembers, rather paradoxically. "I once said that it was the perfect Roses gig. Well, that wasn't true. We played much better later on but I loved the split in the audience!"

John Leckie was absolutely transfixed by the Roses' performance that night. "I'd seen then in rehearsals too, but that was the killer gig, really. I thought they were fantastic and I just couldn't wait to get them in the studio. It was just the right time with the right band. I never doubted that it would be special."

One L. Gallagher, formerly of Burnage, was in the audience too, and it's clear from his memories of the night that the birth of Oasis owed much to the impact that The Stone Roses made that night. "That was my favourite gig of all time . . . killed me dead, changed me fuckin' life. If I hadn't have gone that night . . . and our kid went too, I'd probably still be sitting in some pub in Levenshulme." Liam was famously affected by the sight of the swaggering Brown, stalking the stage with the arrogance of a man safe in the knowledge that he was fronting a band who had signed at their peak, often turning his back, shunning the ecstatic crowd. The sight clearly influenced Gallagher's own surly stage presence.

Ian Brown himself fondly remembers his band's performance that night as one of their best. "It . . . was amazing because we were on top of our game," he recalled. "We were well into the album and we had no doubts that it would be an all-time classic. And that confidence spilled over that night. It was a strange gig in some ways, because the crowd was split in two. There were our fans. Our 'real' fans, who were going mental and then there were the older ones, the ones who had gone to see James, who were on after us. They just stood still, which annoyed me. Nothing against James . . . good stuff, but they . . . represented the other side of Manchester. The Didsbury, Chorlton, veggie-eating side. I've nothing against that, either, but it wasn't us. They didn't know what had hit 'em, that night. I felt really proud."

Inevitably, Gareth Evans made his own idiosyncratic contribution to the night. "We did a number on James at that gig. They have probably never forgiven us for it and I wouldn't blame them, but we had no choice. James were bigger than the Roses at that point. So we pulled a stroke. Well, several strokes actually. First of all I postered all of Manchester and put Stone Roses in huge letters with James really small. They got really annoyed about that. Martine, their manager, was furious. Quite rightly, as we were really the support. So they insisted on going on last, which was fine by me. Sometimes it's better to go on first . . .

"We were supposed to go on at 8 pm with James at about 10.30 pm but there was no way I was having that. First of all I slowed down the soundcheck. It took hours. Then, in the evening I kept the band away from the club and sent a message saying that the band had broken down. By 9.30 pm, the Roses still hadn't arrived. Tim Booth was running around, absolutely furious . . . the Roses finally arrived at 10.30 pm and they played until 11.45 pm. The thing is, and we knew this only too well, that an awful lot of the kids at that gig had to get the last bus home. And, following the Roses, they left. By the time James finally made the stage, it must have been around midnight, half the audience had gone home. The Stone Roses had completely stolen the scene. I don't make any apologies for this. We were desperate to make a big impact that night and everyone says that it was one of the classic Roses gigs."

It was also the night that Roddy McKenna took Andrew Lauder to see the band. Significantly, Lauder was impressed despite or because of the tension. Discussions between the two during the train journey back to London the next day couldn't have been more positive. Lauder stated that he was quite happy to take the band on board but, even at that juncture, seemed to believe that the contract, which had been signed, would at some stage need to be improved in the band's favour. There was an uneasy feeling between McKenna, Mark Farmer and Lauder that, although the band had been signed, the contract was weighted too unfairly towards the label. The company agreed amongst themselves that there would be some kind of re-negotiation. McKenna: "I gave my word to the band, to Gareth, that there would be an improvement of the deal. Back in London, Andrew and I agreed that we had to start looking at the mechanics of this improvement. It was always on the agenda. Right from day one."

However, events now proceeded to take rather a strange turn. Consider the feelings of McKenna, as he stood in a London club, awaiting the appearance of The Stone Roses on stage. Through the nightclub murk, through the bobbing heads of the crowd, he caught sight of Gareth Evans, excitedly chatting to someone who, from the rear, was unrecognisable. As McKenna approached them, a slight chill ran through him. A chill that turned to mild anger as he realised that Gareth was chatting with Muff Winwood, infamous head of A&R at CBS. And, looking round, he noticed there were more senior people, milling around, presumably hoping to pick up the scraps from what they had heard was a dodgy contract. It didn't take long for McKenna to form the impression that Silvertone was being touted as a comparatively small label and that, should things turn bad, 'something' could probably be worked out with someone else.

McKenna: "I challenged Gareth on one occasion. I remember saying, 'What are you doing? We have a binding agreement.' He made a few conciliatory noises but I started feeling a bit uncomfortable. Looking back, I would love to believe that Gareth knew exactly what he was doing. That he knew that he was installing a little insecurity into Silvertone and that it was all part of some great masterplan that would work to his advantage in the future. I would love to believe that . . . but I'm not sure. I'm not even sure if Gareth is sure. Again it was a case of him doing something that worked superbly . . . and it did. It certainly put Silvertone on their toes, made us respect the band a bit."

Clearly, Gareth wasn't 'sure' at all. Why else, for instance, would he continually check his actions with Roddy? It was perhaps a way of refuelling his own confidence. Always a maverick, he had an instinctive, unshakeable belief that his unconventional methods would succeed in the music business. On the other hand, there was always a certain vulnerability to Gareth, as if he was always afraid of going that one stage too far. Endlessly, he would cross refer with McKenna.

"Roddy . . . am I doing the right thing here?"

And then, on two separate occasions:

"Roddy. I haven't got a clue what I'm doing here. I just don't know what I am doing. Am I being really stupid? Will you come and co-manage the Roses?" As McKenna confirmed this unlikely attack of faltering self-confidence to the author, his face broke into a fond smile. Clearly he preferred working with Evans to the usual battle with the archetypal sharp, smart rock band manager. The offer was made, it seems, in earnest, although the band remained wholly unaware of such a possibility.

While acknowledging the scepticism with which many regarded Gareth Evans, John Squire defends the Roses' ex-manager. "A lot of journalists, *NME* people and that, would ask us why we persisted with Gareth and the answer was very simple. We were musicians. We simply wanted to get on with it. We weren't interested in the business side and we weren't interested in business people. So Gareth would just take care of all that and report back to us. We knew what he was like . . . of course we did. But we had a good time with him. He wasn't like a record company man."

In February 1989 the band released their fourth single, 'Made Of Stone', a bona fide Roses classic. The intro was classic Squire – a chiming cascade of notes, setting a reflective, melancholy atmosphere, the flip-side to the 'kiss me where the sun don't shine' arrogance which so characterised their first album. The lyrics had been inspired by a jaunt to Europe that Ian Brown had embarked upon after he finished school, and were filled with an evocative longing: 'Sometimes I fantasise/When the streets are cold and lonely and the cars they burn below me/Don't these times fill your eyes?/ . . . Are you all alone?/Are you made of stone?' 'Going Down' was the B-side, joined on the 12″ version by another experiment in backwards taping, 'Guernica'. 'I Wanna Be Adored', another Roses classic, was originally mooted for the B-side, but was held back as a possible future single in its own right.

The next move was to record their début album. The Roses decamped to London, to Zomba's Battery Studios, which were housed with the parent company's elegant little North London complex; Silvertone were situated, literally, in the front room of an adjacent terrace house. The band were based in a rented house in Kensal Rise for the duration of the recording, the vibe remained firmly upbeat.

Leckie, now a firm believer in the band, held them in high esteem as musicians. "We went in and did four songs immediately. 'I Wanna Be Adored', 'Made Of Stone', 'She Bangs The Drums' and 'Waterfall' . . . pretty amazing, really. I was hugely impressed with the band. All four of them were special. You had a great drummer, a great guitarist who was pulling up all sorts of sounds, Mani was a brilliant bass player and supporter of the whole thing. The chemistry was just right with all four of them. That's what I got off on, really. There was no one in control. It wasn't like The Fall, that's for sure. It was just four, equal guys who had a great feeling of positivity about them." Much to Leckie's surprise, the Roses' commitment to their music extended to some very anti-rock'n'roll behaviour:

"They seemed to think that they were going to make the best record ever. I'd never been with a band who had so much confidence before. They didn't drink, either, which was unusual. I mean I drank more than any of them. They just had a bit of wine with a meal and Ian didn't touch beer at all which was a revelation really."

In short, it was fun. Effortless fun. Five years of stockpiled ideas flowed across the mixing desk with John Squire plucking guitar tricks from his memory. It was as if every second of their struggle had been building for the three sessions that it would take to make the album. The enthusiasm was unstoppable: they recorded through the night, jumping into a taxi at 7 am, to rush back to sleep during the day in Kensal Rise. Each band member was allotted £10 per day for food which, although rather stingy by Nineties' standards, was enough to give them a feeling of security. A second session was recorded at Conk studios, the third at Rockfield, in Wales, where they had their first taste of the rock lifestyle: an in-house cook, the proverbial bag of weed, occasional flashes of speed . . . and recording, recording, recording . . . through the night . . . so sexy, so utterly perfect.

Leckie: "It did seem perfect, that album. I mean we had a few traumas, of course, but there was always this fantastic underlying sense of self-belief. I just think the band knew that they were making a classic album. I really don't know how they could gauge such a thing. They'd never really done it before and, for a while, I thought I must be just getting carried away, y'know, losing my objectivity a bit. But it dawned on me, during those sessions, that this was something truly special. Strange tricks kept coming out of the recordings . . ."

Strange tricks indeed. Listening to a tape of the Simon & Garfunkel-ish 'Waterfall' on a Portastudio, the band reverted to a by now familiar piece of experimentation, played it backwards and – hey presto! – wound up with a rippling, swirling piece of pure psychedelia. This track became 'Don't Stop', the album's pivotal track, literally. Listening to this swirl, on the Portastudio, the band were able to pick out words spinning from the chaos. They returned to the studio and instructed a surprised Leckie to turn the tape over before adding vocals and a forwards drum. "That," Ian Brown later confided to *Record Collector*, "was my favourite thing on that first LP. There's twenty seconds at the end that's killer. The little rhythm that comes in."

The album, like their live performances, opened with 'I Wanna Be Adored', an ominous, throbbing bassline from Mani winding out of the darkness, lit up by golden notes dripping from Squire's guitar. Towards the end of the song, the lyrics changed, gaining intensity: "I wanna . . . I wanna . . . I *gotta* be adored." Brown whispered the words for the most part – the approach that always served his voice best; his vocals were sexy and arrogant, insinuating their way into the listener's consciousness. It was the Roses' clearest statement of intent to date – nothing less than adoration would do for four men capable of creating something so special.

'Waterfall' was another highlight, distinguished by John Squire's tasteful, spare guitar playing. Squire's ability to pick out riffs that became instant classics contributed greatly to the Roses' début, and the riff that runs throughout this track is a case in point. Squire and Reni work well together here, the latter providing a soft, shuffly beat which underpins the track, allowing the guitar to breathe and develop, from the chiming riff to the more funky, wah-wah work out in the lengthy instrumental section which closes the song. Towards the end, crashing cymbals merge with a guitar line that mimics a police car siren. Brown's vocals are gorgeous – softly delivered, wistful, they are a bright-eyed declaration of wonder: 'She'll carry on through it all/She's a waterfall.' The band played the track on *The Other Side Of Midnight,* hosted by Tony Wilson, their first TV appearance. (Photos from the filming were used on the rear of the album and the inner sleeve.) Cheekily, the track is followed by 'Don't Stop', 'Waterfall' in reverse.

One of the most remarkable things about the album was the variety on offer: dance, rock, psychedelia and even folk music (the 'Scarborough Fair' steal, 'Elizabeth My Dear'). Whatever the form, the Roses maintained their feel for a memorable tune. 'She Bangs The Drums', which gave them their first top forty hit, was a slice of pure pop; the song was driven along by Reni's powerhouse drumming, his backing vocals chiming perfectly with Ian Brown's lead; Squire's solo was delicious, a collage of spiky stabbed chords and sinuous runs.

Best of all, though, was the last track. 'I Am The Resurrection' started with the pounding beat of a Motown song, over which Brown delivered some of his most arrogant, sneering lyrics. The lines were drawn out, a coruscating put-down: 'Your face, it has no place/No room for you inside my house, I need to be alone/Don't waste your words, I don't need anything from you/I don't care where you've been or what you plan to do.' In places, Brown's delivery was almost Dylan-esque; there were shades of 'Positively 4th Street' in 'Your tongue is far too long/I don't like the way it sucks and slurps upon my every word.' The lyrics are coolly narcissistic, a cocky statement of independence and superiority that builds through the song until Brown delivers the pay-off line in the chorus, that claim that bordered on blasphemy and that defined the Roses' attitude once and for all: 'I am the resurrection and I am the light', Jesus' words from *The Bible.*

The shock of those lines are barely out, when the song abruptly winds down at around 3.39, dropping just to Mani's loping bassline which introduces a new, funky feel to the track, abetted by some snatches of backwards cymbals. The rest of the track, the best part of five minutes, is pure Roses perfection: Mani and Reni lay down a dizzyingly dance-friendly rhythm section, allowing John Squire to show why he has come to be regarded as one of the best guitarists of his generation. Up until now, Squire had kept deliberately in the background, a few snatched flourishes here and there serving to flavour the track, but nothing more. He opens up in the instrumental jam with some spiky bursts – two guitars, one fuzzy, one pin-bright, working together to provide something as gloriously funky as the groove that Reni and Mani have created. There are little runs of chugging distorted guitar and power chords, rhythms that play off Reni's work, and neat cascades of notes to grace the thundering mass that is being cooked up. Then, abruptly, it all stops: a false coda. Silence reigns. Just when you think it's all over . . . Squire and Reni return for a cheeky little riff, and the whole thing kicks off again, this time to die out in a simple arpeggio of notes plucked on an acoustic guitar. And then the rest of the band come in, Reni picking up the momentum, driving along the spine-tingling rushes of music which gradually escalate, faster and faster, until the song finally fades away, Squire's arpeggio still ringing in the distance, over what sounds like the beginning of yet another jam. Pure magic – if one piece of evidence were ever needed to show a future generation just why The Stone Roses were so special, 'I Am The Resurrection' would do the job fine.

Following the album's completion, Roddy McKenna was given what turned out to be a hugely ironic assignment. For months he had been enthusing wildly about the Chicago house scene, and in particular the way that new Chicago house had managed to speed across the Atlantic, taking up residence, not just in the clubs of Manchester, but across the country. It represented, he believed, a steady flow of innovative ideas which, at that moment, seemed to be right at the cutting edge. He'd spent time, mainly in Maida Vale pubs, chatting to his old Glaswegian mate, Stuart Cosgrove, latterly television supremo, then of the *NME* and a noted authority on the house music scenes of Detroit and Chicago. Cosgrove's enthusiasm lit the fire. McKenna felt that Zomba should set up an office and studio in Chicago but presumed his idea would fall on deaf ears. To his amazement, the company agreed with his Chicago summarisation and asked him to go and set up an office in the city. Stunned by the speed of all this, anxious and excited by his new oncoming challenge and fired, perhaps by the feeling that, after overseeing and approving the Roses album, a certain chapter had closed, McKenna left for the States, his feelings of homesickness tempered by the fact that the company would give him an open plane ticket for both him and his girlfriend. It was a neat set-up and one that few ambitious A&R men would refuse. But it also created a massive twist in the relationship between the band and the company.

The Stone Roses was released, to mixed reviews, in April 1989. It was universally welcomed into the home of every 'Shaggy' looking scally, and then accepted with equal vigour by twenty-, thirty- and forty-somethings who perused the record club adverts in the quality papers. The Stone Roses broke the mould here. Zomba cleverly shunting the record along-side The Carpenters, Pink Floyd and Simply Red, pushing the album to a mainstream market. But despite this, despite the fact that it soundtracked a million student parties and despite the fact that it transcended age and genre with stunning ease, in 1989 very few people truly grasped the sheer perfection of the music on that album. This seems odd in retrospect, as in the intervening years, *The Stone Roses* has become generally accepted as a genuine rock classic, to rank alongside *Sgt Pepper*, *Abbey Road*, *Pet Sounds* and *Dark Side Of The Moon* in critics' album polls. *The Stone Roses* was better than anybody realised at the time. Roddy McKenna: "Of course I knew it was damn good, everyone knew that but, you are right, nobody, absolutely nobody could have known the extent of its greatness."

What must be understood here is the climate into which this glorious album was born. The perimeters of a great Eighties underground rock album had been set, by *The Queen Is Dead*, perhaps, or New Order's *Low Life*. Albums such as these were regarded as peaks. Nobody could ever have expected a band like The Stone Roses to top them. Of course, in Manchester we fell easily for the pure pop rush of 'She Bangs The Drums'. Of course we were seduced by 'Waterfall', complete with its slow, bluesy tail which wouldn't have disgraced a John Mayall album. But we placed the album within the scale of the times. It was local to us. We defended it vigorously as once we might defend Joy Division, or even The Smiths. They were 'our band'. But it was impossible to see beyond that. It was impossible to understand that the hidden gems of *The Stone Roses*, like 'Bye Bye Badman', 'Sugar Spun Sister' and 'Shoot You Down' were trampling into territories that invited comparison with the genuine greats – The Byrds, say, or Simon & Garfunkel. Moreover, in its capacity to simultaneously define and transcend its own time, *The Stone Roses* offers comparison with even The Beatles' output. The Stone Roses were scaling heights that we, as fans, couldn't grasp at the time, and neither could Gareth Evans. Neither could the record company. Neither could the music press. Neither could any of their fans. It happened right in front of our eyes, and we never saw it.

It's all the more surprising, therefore, that Ian Brown himself has reser-vations about that début. "To us, that first LP always sounded flat," he told

Record Collector's John Reed in 1998. "I think Q magazine said it was monochrome and that's how we felt about it. As we were rehearsing, the bass and drums got you in the belly every time but, as it turned into a record, it sounded like another 60s thing. We're not happy with that first LP." Well, if they had reservations at the time, they didn't let anyone know about them. As far as the rest of the world were concerned, the Next Big Thing was here, and it was rose-shaped.

10

THE BIG GIGS

On July 29, 1989, The Stone Roses performed at Blackpool's Empress Ballroom, the first of their three defining gigs (Alexandra Palace and Spike Island being the other two rather perverse venues), and latterly celebrated as something of a coup for Gareth Evans. The venue, being as far from sophisticated London as it is possible to travel, culturally speaking if not geographically, served only to highlight the maverick status of the band, not to mention the manager.

There is no doubt that the idea came straight out of Evans' feverish mind, although originally, his notion had been somewhat more ambitious. Blackpool was to be one of a string of dates beaded around the edges of the country. Gareth Evans wanted The Stone Roses to perform a full tour in decaying British holiday resorts.

Evans: "There is something very romantic about British seaside resorts. Something timeless too. They are either beyond fashion or stuck back in the Fifties, depending on your point of view. But they are also very unpretentious and I thought that would suit the Roses' stance, which was very street level at that point."

The idea was talked up with promoter Phil Jones, an intelligent, London-based motormouth who was fanatical about his music and was then working for JLP concerts in London. The Evans/Jones connection is important – it stemmed back to the time when Jones would pump an endless stream of quality acts into the two Internationals, and would climax with the Roses' legendary Spike Island gig. Jones was given the task of setting up the seaside tour and, inspired by Evans' rather eccentric plan, set about contacting crumbling pastel-painted variety halls in Southend, Torquay, Bridlington and Skegness. Gauging suitable capacities was tricky, for nobody really knew quite how big The Stone Roses were. Secondly, convincing venue owners who were generally hot for Roy 'Chubby' Brown or the Hinge & Brackett Revue, that The Stone Roses would be a lucrative, trouble-free event, wasn't easy. But it wasn't impossible, either. Incredibly, Jones managed to set up the full seaside tour.

It was hard work, fraught with bureaucratic complexity but Jones' persistence paid off. Indeed, the Lees Cliff Hall in Southend had actually started to sell tickets.

It was probably fortunate, therefore, that Jones placed a call to Evans about unrelated International business, only to have the manager casually inform him that, "We don't want to do that seaside thing anymore. We'd just like to play one of them, at a venue where nobody has ever played before. Can you sort it?" Jones, irritated and back-peddling furiously, managed to pull The Stone Roses from the tour in the nick of time (one day later and Britain's seaside towns would have been irreversibly postered), and hit upon the idea of Blackpool, specifically the Empress Ballroom in the Winter Gardens.

Even this one-off proved tricky. Jones found himself standing in the Empress Ballroom, chatting to the nice lady from owners First Leisure, who asked, "Stone Roses . . . don't think I've heard of them. Are they variety?" Nevertheless, she booked the band and Jones, happy in the knowledge that at least one of the seaside gigs would actually take place – and only one month later – left instructions with his colleagues at JLP and left to unwind on a Greek holiday.

On his return at Manchester Airport, with just two weeks to go before the gig, Jones picked up a copy of the *Manchester Evening News*, to discover a large news piece about the gig. Upon calling JLP however, he was informed that they hadn't spoken to Gareth at all . . . or the venue and hadn't progressed in any way with the promotion. Jones: "To be honest, my lot had fucked up. While I was on holiday, SJM concerts had steamed in and had taken over the gig. That was a bit naughty but Simon (Moran, from SJM) was hungry and ambitious. He had impressed Gareth, telling him he was the hot new promoter and, to be honest, he was. I didn't blame Simon although he had the nerve to travel up to Blackpool and just take over the gig. But I was furious with Gareth and Mathew and really lambasted them on the phone."

Jones' outburst actually ended up working in his favour when, out of the blue, Gareth Evans offered an olive branch.

"Well we want to do a massive gig in London," he told Jones. "Somewhere odd, somewhere unique. A real Roses venue. Somewhere that is noticeably bigger than Blackpool. Can you do it?"

* * *

Blackpool today is a grotesque pleasure if, indeed, it is a pleasure at all. Once, before the working class of Lancashire had been tempted towards cheap Spanish sun, it had been the natural magnet for the Wakes week revelries of 'Lancy' towns, where working folk, temporarily freed from their daily drudgery, would wander from slot machine to slot machine, from the Pleasure Beach to Bispham. There was, as they often said, nowt like Blackpool, and its boom time came in the first half of the 20th Century. Indeed, as dour council leaders still relentlessly inform us, it is "still the biggest resort in Europe!" However, Blackpool's image suffered as the century wore on. During the Sixties and Seventies it became, with respect, a cartoon town. To take a day in Blackpool was to shed oneself of all traces and pretences of affectation, all notions of sophistication or cultural aspiration. The joke was to lose oneself in sheer, unrelenting naffness.

It was fun for a while but, during the Nineties, and especially in the south shore Waterloo Road/Pleasure Beach axis, the town's atmosphere had darkened considerably. Giant, brainless bouncers stood guard at the entrances of giant, seething pubs. Gangs of bingeing stag-nighters, collectively stupid and dangerous, would maraud from pub to pub. The guest houses, ostensibly the pride of Blackpool with their matriarchal landladies, would try, ever so hard, to distance themselves from the worst elements but, suddenly, the joke just wasn't funny anymore. The Blackpool of Les Dawson knees-ups, the roly-poly fish'n'chips Blackpool had slowly peeled away and, although it was still possible to have a great day at the mighty Pleasure Beach, it had become more and more difficult to think of Blackpool as anything other than a grotesque caricature. It has been praised for this, for its bawdy gaudy, anti-glamour, for its ". . . full belch in the face of good taste . . .", as noted in the book, *Les Dawson's Lancashire*. But, increasingly, it is an outpost that is woefully difficult to celebrate. To see the magic of Blackpool is to see the fun palaces as crystal rooms. It is an illusion for only the most naïve, only those strangely blind to better things. Blackpool is an inelegant, expensive mess.

The fact that The Stone Roses' finest hour took place in Blackpool, rather than LA, or Geneva, or Glastonbury, or any of those places where rock bands normally enjoy their finest hour, is in itself something of a joke. Perhaps they represented a kickback to days of simplistic hedonism? Whatever, the choice of the town was absurdly inspired. Just one hour from Manchester, it was far enough to warrant a full day out. It also invited fans to simply submit to the town's funfair atmosphere. And that's how it was. A 'nine pints of warm, soapy lager, greasy fish'n'chips, throw up in the Ghost Train' kind of day. A manic Madchester day out. A flash-back to the charabanc and the crate of ale. Ian Brown: "Blackpool was a simple idea. We just wanted to go one step beyond just a concert. We wanted to give people a day out. Have a laugh. We didn't think beyond that, really."

The event was also to prove the pivotal moment in The Stone Roses' story. Pre-Blackpool, they were still struggling hopefuls, still undeniably 'small', and, to some extent, that smallness had given them added potency. Like all rock bands building a solid fan base, they had spent eighteen months developing a 'clubbiness'. And it has been noted that the true size of The Stone Roses' following had remained curiously hidden, uncelebrated even, especially in the south. Perhaps the Roses' fans – be-denimed, Reni-hatted but not always necessarily resplendent in flares – didn't conform to the general notion of rock fans. For a short time, Stone Roses and Happy Mondays fans in the north-west really did resemble the old devotees of Northern Soul. That clubbiness wasn't like donning a long overcoat and going to see Echo And The Bunnymen; it was nothing at all like becoming one of the hairy, spotty, leather jacketed heavy metal hoards. The Roses' following was young, sexy and parochial. But it wouldn't last. Blackpool was a celebration of the end of all that. It marked the moment when the fans let the band float into the mainstream, just as The Clash had moved on from the implosive madness of the small punk venues to scream from the stages of the Apollos and Odeons. Things would never be the same again.

But that glorious day, August 12, 1989, was the perfect pop moment. The Roses brought a wealth of young colour to the pavements of the Golden Mile, long-haired girls in floppy hats, with their swaggering boyfriends, the quintessential heart of 'baggy', echoing that fabulous six months in the mid-Sixties when the entire youth of the nation seemed to undergo a sea-change into early, bright, optimistic proto-hippies, utterly unlike any previous youth cult. And here was the Nineties' equivalent, looking as if they had been snatched out of a Traffic concert at Sheffield City Hall, circa '67. The Blackpool oldies, from beer-bellied forty-five-year-olds to white-haired octogenarians, of which there were many, looked on in disbelief.

The Roses themselves displayed a camaraderie that was ultra-tight and ferociously guarded. Many a music press journalist would come away from an interview feeling highly indignant, hurt even, after failing to make any impression at all against this barrier. They were undoubtedly terrible to interview and, more often than not, retreated into distant silence or chose to shun the journo completely with a barrage of in-jokes. This was a risky business – more and more, they found themselves portrayed, as Jim Cleland noted in *Sounds*, as ". . . just another bunch of dimwit parochials with nothing to say." And yet, to see The Stone Roses among their fans was to see a band with few apparent rock star pretensions. Around the time of Blackpool, I caught them at one of those appalling record signings, at the Virgin Megastore where, shrugging off the warnings from their minders or record company PR people, the band floated among the crowd for an entire afternoon, chatting openly, freely and in a strikingly non-patronising manner.

Nowhere was this more apparent than at Blackpool. It was a day out for band and fans together – at Blackpool, and probably only at Blackpool, for one day, The Stone Roses were small enough to be able to remain amongst friends without becoming patronising or distant and yet big enough to matter. Small enough to be sealed off in Blackpool, but too big to be ignored. Nobody doubted that, within a few short months, the legions who flopped along Blackpool's Golden Mile, all genuinely claiming a friendship, let alone a kinship, with The Stone Roses, would be lamenting the fact that the band had sailed up and away. And that, I suggest, was the true catalystic spark of the Blackpool gig. The sense of here and now, the certainty that it couldn't possibly last. The band would be handed over to an international audience. The band would be omnipresent on a million radios and would become part of the lives of people who had nothing culturally in common with them at all.

It has been previously noted that there was a certain oddness about the disparate blend of Stone Roses fans up until this point. And at Blackpool, as the 4,000-strong crowd tumbled recklessly into The Empress Ballroom, this oddness was strikingly obvious. You could trace it, perhaps, back to the days when Gareth would adopt his rent-a-crowd technique, all but press-ganging people to stand in attendance at The International. You could look further back, to the swell of Perry boys discovering The Chameleons. You could see these same people, in tow with their girlfriends and younger brothers, arriving wide-eyed and cheery at the Empress, mingling with students and punks and Goths and casuals and, dotted around, familiar faces from old Manchester days, from distant gigs of The Fall and New Order. Further back than that, I'd suggest, the older sections still grubbing around, 13 years after pogoing to the swirling sound of Buzzcocks. That was the thing about Blackpool. The crowd.

United by The Stone Roses. United in a celebration of . . . Manchester? No, not really. It was a celebration of *a* Manchester; a kind of dreamstate city, full of buddy buddy chumminess, a 24-hour party city. A city of exquisite innovation, of cultural sharpness and beautiful football. It didn't exist, of course, at least not without being shackled to a darker antithesis. But, for one day, in Blackpool, the pressures and torments of the real life Manchester could be left 60 miles down the M6.

"Manchester . . . in the area . . . international . . . continental . . ."

Ian Brown's words swam over a football-style mass sway, a thousand fingers held aloft, pointing to the sky, all loving this hyped up, super-arrogant shadow-boxing popster. Riding on the grumbling swell of Mani's infectious bass, 'I Wanna Be Adored', the most tentative of anthems, emerged boldly from the shadows, inducing a jovial hysteria that would never be seen again at a Stone Roses gig. It was no surprise that John Robb chose to open his Roses book with a lengthy appraisal of this particular gig, correctly suggesting it to be the band's finest live performance. There were so many reasons why that was the case, but it was mainly because that gig saw the band perched on the very brink of greatness, and only those completely in the know, only those enjoying that dancing frenzy in the Empress Ballroom, knew just how potent that little collection of songs actually were.

Gareth Evans: "The Stone Roses still had an awful lot of doubters. A lot of detractors. Right across the country. I knew that. I knew there was a reaction against them in London too. This would change, I had no doubt about that but Blackpool was something different. It was almost like pulling the band back from all that hype and letting them play to their own. To the people who knew them and had helped them build to this day. It was a thank you and a goodbye, I suppose."

The evening's special frisson was sustained long after Mani's wandering bass line heralded the oncoming of 'I Wanna Be Adored' and latched on to the mass audience heartbeats. The gig was won from that moment, even before Squire's metallic guitar ushered in Brown's ever subdued vocals. True enough, it wouldn't have mattered how well the band performed that night as, in a sense, the actual set was merely the climax to a full day and, frankly, most memories are fogged by time and overindulgence on the day. Which is why, as we remember an awesome, note perfect 'Waterfall', on which the band always relaxed into an effortless groove, the truth may well have been somewhat more shambolic. 'Made Of Stone' and 'Elephant Stone', twin sisters of the Roses classic set, came teasingly back to back, while 'Sugar Spun Sister' yearned for a large stadium. There was no doubt that The Stone Roses, who also débuted 'Where Angels Play' that night, had started to produce a sound that couldn't be contained by such a small arena. And that was the true point of Blackpool. It was a pressure cooker on the brink of explosion.

* * *

"It's a fucking nightmare, Madchester, you go down to The Hacienda and there's all these guys in their mid-thirties, suddenly wearing Day-Glo T-shirts and dancing very badly. Same guys who used to go to punk gigs. They are pathetic. Madchester is pathetic. That's why I moved to fucking Edinburgh . . . to get away from all those cunts." Mark E. Smith.

Smith had a point. While the entire city celebrated (though what it was celebrating wasn't exactly clear), Smith saw the intelligence of the Manchester scene draining away in a dizzying mess of headlines. Walking along Whitworth Street, or Deansgate, or even through dank, unlovely Piccadilly, gave you the odds-on chance of an encounter with some eager film crew, hastily assembling footage for some projected 'Madchester' documentary that would never get made. Alternatively, there would be some industrious hack, haunting the café bars, scribbling down notes, affecting a Paul Theroux worldly travel writing stance, attempting to pin down the heart and soul of Madchester. And the city that eventually emerged, via a hundred of these pieces, remained largely unrecognisable. A mythical city emerged from the blizzard of journalism which descended on Manchester, grafted from the chemically assisted musings of a thousand students, all ready to spew forth tales of a dance trance nirvana, of a city of strobe lights and Orangina, of an encroaching café bar network. A sci-fi vision of a hypnotic, pulsating, vibrant scene. But few people, other than Smith, noticed that in the heady rush to sample a peaking city night life, the enchanting post-industrial arrogance that had always marked the city's character was silently draining away. The point needs to be made. Madchester was a state of mind. An exciting, numbing, dizzying state of mind, for sure, but it wasn't the soul of a city.

If one is to be pedantic about this, it all began as a marketing joke. *NME*'s Danny Kelly, among others, would claim the dubious honour of burdening the city with the 'Madchester' tag, but the real source stems from the fevered mind of Factory film maker, and one half of The Bailey Brothers, Keith Jobing. After a tongue-in-cheek suggestion by Jobing, Factory produced three daft T-shirts. The first, a curiously vicious take on the government's Anti-Heroin campaign read, 'JUST SAY NO TO LONDON'. The second, and most idiosyncratic, shirt bore the inexplicable legend, 'MADCHESTER. NIGEL MADSELL FROM THE ISLE OF MAD', while the third adopted the title of The Bailey Brothers' never-to-be-completed filmic tale of joyriding, 'MAD FUCKERS'. And that, basically was that. Despite the heavy protestations of Happy Mondays, Factory Records insisted on calling their groundbreaking release, 'The Madchester EP'; the image of a city insane, simply mushroomed overnight, and 'MADCHESTER' screamed from a million unofficial (and all too swiftly shrinking) T-shirts.

★ ★ ★

After Blackpool, the Roses set off on their first European tour. Five coaches of British fans accompanied them, as they played in Valencia, Barcelona, Milan, Ghent, Hamburg and Amsterdam. The highlight came when the band played *Les Inrockuptibles* festival at La Cigale, in Paris, with Liverpool's brightest hope at the time, The La's, and indie darlings Felt.

After Europe came Japan, though the band had initially declined to go

The early Stone Roses as a five piece piece, left to right: Ian Brown, Andy Couzens, Pete Garner, John Squire and Reni. *(Retna)*

Ian and John flank a 'Pollocked' guitar, September, 1987 *(Ian Tilton/SIN)*

Performing 'Waterfall' on *The Other Side Of Midnight,* hosted by Tony Wilson, their first TV appearance in late 1988, left to right: John, Ian, Mani and Reni, with Cressa behind the amps. *(Ian Tilton/SIN)*

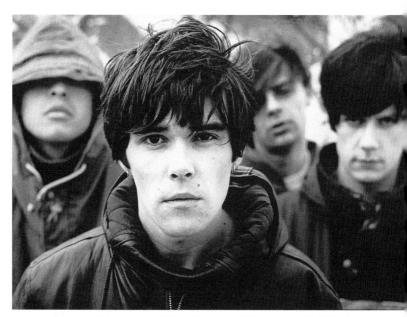

Reni, Ian, Mani and John, February 1989. *(Steve Double/SIN)*

The Roses with Cressa (top left). *(Chris Clunn/Retna)*

Through the Pollock glass: Reni, Ian, John and Mani in August 1988. *(Ian Tilton/SIN)*

John, Reni, Ian and Mani in Manchester, February 1989. *(Steve Double/SIN)*

Backstage at Blackpool Winter Gardens, summer 1989, left to right: Reni, Cressa, Ian and John. *(Ian Tilton/SIN)*

Ian on stage at Glasgow Green, June 1990. *(Ian Tilton/SIN)*

John on stage at Glasgow Green. *(Ian Tilton/SIN)*

The Spike Island press conference in the Piccadilly Hotel, Manchester; left to right: Mani, Ian, Reni and John. *(Ian Tilton/SIN)*

Stone Roses manager Gareth Evans (left), pictured in 1998 with Michael Slater of the Professional Golfers Association (seated alongside Gareth) and entrepreneur Peter Greenall, also known as Lord Daresbury. *(Gareth Evans collection)*

The Stone Roses backstage at Reading, August 1996;
left to right: Ian Brown, Aziz Ibrahim, Mani and Robbie Maddix. *(Retna)*

The Roses' swansong: Ian Brown on stage at Reading. *(Rex)*

John Squire on stage with The Seahorses at the London Forum, June 1997. *(Steve Gillett)*

Ian Brown as a solo performer, at Glastonbury, June 1998. *(Angela Lubrano)*

Gone but not forgotten, The Stone Roses, pictured in Seattle in January 1995.
(Marina Chavez/SIN)

when the promoter had refused to cater for their entire entourage (14 strong). He changed his mind when *The Stone Roses* shifted 20,000 copies in the Far East in its first week. The band encountered gratifyingly full-on adoration in Japan; mobbed like major-league stars when they touched down, four dates in Tokyo and Osaka sold out in four days, and 14 pages of one issue of Japan's leading rock mag were devoted to the new fab four. The Roses' machine was gaining momentum.

Roddy McKenna was in a curious situation, zipping back and forth across the Atlantic, visiting his girlfriend and family in Britain on a regular basis, as well as keeping firm tabs on the increasingly awkward balance between Silvertone and The Stone Roses. In October 1989, he returned, jet lagged and rather confused by Gareth Evans' endless calls from deepest Cheshire. Absurdly, he still felt as if he was the only true link between the company and the band, and most definitely the only 'warm' area, a middle ground, where the trust from both sides came closest to meeting.

Despite the uncertain messages he had been receiving from both sides of this divide – the reports from Silvertone almost always conflicted shockingly with those from Evans – he nevertheless decided to visit Battery Studios where the band were deeply involved in the recording of the next single, the curiously pedantic 'What The World Is Waiting For'. Four months had been spent honing this record and the band seemed content that some kind of perfection had been attained. McKenna shuffled into the darkened studio and, through the gloom, noticed the illuminated heads of the band, all nodding appreciatively to what appeared to be a completed work, though it was not 'What The World Is Waiting For'.

Not wishing to disturb the intense atmosphere, McKenna settled down next to the mixing desk and, through his dizzying jet lag, found himself soothed by one of the most remarkable slabs of golden funk he had ever heard. It was incredible. This song dripped from the speakers . . . a gloriously crystal clear guitar pumped along by a bass line that James Brown would have murdered for. McKenna was stunned. The maturity of this music washed across him in an instant, effectively trashing the reservations he had been storing up about 'What The World Is Waiting For'.

"What exactly is this?" he asked. (It might be noted that for some time, Gareth Evans and the band had been working on renegotiation of their original contract; the atmosphere in the studio was warmly welcoming to McKenna.)

"Oh it's just the B-side of the single," came a casual reply.

"Is it fuck!" replied McKenna. "This is brilliant, this is possibly the best thing you have ever done. It's got to be the A-side. It would be criminal to lose this and, to be honest lads . . . can't you see? It's miles better than 'What The World Is Waiting For'."

The band seemed stunned at first. Their dabblings with funk had been largely experimental, intended only in hinting at a future direction, at musical depth also; "That was the first one we wrote over loops," Brown told *Record Collector* in 1998. The song, such as it was, that had been built on the top of this striking backbeat was, to say the least, slight. But it didn't matter. This was something else. It was the sound that Happy Mondays would always be striving for. No Mondays put-down intended, their failure to reach the levels of musicianship that existed in their heads, created an ever-striving sound, and it was that failure that, ironically, gave them an essential edge. The equation is simple. If a band wishes to emulate and build upon the magical sex-fuelled funk of George Clinton, of mid-period Sly and The Family Stone, of Brown himself, then it is simply going to have to fall way short, though it might create something utterly new in the process (cf. The Mondays). Only very few British bands – The Incognito/Light Of The World/Beggar And Co – had managed to come close and sound convincing. It was certainly not a feat that one would expect to flow effortlessly from the newest, baggiest bunch of Manc scallies.

McKenna was knocked out by the track and communicated his enthusiasm back to Silvertone. This song, 'Fools Gold', would be a classic. The track was a strong echo of the latter-day, post-Northern Soul All Nighters, which took place, not in some parochial outpost, but deep in Manchester clubland in the late Seventies, just as punk had softened into New Wave and seeped fully into the mainstream. These funk parties – which would also, coincidentally, provide the inspiration for Factory's great lost act, A Certain Ratio – would reverberate to a flat constant, Clinton-inspired funk that was, in a sense, clubland's great secret. Beyond the pages of *Blues And Soul*, this music never found any kind of music press representation. It was high fashion, low hype, and would forever be heard pumping out of the speakers in the most fashionable city centre clothes shops and hairdressers. One recalls also a magic occasion in 1979 when Clinton's Parliament/Funkedelicament Thang tour arrived at Belle Vue Kings Hall, to massive and wholly unreported audience fervour. Undoubtedly the first stirrings of what became New Romanticism was born from this fashionable underground scene.

It is to The Stone Roses' credit that they fully understood the quiet significance of funk and jazz funk – from the dense, dark musical ramblings of Miles Davis to, his very antithesis, the avant-garde attack of the great mid-Seventies German band, Can. The Tony Wilson-endorsed theory that, "Manchester creates great bands because the kids have great record collections . . ." was certainly true in the case of The Stone Roses. The reference points in 'Fools Gold' were immaculate. It would become the most radical, understated, tasteful sound of the baggy era.

McKenna was stunned by 'Fools Gold', and the fact that it instantly pushed the band away from any connections with the influence of The Byrds or Love. In striking that delicate balance between rock and dance, the song was announcing The Stone Roses as a band of the Nineties, if not *the* band of the Nineties. His enthusiasm convinced both the label and the surprisingly reluctant band into allowing the song to share a double A-side with the more straightforward 'What The World Is Waiting For'. A daft decision, if the truth be told, as, in the world of record promotion, there is no such thing as a double A-side. Any record plugger will agree that the first twenty seconds of any record are the most important, for it is during that lead in that it manages to secure continued radio play. And since The Beatles it's rare that any plugger successfully flipped a record over when the initial A-side begins to falter. (Although The Spice Girls and All Saints have latterly achieved such success.) It's a different story in the dance arena, where excellent B-sides can be picked out by astute DJs who, merely by repeat playing, can set a domino effect in motion. And 'Fools Gold' screamed for a Dave Haslam or Graeme Park to really get hold of it.

Whether this was a possibility acknowledged by Silvertone or not remains uncertain, but the white label was handed across to publishing and music industry plugger Gareth Davies, amiable partner in the London-based promotion firm of Beer Davies, who took it on himself to shunt the double A-side to television companies. By this time, *The Stone Roses* had earned a silver disc, having sold 75,000 copies (in retrospect, and in the wake of Oasis mania, an astonishingly tiny amount for such a record) and Silvertone believed that album sales would swell in tandem with the new single if the band could attain reasonable television exposure.

Securing that television exposure was Gareth Davies' task. Davies astutely took the disc not just to the usual plethora of rock chart shows, but to more discerning arts shows as well. The Manc ethic, he reasoned, might just appeal to art show editors wishing to cash in on the working-class chic of the band. Horrendously patronising indeed, but Davies knew that the biggest Manc band of all would stimulate the stifled imagination of the Hampstead beardies, and perhaps help them reach respectable viewing figures for a change. In particular he targeted BBC2's *The Late Show* which, under the guidance of Mark Cooper, had allowed rock music to seep tastefully into the format on a regular basis. Cooper, an ex-music journalist, was never going to allow *The Late Show* to suffer from the same degree of haughty patronisation that had plagued *The South Bank Show* whenever they attempted to accommodate rock music into the programme.

Davies was fully aware of the difficulties involved in putting The Stone

Roses on live television. For a start, their sullen arrogance, which worked perfectly well at gigs, didn't necessarily sustain its charismatic edge in the full glare of an empty TV studio. This could be damaging for both band and the ongoing reputation of Beer Davies. Nevertheless, when *The Late Show* actually started to return his calls and, indeed, enthuse wildly about the glorious bass driven funk which characterised the new Roses single, he began to feel that something interesting might be taking place. Although confused at first, it dawned on Davies that they were actually talking about 'Fools Gold'. Further responses secured this enthusiasm, and Davies telephoned Andrew Lauder and convinced him – much to the chagrin of McKenna, who had been pushing Lauder for more than a month on the same matter – that 'Fools Gold' should be granted A-side status. Thus, a record that went against the rounded songwriting tradition of The Stone Roses, and was never intended to be an ear-catching A-side, provided the band with their very first top ten hit.

The band's *Late Show* appearance is now legendary. On the day, Davies' nerves were not helped by the band's stubborn refusal to co-operate with, as they saw it, the pedantic and unsussed 'professionalism' of the studio crew. Time and time again, as the hapless director issued fairly standard instructions, the band would just stare blankly, close ranks in their customary manner and proceed to ignore completely any studio guidance. Nobody, they reasoned, tells The Stone Roses what to do. Gareth Evans didn't help matters, repeatedly bursting into the line of fire, chastising camera crews who, perhaps understandably, believed they knew a lot more about filming a live band than this volatile and unreasonable band manager. In their eyes, Gareth Evans was the archetypal agent of smarm, whirling around in a constant pique of bluff and interference.

When, after hours of run throughs, they finally burst into action in front of live cameras, the sound was still predictably feeble, the band themselves predictably surly, turning away from cameras honing in for the obligatory close-ups, deliberately going against every aspect of the day's direction. Which, in itself, was highly entertaining. However, the true drama occurred less than a minute into the song, when the Roses' amplification proved too much for the Beeb's power supply, which cut out – all sound abruptly ceased, leaving the band suddenly strumming silent guitars and Ian Brown monkeying it up to no effect at all. The entire affair edged at once into areas of captivating uncertainty. A twitchy Tracey MacLeod was ushered in front of the band to explain the problem to the audience, noticeably wincing as Ian Brown paced the studio behind her shouting, "Amateurs . . . amateurs . . . we're wasting our time here, lads."

Evans is very clear about the impact of the Roses' appearance that day: "That entire thing was completely, utterly, engineered by us. By me. It was a scam. It was as simple as that. We sat around and planned it. I know it's corny but I knew that the stories of great rock bands, from The Rolling Stones to The Sex Pistols, always included some kind of legendary television appearance, where something goes horribly wrong . . . It was no different than Jimi Hendrix on *The Lulu Show*. And where better, for this to happen, than on *The Late Show*. A really middle-class programme that didn't suit the Roses at all. How could they have gone on there and smiled sweetly and played the game. The BBC Arts thing was horribly patronising towards bands like the Roses. So we just wanted to stir things up. And, of course, it worked better than I ever hoped it would. The Beeb may have complained but they knew, deep down, they knew it was the best thing that ever happened to *The Late Show*. To this day that is the performance that people still talk about. It may not have exactly been The Sex Pistols on Bill Grundy, which is what we really wanted, but it made BBC Arts worth watching for a while and that can't be a bad thing. And it was exciting on the day. You could just feel the tension building, great fun really."

And, according to accounts of McKenna, Evans and a plugger who wishes to remain nameless, understandably so, somewhere in the home counties, a faceless geek from the top of the BBC's curious hierarchy switched off his television and made a mental note to do everything in his admittedly diminishing power to prevent The Stone Roses from getting another second of BBC Arts coverage. At a lively and impromptu meeting, conducted the very next day, this point was pushed across, and most forcibly.

★ ★ ★

"We want to play somewhere in London . . . somewhere unusual."

With Gareth Evans' words still ringing in his ears, Phil Jones replaced the telephone receiver, glanced across his desk at JLP Concerts and noticed a leaflet that had arrived that morning from Haringey Council. 'After extensive renovations Alexandra Palace is now available for hire.'

Alexandra Palace? The Ally Pally? Could there be a more perfect venue for The Stone Roses? Jones immediately called Gareth back with his idea and, within two hours, Gareth called back to say that the band really liked the idea, and asked Jones to get things organised. Naturally, it wasn't all that straightforward to sort out. Jones went to meet a sullen gathering from Haringey Council, all of whom were extremely concerned about just what 7,000 rave kids – they had read the warehouse party scare stories in *The Sun* – might do to their beloved, recently restored historical building.

Jones: "The renovations were lovely. It was extremely posh and, to be honest, I shared their concern, although I didn't show it. It was a fantastic building and for the Roses to play in there as they had never really played any dates of significance in London before, I knew would be a real event. I assured the Haringey people that nothing could go wrong and the date was swiftly agreed. The thing is, we were prepared to pay the money for the hall, which was a considerable amount. I'm not sure how many other takers they had, but they were still worried. They didn't know who would turn up. And neither did we. Did The Stone Roses have a big following in London? This had simply not been tested at all. In that respect I think we took a massive risk there. To sell 7,000 tickets you have to catch a band who are really at a peak."

To add to Jones' angst, he saw in *NME* that Happy Mondays were performing at Manchester's Free Trade Hall on the very same night. This was indeed a worry. Surely that would tempt music-loving scallies to remain in their home town? With this in mind, he opted for a poster blitz on London – huge black and whites advertising the Roses at the Pally. Whether this would have been effective or not is not known. For all 7,000 tickets had been sold before a single poster hit a wall. (In fact, all the posters succeeded in doing was to cause a log jam of desperate phone calls to the JLP office.) The promoter tried to persuade the Roses to play three or more nights, which they could have sold out easily. "As it turned out it was to be the most stressful event I have ever been involved in," he admits now. "I realised this, halfway through the day, as we were preparing the venue. I was attempting to organise things, while the people from Haringey were constantly demanding me to sign all kinds of things. I just kept signing away, hoping they would just sod off and leave me to do my job, but they kept coming back. It was officialdom gone mad."

With a crowd already milling around the park – another distinctive baggy invasion of Reni hats and flares drifting through the streets of Hornsey and Wood Green – problems were beginning to crop up from the stage, centring on the lighting rig. The lighting team had come down from Manchester but, for various reasons, had hired hydraulic trusses from London. Jones: "The fact is they didn't know how to use that equipment. They were trying and trying but, by 4 pm, were still not done and I was screaming at them, really screaming which is very unusual for me. I'm not pointing the blame at anyone but the fact was that the delays into the lighting rig meant that everything else had to be done in a rush."

'Everything else' included the soundcheck. This was a room that hadn't hosted a music event for years – and, if one scans stories about the psychedelic glory days of the Ally Pally, when the likes of Pink Floyd and The Soft Machine graced the venue, or when Led Zeppelin sold out two shows there just before Christmas, 1972, the recurring theme is always the appalling nature of the sound. Clearly, the occasion demanded an exhaustive soundcheck. However, despite having to squeeze said soundcheck into less than two hours, not nearly long enough to iron out all potential problems, Phil Jones paced around the hall during the final couple of numbers and pronounced himself completely satisfied. It was a good sound – solid, discernible. With the bodies of the audience softening the brittle edges, there seemed little doubt that Ally Pally would prove an excellent venue.

However, when the doors opened, and 7,000 excitable baggies flooded in, Jones was disturbed to note that the audience, despite being loosely assembled, barely stretched halfway to the back of the room. Promoter's logic instantly informed him that, at least another 4,000 people could have comfortably settled into that vast gap and, at the back of his mind, calculations began to fire off. But his thoughts weren't merely monetary. He knew full well that such a gap, ending, as it did, in a sheer 'bouncy' wall, could well cause severe sound problems.

That night the band were plagued with problems. The warm-up DJs had uncharacteristic problems with jumping records, which hardly got the crowd into the right mood. The atmosphere was little improved by the Roses' appearance. During 'This Is The One', feedback and an echoey rumble swamped Brown's barely audible vocals. One song into the gig, Jones wandered through the crowd, and noticed frustrated glances among the kids towards the rear of the venue. At first he couldn't grasp the problem. Then it dawned. The sound engineer, seeing the gap at the back, hadn't bothered to set the 'delay' for the back of the hall. In effect, this meant that the audience was receiving the sound from the front, which then went to the back of the hall, bounced off the wall, and hit them again, from behind, half a second later. This wasn't a case of a muffled PA, it was a sharp, powerful PA hitting the audience from two separate directions, causing a severe echo which soon dulled into a completely indecipherable mush. Two-and-a-half songs passed by before Jones, realising the problem, screamed for the soundman to "Turn the fucking delay on!" In an instant, a flick of a switch repaired the sound. From this point on, things did improve: 'I Am The Resurrection' and 'Fools Gold' were strong, the Roses' ability to jam solidly saving the day, on balance. "We made the mistake of using our mate as the sound engineer," Ian Brown conceded in 1998. "He'd done the tour but the place was too big for him . . . But the atmosphere was great."

Alas, The Stone Roses at Ally Pally will be forever remembered as a gig dogged by that appalling sound. No reviewer present that day seemed to notice the violent change, from muddle cacophony, to powerful harmony, which allowed the remaining eleven and a half songs to flow by with acceptable clarity.

* * *

Nowadays, it is regarded as a classic interview by a renowned rock writer undertaken on a noteworthy occasion. That was the intention. To stamp the word 'legendary' onto the article. For the writer to steam in and steal some of the thunder, to exaggerate a little, maybe tweak bits here and there; maybe prove himself bigger than two bands, one city, one scene.

The writer was Nick Kent, formerly of *NME,* latterly of Paris, fleetingly a Sex Pistol and one-time mate of Keith Richards . . . the CV of rock star matiness is endless. The feature, commissioned by Sheryl Garrett for *The Face,* was admittedly a fine idea. To prise Kent away from Paris and into the *Top Of The Pops* studio where he could capture a unique moment – the evening of November 30, 1989, when Happy Mondays and The Stone Roses both appeared on the same *Top Of The Pops.* The charts also included 808 State's seminal dance track 'Pacific State', Electronic (Barney from New Order and Johnny Marr) and Morrissey's 'Ouija Board, Ouija Board', while the Inspirals topped the indie charts. Manchester was, indeed, in the house.

To be fair, patches of Kent's text are truly mesmerising. In particular he notes the intense bond between the two bands, leaving the reader to search, vainly in this reader's case, for similar recent cases of brotherly musicianship. (Teardrop Explodes and Echo And The Bunnymen, perhaps.)

"They're the only other group we can just sit down and have a drink with, like," Ian Brown commented. "The Mondays and Stone Roses have the same influences, really, 'cos we've all been to the same clubs. Blues nights, reggae nights, house nights, a bit of Parliament, a bit of Funkedelic. We're all takin' it from the same record collections, just doin' it up different." (An ironic comment, in retrospect. Gareth Evans spent considerable time keeping the two bands apart, for fear that the Mondays would spike the Roses' drinks before they went on stage.)

The Mondays' frontman was equally complimentary about the Roses. "Y'll find no rivalry here, pal," Shaun Ryder stated. "Well, the only rivalry 'tween oos and the Roses, like, is over clothes, really. There's always been a bit of a race on to see who's got the best, flashiest clothes, right . . ." As he got into his stride, Ryder's characteristic style kicked into overdrive, and it became clear that the supposed rivalry between the two bands, like that between The Beatles and the Stones in the Sixties, was mostly publicity hype: "They're dead brilliant, Stone Roses. They're more tuneful than us but we're a top band too so it works great together, I reckon. I mean, I can call 'em mates. Ian. Fookin' Manny. Rhemmi![23] Friends, y'knowharramean. And particularly fookin' Cressa, man! Whooray, we taught 'im everythin' 'e fookin' knows."

---

[23] Throughout Kent's article Reni was spelt Rhemmi!

Ian Brown was at his most arrogant when Kent questioned him about the Roses' ambitions. "Being bigger than U2? Well, they're empty anyway. What does all that emptiness say to all those people? But yeah . . . I think we can deliver on that."

When the subject of drugs came up, Kent noted that Gareth Evans leant over to whisper something in the ear of Tony Wilson, after which the Factory man noticeably stiffened. What Evans actually said (he would later claim that it had been a joke) was that if Wilson mentioned drugs in context with the Roses, he would shoot him. A fact that was relayed to Happy Mondays. "Yeah, but the thing was," says Evans, "that the Mondays then brought me a gun! Ha ha! That's true. They were joking too, of course. Well, I think so, anyway. Tony knew about my . . . old connections, so maybe he took it a little too seriously." (Kent had himself dropped an E as part of his preparation for the feature, though one can't help thinking he was a little late coming to the fair . . .)

But if Kent's article acknowledged the unshakeable camaraderie between the two bands, it also did them and Manchester a genuine disservice. One comment in particular drew a storm of protest – the author's assertion that Factory boss Tony Wilson had joked about the death of Joy Division's Ian Curtis. "I have absolutely no problem whatsoever with any of these guys dying on me," Wilson was alleged to have said. "Listen . . . Ian Curtis dying on *me* was the greatest thing that's happened to my life. Death sells!" *Face* editor Sheryl Garrett later admitted that the quote was simply made up to add spice to the article, but that confession was unlikely to appease those concerned. Indeed, at the Spike Island press conference, Ian Brown commented, ". . . we do not have a grudge against anyone apart from Nick Kent because he's a liar . . ."

Another waspish touch by Kent was to relay their speech in monkeyish fashion, throwing in the obligatory 'fookin' to illustrate northernness and therefore, in the eyes of that particular writer, parochial stupidity – a rather cowardly tactic. Although they would deny it, the article hurt the Roses, the Mondays and Factory (Wilson had to contend with calls from understandably hurt members of Ian Curtis' family); they had been attracted to the idea of the interview by the sheen of genuine quality that, to his credit, graces most of Kent's work.

Of more interest than the controversy, perhaps, was the emergence of The Stone Roses' anti-Rolling Stones stance, which strongly echoed John Lydon's comments about ageing rock stars a dozen years before. The rumour was that Mick Jagger, having been ". . . Knocked out, maan . . ." by the Roses' album, had reportedly offered the band some global support spots on The Rolling Stones' tour. Needless to say, the band took great delight in being seen to publicly snap at Jagger's feeding hand. In the *Manchester Evening News*, Ian Brown stated cockily, "We are far more important than The Rolling Stones . . . they should be supporting us. Not that we'd let them." This was exactly the sort of comment that a maverick pop icon should come out with, although the cynic might argue that when The Stone Roses have recorded a further 28 albums, remained the biggest drawing touring act in the world and maintained a staggeringly high profile for 26 years, then maybe they could justify such an attack. To Kent, arguably the world's most devoted Rolling Stones fan, Brown revealed, "We said no (to the Stones) 'cos everyone else'd say yes. We're against hypocrisy, lies, bigotry, show-business, insincerity, phonies and fakers . . . There's millions of them and they're all pricks. People like Jagger and Bowie . . . they're so insincere now they're just patronising."

With the benefit of hindsight, it seems unlikely that, even if The Rolling Stones' agent had managed to twist the ears of Gareth Evans, informing him no doubt of the tidy sum that would come his way should his sniffy little charges sink to the depths of supporting The Rolling Stones, he would have bowed to the 'moral' stance of the band, and continued to shunt them around the mid-size venues of Britain, despite what he said at the time. And what he said was this: "We said no because we were always going to be the biggest band in the universe. We knew that. We didn't want to be pushed around by them or anybody else."

The author quizzed Evans when the story broke, suggesting that a support spot with The Rolling Stones would be a hugely lucrative stepping stone to that coveted 'top spot'. Wouldn't such a platform give The Stone Roses a chance to show how good they really are? Evans' response was characteristically confident: "We'd have blown them away, wouldn't we?" Well, maybe. Then again, given that the Stones would have all their showbiz armoury on display and, of course, would be performing to a mass of adoring folk who had each coughed up £30 for the experience, maybe not. Perhaps a sullen Ian Brown on an anti-rock star rant wouldn't win the sympathy of such a crowd . . .

At the time, the story gave the band a lot of good copy, and spread the word that there was a new band with serious attitude in England. But as to there actually being any *truth* in it . . . In 1998 Evans cheerfully admitted to the author, "Yeah . . . yeah . . . that was a scam, too. I don't deny it. In fact we sat in The International trying to think which band we could refuse to support.

"I think I'd seen a newspaper article about the Stones, or maybe Mathew had mentioned it to me and I just thought, 'Well, that's it. We'd be really indignant towards them'. I don't think The Rolling Stones knew anything about it, or who we were, really. For us, it was just a way of drumming up a bit of press. It had no more meaning than that. I would have done *anything* . . . to keep The Stone Roses in the press at that time."

Evans' motivation, according to the man himself, derived not only from the need to raise the band's public profile, but also from their early, unsatisfactory contract with Zomba. "I was putting everything into raising the band's profile so it would help us renegotiate the contract. I knew that bands only get one stab at this kind of action and if we allowed it to drift, as bands do all the time, we would sink back into the mire . . . You have to catch everything that's going for you while it's there, or it just goes away. And if that meant occasionally offering myself up for ridicule, so what? To tell you the truth, the press loved me. They still do. Because I give them stories. Always have done. Always will."

The band were in the studio again in December, to start work on their follow-up album. The end-of-year listings in the music press left little doubt as to who the people's favourite was. *Sounds* made The Stone Roses best LP of the year, *NME* awarded them three of the year's top four singles; *Melody Maker* readers made the LP one of the top twenty albums of the decade.

* * *

Paul Birch and Dave Roberts, the twin powers behind FM Revolver's idiosyncratic but lucrative little set-up, naturally felt aggrieved when The Stone Roses haughtily brushed them aside in the hunt for larger deals. It's difficult to blame the company for repeatedly attempting, as they did, to push 'Sally Cinnamon' back towards the charts. By their standards, a bulging wad had been sacrificed in the initial scramble for chart action, and they had seen precious little return for their investment. They had contractual possession of a song of genuine quality. Frustratingly for them, despite the rapid ascendancy of the band in question, and the speed with which 'Sally Cinnamon' had flown from record counters, the true prize – a major top ten hit – had failed to materialise.

Birch and Roberts, whilst acknowledging that their outfit could not accommodate the band should they take off on a large scale, had believed that a slice of loyalty would have given them one or two large hit records, some recompense for their initial payout. After all, Gareth Evans had approached FM Revolver with the Roses at a time when no other record company seemed remotely interested in them. At the very least, the two felt that their company deserved the chance to latch onto the band's latter success, re-release 'Sally Cinnamon' and try, this time with a hastily assembled and rather shoddy video, to make the charts (the re-issue in fact just scraped the top 50, making 46).

As far as the Roses had been concerned, FM Revolver were simply inadequate – a small-time, small town outfit, barely worth bothering about once the larger fishes had started to bite. Gareth Evans, it must be said, failed to return any of Birch's calls which may seem churlish but, frankly, is standard music business practice. It was Evans' job to brush aside the smaller company in favour of those which could actually take his act somewhere. The Roses themselves saw the re-release, delivered without their consent and promoted by a video that, as they saw it, undermined their artistic standards, as the work of charlatans. In their eyes, FM Revolver had betrayed them. At an International Club band meeting, their fury spilled over into a mess of juvenile plans for revenge. On January 30, 1990, as The Stone Roses travelled from Manchester to the studios that had become their second home, Rockfield in South Wales, events took a dramatic turn.

In view of the personalities involved it wasn't difficult to predict that something might happen, especially as, en route, the band would skirt Wolverhampton and the nerve centre of FM Revolver. With vengeance on their minds, and with Gareth's blessing, they slipped off the M6 and paid an impromptu visit to Paul Birch and his girlfriend Olivia Darling. What happened next was both cruel and ironically apt as the four Roses, led by Ian Brown, swamped the FM office and Birch's Mercedes Benz with a colourful blue and white Pollock-style paint job, causing £23,000 worth of damage. The band saw it as an entirely justifiable artistic statement. They knew full well that the action would garnish their already high-profile PR image with lashings of press reports, local and national. Indeed, as the police intercepted them arriving at Rockfield literally covered in paint, they were also aware that a court appearance and a hefty fine would follow.

They did. In March, the band dutifully attended Wolverhampton Crown Court, where they glowered at the assembled hack pack, the loyal fans, fascinated by the sheer daft drama of it all, and the judicial figures around them. The judges warned the four that, "your deplorable actions were immature to the point of childishness and will not be tolerated", while the press afforded the band a healthy splattering of PR that, in terms of financial worth, mocked the £3,000 plus £95 costs that each band member was fined. Ironically, in court the judge had told them, "I think a prison sentence might lead to notoriety for you and ultimately be to your benefit, and I certainly don't want to contribute to that." On leaving the court, the band posed on the steps, giggling as if they had just raided the local sweet shop. They felt they had won.

* * *

Flamboyant promotions supremo Phil Jones, flushed by his success at taking the Manchester Festival from a small scale, rather grubby little arts bash to one of the most celebrated events of the festival season, had returned to Manchester from a brief spell in London, and settled into the lively bohemia of Chorlton. By day, he was surrounded by bureaucrats – nice bureaucrats, but nonetheless, rather lacking in the spirit of rock'n'roll. As an antidote to this, he treasured his continuing liaison with Gareth and Mathew, becoming third partner in GM (Gareth and Mathew) Promotions (though nothing was signed and no percentage was on offer).

Jones: "I was quite happy to accept that loose situation. It was a break from my day work and quite exciting, to be honest, because, by now, the Roses were really exploding everywhere, so no one could tell what might happen next, what with Gareth's loose cannon approach and the sudden power that he had been given. And I liked him, to be honest. It was always fun."

If The Stone Roses were going to top the Ally Pally bash, and they intended to do just that in the spring of 1990, then this time the venue would have to be very different, and quite extraordinary. The initial brief, delivered to Jones by Gareth and Mathew, was to find somewhere within an 80-mile radius of London. The search began. As word seeped out, Mathew Cummings started to receive the strangest phone calls: "Hi . . . yes, I own a disused speedway track in Southend, would you put the Roses on?" "Hello, I'm the owner of a caravan park in Llandudno." After a torrent of dubious offers, Evans and Jones took Gareth's Range Rover and toured a series of bizarre locations in Essex. It was quite romantic: clandestine meetings with gypsy crews whose caravans were scattered across dust tracks, speedway tracks, hollowed out, deserted quarries, and giant crumbling warehouses. They saw all manner of bizarre locations patrolled by equally bizarre characters who claimed dubious ownership. Although most of these meetings had something about them to make them memorable, practically all the locations were unfeasible, if not downright dangerous, and nothing quite fitted their requirements. The venue would have to be large enough for 30,000 people. It would need a willing and enthusiastic council – and Essex Council, allergic to any traces of the new 'rave' culture, were intensely paranoid – and, perhaps most importantly of all, it would have to be truly evocative. Someone suggested the original site of the giant Isle Of Wight festivals of the early Seventies, or re-staging Bickershaw in Lancashire, but neither seemed quite right. Somewhere, out there, was a place, a space that was weird, unforgettable and safe.

The site they eventually selected was Spike Island, best viewed from the hills which rise to the south-west, out of flat, lush, wealthy Cheshire and into the rolling pastures of Gwynedd. From any vantage point, up there, a glance to the north will arguably reveal the oddest and most diverse view in Britain: Liverpool's silent grey towers to the north-west, Manchester's dour sprawl to the east, a solid stretch of conurbation between the two, softening to a gentle greenness in the south. All this, with Deeside to the fore, framed – on a clear day at least – by jagged Cumbria, the flat-topped Pennine moors and, to the east, the Peak District. It still seems inconceivable that such a small area has spawned so much in the way of internationally recognised youth culture, from Merseybeat, kicked into gear by sailors bringing sacks of heavy vinyl discs in from New York, through punk and Madchester, to Oasis themselves.

But a truly surreal edge is provided by the sight which lies directly in front of you from this Clwyd hill. An intense concentration of industrial plants, more nightmarish moonscape than landscape; a mess of pipes, chimneys and cooling towers, of startlingly jagged structures and rickety contraptions. Naked flames blast away, and mysterious gases, rising from a million outlets, form a massive haze which hovers above the scene. At twilight it becomes even weirder, as the whole scene greys into a background pierced by clusters of yellow lights.

It was a scene that Gareth Evans knew very well indeed, having skirted back into the north-west, from his yacht moored at Conway in Wales, countless times. When The Stone Roses stipulated that they wanted to "hold their own festival, not near London but somewhere between Manchester and Liverpool" his imagination was immediately fired into action: it would be the chemical generation, raving away beneath the chemical towers. It was a striking vision that just wouldn't leave him. Somewhere down there, amid that surreal landscape, The Stone Roses could perform in front of their own little Woodstock. Just imagine! It would be a visual feast, unlike anything any of their contemporaries would attempt. It would even smell weird.

Evans remains adamant about the inspiration for the idea. "Spike Island was totally my conception. Totally. Beginning to end. Obviously, an awful lot of work was done by Mathew Cummings and Phil Jones . . . but I had been thinking about Spike Island for a long time. In my head I'd say two years. In the later stages I had to go to so many public meetings. You wouldn't believe the bureaucratic nightmare involved in staging it. That gig didn't just 'happen'. It took a long, long time to get that planning permission. At one meeting with councillors, people turned up with banners saying, 'Mr Evans, Impresario' . . . I'm not even sure what that means . . . 'Go back to London'. Go back to London? I took great delight in informing them that I lived in Knutsford, 14 miles away, also in

Cheshire. I put Widnes on the map for them. All they had, before that, was a lousy rugby team."

In conversation with the author, Evans readily brought up a point that is often forgotten when Spike Island is discussed. "You know, that area is the most polluted ICI site in Europe. So I had the idea [prior to U2's anti-nuclear jaunt to Sellafield] . . . for The Stone Roses to go on this campaign against pollution. This was going to be the central issue. The very point of Spike Island should have been to attack the notion that, in chemicals, anything goes just as long as it makes money. It was a very rough site. It was industrial, factories all around. It was where Saddam Hussein bought the gas that killed the Kurds. Remember that gas? It came from around Spike Island, man. I hoped we would get loads of press on it all. I wanted it to be the biggest issue of all."

It's worth noting that two previous attempts to fuse the rock audiences of Liverpool and Manchester, by concentrating on mid-Lancashire, had ended in disaster. The 1971 Bickershaw Festival, organised by Jeremy Beadle, saw a line-up that included The Grateful Dead, Country Joe McDonald and Brinsley Shwartz risk certain electrocution as they slammed away under a torrential downpour before a mass mud bath framed by slagheaps. It was an organisational disaster that saw Beadle emerge from the day considerably poorer for the experience. In 1979, Factory Records of Manchester and Eric's of Liverpool (Tony Wilson and Bill Drummond respectively), attempted to celebrate the parallels between the cities by putting Joy Division, Teardrop Explodes, Echo And The Bunnymen, The Distractions, A Certain Ratio and Elti Fits together, amid similar slag heaps, in the mid-Lancs mining town of Leigh. Although an artistic triumph, hardly anyone bothered to attend, and those who did were roughly hassled by an over-zealous police unit hungry for drug busts.

But Jones and Evans weren't concerned with these previous failures. This, after all, was a different era. The Madchester audience alone had swelled to city-bursting proportions and The Stone Roses were so per-fectly balanced at the very forefront that, in terms of attendance figures, their only problem would be one of keeping the numbers of ticketless hopefuls to a minimum. How big could it be? Well, how many people can you cram onto Spike Island? It would be a pilgrimage of baggy, the defining moment of the era, part rock concert, part rave, part festival. In February, amid freezing conditions, Jones, Evans and Roger Barrett paced across the site of Spike Island. Jones himself was absolutely delighted with the venue:

"It did seem very simple at that point," he explains, "because it met all the necessary requirements. There was enough exits and entrances. It was large enough and it had been used before, as the site of the Halton Show, a very weird folksy, hippie-type fest which, apparently, had attracted huge amounts of people. Plus the council chaps, who we met that freezing day, seemed very excited about it all. They were Stone Roses fans. It was the biggest thing ever to happen to Widnes."

Naturally, with any event of this size and nature, objections soon bubbled to the surface. The main problem with Spike Island was that, contrary to popular rumour, it wasn't surrounded by a vast area of open land, but was extremely close to the town centre. When Jones and Barrett drew up a proposal for the licence, and duly presented it to the council meeting, their fears about possible objections were justified.

"We will have drug addicts pissing in our gardens," came the cry from one aggrieved resident. "It will set a terrible example for the children of our town," said another. The *Runcorn Observer*, naturally keen to represent the views of its readers rather than alienate them, went into headline overdrive, encouraging the paranoia with horror stories about thousands of drugged-up youths descending on their town. Indeed, when Phil Jones next met up with his wife's grandmother, a resident of nearby Frodsham, she seemed unnaturally upset about this 'forthcoming invasion'. The couple didn't have the nerve, or the heart, to tell her that Phil was actually the man who was organising this terrible event. The police too, again alerted by tabloid rave scare stories, remained intensely suspicious, subjecting Jones to rigorous demands. How, for example, would 30,000 kids manage to travel to and from the venue? Would they all trample through Widnes? Where will they relieve themselves en route? Will they leave lots of litter in the town centre? Is there going to be adequate public transport? Will the motorways become clogged? The general nervousness emanating from all corners of the authority was simply deafening and also quite needless. Practically all the Spike Island tickets would flow out through a coach transport connection. The kids would be bussed in and bussed out again. Simplicity itself.

By word of mouth, and through one solitary advert in *NME*, 29,500 tickets flooded out of Phil Jones' office. Not bad. Could another band in the country at the time have inspired such advance sales? Undoubtedly not, and the Evans plan, to hit Zomba with the renegotiation at precisely the right time seemed to be coming together with dizzying speed. Evans took the band to view the site; if anything, their enthusiasm was intensified by the strange backdrop.

"I don't know how you fucking pulled this one off, Gareth," Ian Brown informed his manager that day, "but it's just perfect."

Not perfect, perhaps, for the roadies who, while working during the week before the event, beneath blistering sunshine, found their bare backs turning a curious shade of yellowy red. It was sunburn, of sorts, but not at all like the sunburn they had experienced the year before, in Lloret De Mar. Rather than turning slowly brown, their skin seemed to halt at a Day-Glo yellowy hue, and begin to itch and blister. Some of them, understandably worried about this effect, took time off to consult a local doctor in Widnes. They were greeted with a knowing smile, and were told that it was a simple case of 'Widnes disease'. (Meaning, they had been exposed to an unidentifiable chemical present in the atmosphere above the site, which had this mysterious effect on the sun's rays.) Needless to say, Spike Island was spared the sight of exposed roadie flesh and bottom cleavage from that moment on.

Jones confirms the story: "Well, I spent four days on that site and it was pretty hot for that time of year but I certainly did start blistering in a weird kind of way. Some people thought the roadies were playing on this a bit but I know they were genuinely worried. These weren't a bunch of softies. They had worked, outdoors, all over the world and nothing genuinely bothered them. There did seem to be some kind of chemical haze hovering above that site. You could see it. The sky wasn't the right colour. And there was that strange smell, but you would expect that at a chemical site. But God knows what they pump out in those places and you could definitely feel something strange burning into your skin. That wasn't a made-up story. It was a genuine fear. It's ironic to think how the local people, the local media were so worried about the harm *we* might bring to the area when there is stuff like that going on all the time."

Inevitably, further problems arose, which centred on the delivery of GM Promotions' cash payment to the PA company. In short, one day before the gig, it had failed to materialise. In the grand tradition of Evans and Cummings, it would come – it always came – in the most bizarre manner. Thus it was that at the eleventh hour, sound engineer Danny Mackintosh found himself walking into a clandestine meeting with Mathew Cummings, at a deserted Widnes bus stop, where Cummings handed over thirty thousand pounds in a plastic carrier bag. Mackintosh might have been forewarned. Mathew Cummings was well known for 'plastic carrier bag syndrome' and one always wondered how Manchester's multitudinous muggers hadn't honed in on this curious habit. Perhaps the idea was a simple bluff. No one, after all, would actually expect to find large sums of money being carried round in a plastic bag.

The author can still recall a related incident, which took place in the office of the Manchester music magazine *Muze*, of which I was the editor, in 1987. Gareth and Mathew had been semi-regular visitors –

possibly, we thought, considering ploughing money into the ailing mag. One day, after a particularly frenzied meeting, Mathew and Gareth left the office and, hours later, we noticed that Mathew had left his plastic bag in the corner. Peering into the bag, we were stunned to see it crammed full of twenty pound notes. £10,000, at least . . . well, that was our rough estimation. And Iggy Pop had performed at The International the night before. We called Mathew who took a further two hours to sneak back into the office, exclaiming, "I'm always leaving my bag everywhere. Thanks chaps." Genuine carelessness? Inconceivable unprofessionalism? Possibly, though Gareth later offered a wry comment which encapsulates the idiosyncratic nature of GM Promotions perfectly: "Oh yeah, we did that as a tester, really. To see if anyone would take any of the money. It's a good trick." Such is the strange psychology of Gareth Evans.

* * *

It was, of course, Gareth's idea. On the day before the gig, with the world's music press already assembled in Manchester, Gareth Evans staged a press conference within the catacombs of the Piccadilly Hotel. The Piccadilly is a large, featureless concrete slab, famed for its appearance in the Albert Finney film *Charlie Bubbles*, and for little else. It remains a curiously soulless hotel, affixed to another numbingly tedious rectangle of concrete, which in the Seventies was intended to provide Manchester city centre with a modern shopping plaza. Needless to say, long before the end of the decade high rent and low patronage had forced all the retailers to depart, leaving Piccadilly Plaza as little more than a cavernous shell, filled with discarded crisp packets, hillocks of fag dumps, the omnipresent stench of stale urine and Piccadilly Radio. And, until the hotel rebuilt its frontage at the start of the Nineties, the only way to emerge from hotel to street was to drift through this nauseating gauntlet.

The hotel had a curious place in the rock and showbiz history of Manchester. Being placed directly above the Piccadilly Radio studios meant that there always seemed to be a DJ holding a pre-interview chat with a visiting rock star in the bar, or a football team shuffling clumsily into one of the lifts. It was low-brow and high-cost and seemed quite the perfect concrete monument to the architecturally philistine Seventies. A first time visit to Manchester, beginning with a check-in at the Piccadilly Hotel, gave the immediate impression of a city blessed with all the architectural allure of Gdansk. It is a tourist's nightmare. It was Gareth Evans' dream.

"The idea was for the Roses to use the press conference to make a stand against pollution," he says today. "All those reporters, from America, everywhere. And they [the Roses] were boring. I should have done the press conference . . . But John Squire once said to me, 'Could you take a lower profile, Gareth?' I now realise that maybe he was jealous. Perhaps that held me back . . . I've only just realised this [1998] but John definitely struggled very hard to pull me out of the spotlight. And you can say what you like about me, maybe I bullshit a bit, maybe I spin yarns, but I should have done the press conference. That was a mistake on my behalf. At least it would have been entertaining, no one could deny that. It would have been a lot more fun than those boring bastards." Evans has a point. The Roses were less than scintillating in interview, frequently resorting to grotesque face-pulling when questions bored or angered them.

"Why do it? Why do it, Gareth?"

It was a good question. The only good question of the day, really, delivered by a sweet girlie fanzine scribbler who knew more about the band than anyone else present. Evans blushed with pride, stood back, opened his palms, as if to say, "Look at this. It's magnificent, isn't it?" It was anything but magnificent. Faced with a monosyllabic band, the assembled hacks, melting in the intimidatory atmosphere, shuffled uneasily, glanced at their empty note pads, searching long and hard for some kind of relevant opening gambit. It wasn't really the journalists' fault. There really wasn't anything to ask. And so the entire thing kicked along, as expected, with standard press conference probes coming from the writers from Spain, Australia, New York and – gasp – Fleet Street.

The occasion could have set a benchmark for pointless press conferences. Indeed, it has been suggested elsewhere that the whole fiasco was absurd enough to stretch into the realms of weird parody. A few choice snippets:

Linda Duff, falling into time-honoured *Daily Star* tradition, plucked out the standard query, "What will you be doing in five years' time?"

It was the kind of question one might have asked Duran Duran, half a decade earlier, when compiling a 'Personal File' for *Smash Hits*.

"What a stupid question," sneered the professionally bored Brown, leaving it at that.

Journalist: "Do you think you are the new Rolling Stones?"

Brown: "This is 1990, isn't it? So I say to you, the Rolling who?"

It was grim stuff. At one point, a photographer with strong Manchester connections demanded of the assembled hacks, "Why the fuck are you all here? Why are you so afraid to ask the band any questions?" This, in itself, was rather naïve. The hacks were there because they had been invited. It was their job. It would have been better to ask the band why they had instigated this fiasco in the first place.

Ian Brown responded with the anticlimactic, "It was our manager's idea," which Gareth Evans followed up by announcing, rather unconvincingly, "It is great, the centre of the world. You don't get better than this."

Perhaps the most notable moment came from Frank Owen, one-time singer with Manchester band Manicured Noise – which had once featured Morrissey as fey vocalist – and now writer for the New York-based *Details* magazine.

"This is fucking bullshit," Owen declared, exasperatedly. "You are treating these people like fucking shit . . ." At this point a friend of the band, clearly inebriated, started pushing Owen in the chest, telling him to shut up. "No, you shut up, you dickhead," replied Owen, to assorted cheers. He continued, "You are behaving like pigs to these people. Why are you dissing all these people here?" The confrontation which, doubtless, had Evans rubbing his hands with glee, bubbled momentarily towards ugliness, and then subsided. Brown asked Owen, "Are you still upset?"

"Yeah, I'm fucking still upset. These people have come all this way and you won't answer the questions properly."

One can only conclude that the press conference wasn't given at the request of the journalists. It was instigated by Gareth and, therefore, the band. Why instigate a press conference when you have no particular news or angle to stress? It was sheer naïveté, that's all. An intelligent option might have been to invite the hacks with the purpose of talking about live open-air gigs and why Spike Island had been chosen as a venue. Simple. But all it did was highlight an odd fact about The Stone Roses. However brilliant they could be, beneath the dipping melodies, the glowing bass lines, the sardonic vocals and the stunning drums, they came across all too frequently as 'four dull lads', to quote *Melody Maker* journalist Jonh Wilde. That was their one glaring weakness and Gareth Evans, seeking controversy, had achieved nothing other than to throw a dazzling spotlight on that one undeniable fact.

* * *

On the day itself, there should (legally) have been 30,500 people packed on to the island. (Council stipulations allotted a space of 1/2 square metre per person.) Although nobody quite knows how many tickets were actually sold, a rough guess might add a further 5,000 to that number.

Jones: "There were definitely a lot more people there than there should have been. It was a worry to me. It was getting extremely crowded. The biggest mess was the backstage area. There must have been 5,000 guests at that gig, probably the biggest guest list in the history of rock."

And outside, to everyone's annoyance, unofficial merchandisers avoided police patrols, selling cheapo 'baggy' tack by the sack load. More worrying perhaps, were reports of people having their food snatched from them by overzealous security, which angered the band though Jones maintains, "Obviously I heard those reports but, if it did happen, it was nothing to do with the official line on things. We never told anyone to snatch food. There was a problem with drink because, again, that was a council stipulation. But not food . . . You learn all the time with gigs like this, simply because we hadn't done anything like it before. I know, to this day, that there are Stone Roses fans who are angry about that situation and I can only say that we got that aspect wrong. We should have exercised tighter control over the security staff . . ."

Of more worry to Jones was the sound that, during the long afternoon and evening which preceded the Roses appearance, hovered dangerously close to the council's agreed noise limit. The council were busy, too, with officials wandering through the town the whole day long, holding sound metres aloft and in communication with their leader ("A real nasty piece of work he was" – Jones) who wandered around the inside of the venue. If the sound had wavered over the level, the council would have had every right to pull the plug or, more probably, sue the promoters after the gig. The officials appeared to be salivating at the prospect.

As part of the day's entertainment, the Roses had instructed Jones to set up, "some kind of drumming event" and the only thing he could think of was the great Thomas Mapfumo and his Drum Orchestra. Not, perhaps, the most instantly obvious attraction for a crowd comprising, or so it seemed, of a large number of débutante gig goers, but the vibe seemed loose enough. Of more worry, perhaps, were the gut-wrenching bass lines of Jah Wobble, whose set – which seemed to set the whole of Widnes a-quiver and sent the sound metre team into a frenzy – was fed through Gary Clail's celebrated On U Sound system to awesome effect. Nevertheless, the bone-crunching dub served only to confuse large numbers of the crowd and their disapproval was heightened further when, post-Wobble, a DJ began pumping Chicago House across the gathering. Indeed, it was only at 5 pm, when DJ Dave Haslam played it completely safe, punching out tunes by James, Happy Mondays and Inspiral Carpets, that the swell of dissatisfaction subsided mercifully into a kind of collective calm.

And that, perhaps, was the point of Spike Island. A gathering rather than a gig. A day trip built from the foundations of that day spent wandering along Blackpool prom, spreading colour and vivacity. Spike Island was a mass charabanc outing culminating in a rave beneath the chemical towers. Whichever way you looked at it, even from the gushing sycophancy of the backstage area, it was a landmark event. Of course, not everyone has fond memories of the event. Speaking in *Uncut* magazine almost a decade later, Ian Brown remembered both the day, and his then-manager, with precious little affection.

"We had a wanker [Gareth] running it. We trusted him. We are not the kind of people to put on a show where people have their sandwiches taken off them at the gate. That reflects on you. The kids think, 'Oh they're doing that'. The way people were treated on that day was despicable. The sound wasn't good 'cos he didn't spend any money on the PA. Another thing. We never helicoptered into Spike Island. There was a chopper, but it wasn't us. We got a bus."

The Stone Roses were actually supposed to be arriving by helicopter but, after the first chopper, bringing a selection of Gareth's friends, had landed, and had nearly caused a riverside crush, Jones immediately objected to further helicopter trips, forcing Evans to bring the band in by bus. Whether people were treated despicably on that day seems to be a matter of some debate. Although many were clearly aggrieved, more by the length of time they had to wait for the band than by any maltreatment by security, the majority (including future Oasis rhythm guitarist, Paul 'Bonehead' Arthurs, trivia fans) entered the camaraderie spirit of a day out by the swelling Mersey. Indeed, the river was rising to an extent that caused Phil Jones serious concern. "I was terrified. Halfway through the day I noticed that the river suddenly seemed incredibly high. I mean, dangerously high. I checked and nobody at the council had mentioned the spring tides, which were common and could so easily have swamped that entire island. This was a serious concern. Most people didn't notice it but it was creeping higher and higher all day. We employed teams of frogmen, and even the look on their faces showed concern. I thought we were going to have to start pulling masses of bodies out of the river. Thankfully, as the evening wore on, it seemed to abate. But it was a close shave. I wouldn't like to know just how close it was."

And after all the hassles with councillors, security and spring tides, the band's performance, dulled by the strong wind and the PA which couldn't effectively combat it, was not one of their finest. They had just returned from a triumphant trip to their beloved Stockholm and seemed somewhat jaded. Perhaps their confidence had been undermined by the Piccadilly Hotel press conference. That said, it's difficult to imagine anything less than a fired-up performance in front of thirty thousand revellers who, frankly, were past caring about the standard of the sound, or performance. Spike Island had become a symbol of the new generation, the fabulous fusion of rock and dance, of gig and rave, of Sixties and Nineties – a big new adventure for youth culture. Would it matter, in the end, that Mani's bass was booming across to Frodsham, effectively missing the crowd entirely, or that Brown deliberately kept silent between songs, maintaining a Lydon-esque cool that wasn't entirely convincing. But the people in the crowd, the people who actually paid for the whole damn show, had themselves a good deal more fun than the pop stars, hacks, soap stars and sundry sycophants gathered backstage. And I speak from personal experience.

Phil Jones: "Do you want to know what the best thing about Spike Island was? It was the lighting. The lighting was spectacular. The finest you could imagine. Looking at those kids out there. They were in a state of rave, looking genuinely gobsmacked. Truly, it made Pink Floyd seem small time. I was very proud of that lighting. I doubt if it has ever been bettered." Probably not and what's more it finished in a flurry of fireworks that will be bettered only on Millennium night. Multicoloured explosions, zipping trails of brilliant white, illuminating everything from Deeside to Merseyside, signifying a logistical triumph . . . and one hell of a party.

And after such a party, the comedown was inevitably severe. Punters crawled out of Widnes, attempting to get back to The International where, standing by the bar, soaking in the post-Spike vibe was rather like watching the sun rise after three days without sleep. Weary bodies drifted into the club, grabbed a beer and fell into little huddles, swapping anecdotes, building the foundations of Spike Island folklore.

By its very nature, the day helped The Stone Roses blast their way well and truly to the heart of the British media. The week following Spike Island saw every broadsheet in the country publishing lengthy, often ludicrous, articles about the new culture, about 'Madchester', about the flowered and flared generation that offered so many convenient parallels with the Sixties. It was an editorial dream, of course. Moreover, here, at last, was a youth culture that the parents could relate to. But Spike Island also marked the moment when the music media's attitude to baggy culture began to change. As, across the city, the honest if unthinking laddish mode of Happy Mondays would hand an arsenal of ammunition over to a pre-*Loaded* pro PC media. It was difficult, in those days, to admit to laddish heterosexuality without being immediately seized upon by absurd guardians of political correctness. As such the whole Mondays Madchester scam spiralled into darkness, and you could practically sense the hipness draining away from both acts. It wasn't necessarily anything to worry about, for The Stone Roses, if not the Mondays, had ballooned to proportions that even the mighty *NME* couldn't seriously dent.

Ironically, as it was becoming clear that Spike Island was the pivotal hinge in the Roses' British fortunes, the shockwaves from the gig were spreading across the Atlantic. America, not noted for swallowing British hype, seemed to be readying itself for a sizeable invasion, and the influential college radio circuit was starting to feature Roses tunes. This did, it has to be said, cause a good deal of initial confusion. The Stone

Roses, and Madchester beyond them, had been thoroughly sold as the source of the new all-encompassing dance craze, and here they were, the biggest band of the whole new caboodle, sounding like . . . The Byrds! Rodney Bingenhiemer (Los Angeles KROQ DJ, noted music and party organiser): "Yeah . . . The Stone Roses . . . that shocked us all a bit . . . man. Fantastic band, that was always obvious and we had been playing Manchester stuff for a long time. The Smiths, New Order. But, well, to us this sounded incredibly retro. Not Manchester at all. Which was really odd. It was like a bit of LA, coming straight back at us. That said, we loved it. There are always lots of British bands attempting to come over, but this seemed like the big one."

If Spike Island had seemed like a bit of an artistic disappointment, then the band's next gig, in a huge tent in Belfast (Evans: "Let's play in a lot of Big Tops!") was to provide an unlikely high. Under canvas, the Roses' sound made an infinitely greater impact. Manchester acts have traditionally gone down well in Belfast, partly, one senses, because 'Irishness' has been seeping into Manchester for a century and a half and has always reflected strongly in the music of the city (even if the Roses, as it happened, were considered to be the most 'English' band since The Jam).Their scintillating performance was repeated the following night in Glasgow, and Ian Brown would later admit that the two gigs seemed to merge into one wild celebration of uncritical crowds who had come to dance and lose themselves. There is no doubt that the band enjoyed being freed from the tension of playing at Spike Island. That gig had been building for several months, not just physically but in their heads. Once past it, once over that unrepeatable hurdle, a simple thing like playing a gig in an enclosed space seemed refreshing.

In *The Stone Roses and The Resurrection Of British Pop*, John Robb hints at a strange sense of anti-climax which surrounded the Glasgow dressing room (actually, a caravan) after the gig. The band sat around, curiously silent and somewhat drained, as if an end of sorts had just been reached. In retrospect, it seems so obvious to point out that The Stone Roses had tipped over some kind of artistic and, most certainly, commercial cliff face. The two gigs, Belfast and Glasgow, were performed in a rush of post-Spike momentum, a joyous euphoria, where everything seemed quite perfect and no one noticed that, with Spike, they had reached their peak. It couldn't be bettered. One hour later, at the Sub Club, The Stone Roses' after-show party exploded with unrestrained vigour, but within the band itself, there bubbled a myriad of insecurities which had hitherto been kept down by the Roses' all-for-one camaraderie. At Glasgow, the euphoric shows were not an example of a band who had reached a state of musicianly exuberance at all, they were a band whose true energy had just been spent. It was temporary euphoria, a wonderful afterglow follow-ing the main event, but not a springboard on to greater things. Gareth Evans noticed it. He hadn't thought of it before, when Spike Island was absorbing all his attention, but, suddenly, he wasn't quite sure what to do any more. There was a dizzying sense of . . . an end.

A new single, 'One Love', which should have been the killer punch after the stunning 'Fools Gold', reached number four in July 1990, but it was generally regarded as a let down. The sentiments were fine – 'One Love/We don't need another love/One love, one heart and one soul' – but the music – a shuffling George Clinton-esque jam – didn't do them justice; it was, arguably, their least effective single to date. It didn't matter: the Roses' momentum was enough to carry the record; sig-nificantly, 'One Love' still stood head and shoulders above the handful of bands who were gathering at the bottom end of the charts, all beginning to adopt the Roses' image – flop-fringed, sullen-faced and baggy of trouser.

The single's release had been delayed for the most bizarre of reasons, a famous incident which coincided with a visit Evans made to John Squire's abode. Whatever people in Manchester may have thought about Gareth Evans, be it justified or otherwise, on one subject, everyone agreed: he devoted an awful lot of time to his son, Mark, a 'Down's syndrome' child. And in the early Nineties, Down's syndrome children were still suffering from a huge wave of ignorance and prejudice. Even the medical world was only just coming to terms with the true status of such children, who needn't necessarily be lacking in intelligence at all; indeed, during the Nineties, more and more Down's children have been achieving goals that had previously seemed unattainable. Gareth Evans couldn't care less what anybody thought – he adored his son (still does) and has never lost sight of that potential. A few years before, Gareth and Mark were refused a table at a Manchester restaurant one lunch time because of Mark's condition. Understandably, Evans went berserk, and the incident threw him onto the defensive whenever he experienced such prejudice.

The Stone Roses were fully aware of Gareth's devotion to his son, and generally respected him for it. This made it all the more astonishing when Evans arrived at John Squire's house in Chorlton-cum-Hardy one breezy afternoon, to discover the guitarist sitting in his darkened front room, watching old footage of Nazi concentration camps on video, and in particular, one in which Down's children were being escorted into gas chambers. Fighting a feeling of nausea, Evans flicked through the video boxes. "How did you get these?" he asked, genuinely shocked, ". . . and what's more . . . why are you watching them, John? They are sick. How can you sit there and watch this stuff? How can you have it in your home?"

Squire looked up slowly, and replied, "Oh there's a lot you don't know about me, Gareth." His gaze returned to the screen. It may well have been an act, and perhaps, in some way, Squire was using the occasion to hit back at Evans in the only way he knew would make an impact. After all, he knew about Gareth's son. He knew Gareth was coming round to the house. How could he have not realised that the videos that he was watching might cause offence?

The incident remained lodged in Evans' head and resurfaced when he saw Squire's completed artwork intended to accompany the Roses' 'One Love' single, artwork that was far enough down the line for sleeve and T-shirts to be stacked and ready for shifting to retail outlets. But Squire's discreet artwork couldn't disguise the startling fact that, screaming from the T-shirts, and from the single sleeve, was a definite Swastika. (Indeed, one wholly innocent Stone Roses roadie was surprised to find himself refused entry to The Hacienda because of his 'One Love' T-shirt.) How could Squire have been so naïve? Was it merely a punkish attempt to shock? And Zomba, of course, was a heavily Jewish record company! (Although, according to Evans, it was mild embarrassment that permeated that office rather than any real sense of outrage.)

John Squire's reply was simple: "Hitler isn't the only one allowed to use a swastika." Which, while true, doesn't alter the amount of hurt that using such a symbol is guaranteed to cause.

Squire still maintains that the swastika image was entirely accidental. To his credit, he immediately agreed to redesign the sleeve, splitting the image until it repeated harmlessly across a collage of squares. Ian Brown: "It was an accident. And we certainly didn't want some kid getting beaten up for wearing one of our T-shirts, in Barcelona or anywhere else. 'One Love' was certainly good enough to make it without that kind of crap." This in itself was a curious statement. Although one doesn't doubt Brown's sincerity, it might have been more appropriate if he had said that the band didn't wish to cause offence to anyone who might be sensitive to that particular symbol. Moreover, back in his scooter days, when he had a taste for all things Oi, Brown did have that swastika tattoo. In his defence, this wasn't something he was particularly proud of, nor had he ever attempted to deny it or keep the fact hidden. It was just there, a reminder of a different time. And now, weirdly, the swastika had made a fleeting reappearance in the story of The Stone Roses in connection with a song which preached brotherly love for all.

Intriguingly, 'One Love' might be regarded as the band's most significant incursion into 'black' music. "No one can say we can't do it, man," Ian Brown asserts vehemently. "No one can say that we are just kids

154

playing around with a music form, because we have put in the hours, the years . . . the work." True enough. The celebrated 'effortless' feel of 'One Love' and, indeed, 'Fools Gold', wasn't achieved by a swift career-boosting change of direction. It was attained by a deep understanding of the form and the ability to blend elements of funk and guitar rock; indeed, one might perceive Cressa's influence here too, the Roses' guiding light and omnipresent bearer of sound advice.

11

THE ZOMBA DEBACLE

Gareth Evans, arch-wheeler and dealer, hadn't lost his knack for scams and stories. His latest idea was as barmy, and as strikingly memorable as any. "I sent Ian and John to the Mull Of Kintyre. They were happy to go because of the Paul McCartney thing. But I sent them there to write songs. That was the point. People write songs in Kintyre. Actually, do they? I had no idea where the place was, or whether it was truly evocative, or whatever. I just liked the idea of them in this remote place, with mist and heather and sheep and sea, writing songs. I just thought it had rock star class . . .

"It sounded good when I was in meetings, in London, and could say, 'They are in Kintyre.' It was as daft as that but there was something sort of anti-cool about it. They liked that, too. They went willingly. I think they liked to think of themselves on the scale of The Beatles." A novel idea to say the least, but Evans had plans to add a distinctive twist to the story. "My scam was to take it one stage further. My scam was for them to go fishing or something, go out on a boat and for Ian to be washed over-board. Not really but, as far as the press were concerned, yes really.

"The local press could have picked up on it first. Then the *NME* would have been alerted and then the national tabloids and all of that. It would have been fantastic. Front page stuff, banner headlines. A sense of unreality. All the best bands have that, and imagine the mystique created by a lost Ian Brown . . . They would have been just enormous after that." As it turned out, the idea foundered, because of Ian Brown's reluctance to go through with it. Understandably, Brown felt that if it went wrong, and they were found out, the Roses would have looked ridiculous. But what a scam . . .

* * *

Record sales, although not enough to push the band into orbit, were certainly substantial enough to make the shortcomings of the Silvertone deal known, in the business at least, as a precariously small affair. It was certainly a deal that appeared incapable of promoting a band who looked, for the first time, as if they may well deliver on Ian Brown's expectations to eclipse U2. Gareth Evans, of course, was fully aware of this and even if he hadn't been, the fact that his telephone had started to glow red-hot with calls from record company big wigs, was enough to convince him that the major players were interested in his band.

Evans: "I spoke to everybody. Every top man in the record industry was on to me apart from Zomba, really. After Spike Island they seemed to think things were ticking along nicely, but . . . all kinds of people were telling me that The Stone Roses needed to improve their deal. It was confusing. I was waiting for Zomba to call. They never did. Other people called, all the time. It struck me as very odd indeed."

In Britain, Roddy McKenna had existed as a firm link, as the only firm link, between the band and the record company. Indeed, with McKenna out of the picture, the bond was, to say the least, shaky. In fact the company's only personal connection with the band was via Gareth. Other than through Evans or McKenna, they never spoke to the band at all. They would convey messages to Gareth, he would go to the band and vice versa. Now whether Gareth used his position as middle man to tinker with communications is open to speculation. When I asked him about this, he shrugged and offered me the look of a chided Labrador puppy. ("I would never have thought of tinkering with the truth.")

In retrospect it seems hardly surprising that from the moment McKenna left, cracks started to appear in the relationship between band and record company. How ironic that, just as the band began to attract world attention, the one man who could hold things together was shunted from the scene. How did it happen? Surely Zomba realised that, with enormous amounts of money at stake, an awful lot of heavy duty vultures would start pecking, and that Gareth's apparent eccentricity would seem like a gift to these vultures? That, with a little work, a few neatly placed words, a push here, a stab there, it would be relatively simple to plant the notion that Silvertone just weren't up to the task. Planted and nurtured until the band were ripe for the picking. A new management company with links in the American record industry perhaps? Well, it happens with most bands and, not since the Sixties, when artists would sign away half their life's work for two pints of bitter and the chance to get on to vinyl, had a major British band seemed contractually so naked. And with Gareth being the only factor holding the whole thing together, is it any wonder that things soon started to fall apart?

Zomba were obviously not quick enough off the starting blocks to improve their existing deal. With the band's escalating profile, with all the attention they were now getting as the UK's biggest band, how could the company be so confident that they would hold on to them? Admittedly, as

American interest began to build, and the relationship between band and company began to shake, Zomba became increasingly uneasy and attempted to paper over the cracks. At Christmas, for instance, the company authorised a special bonus payment for the band, simply as a show of good faith. This amount – reports put it between thirty and forty thousand pounds – was duly handed across to Evans.

With McKenna out of the picture, Gareth Evans was the only link between the Roses and Zomba. McKenna: "There were obviously massive cracks between the label and the band and I don't think it helped when I was out of the way. I mean, there was hardly any contact at all, which was pretty weird. But I had to come back to the UK that January (1991) and I met up with Andrew to discuss the Roses' problems.

"The thing was, the label didn't really know how the band were feeling. Whether they were happy or not. They only had a lot of short, surreal calls from Gareth to go on . . . it was getting really serious. But, to be fair, Gareth had always been straight with me in that respect. He had said that, any time I wanted, I could go and see the band and that I didn't have to go through him first . . . So I took him up on his word. Me and Andrew travelled to Manchester to meet the band. It was a good meeting, I seem to remember. They didn't seem to be all that unhappy and we got on pretty well. But at the end of the meeting, I can't remember whether it was me or Andrew, but one of us said, almost matter of factly, 'Oh, by the way lads, did you get that Christmas money?' They looked a bit strange and then said, yes . . . and they claimed that they had received £500 each.

"We couldn't believe it . . . well, perhaps we could. That's how it was, having Gareth involved in the grand plot from, as far as Silvertone were concerned, the very beginning. I'm not saying, here, now, that Gareth stole that money. It wasn't like that, it really wasn't. The whole setup was more complicated. The money went to The Stone Roses . . . somewhere." Realising just what he has said, McKenna then backtracked, slightly. "Well that's exactly how it happened. And the band didn't seem particularly upset about it. And don't get me wrong. I was never anti-Gareth . . . quite the reverse. I respected and still respect him. He has that power and naïveté and, put together, it can sometimes work very well. You must always remember that Gareth had seen a lot of bands and he definitely saw something special in The Stone Roses. He knew he was going to take them all the way.

"Whatever business arrangements he had with that band, he had a definite passion for them, make no mistake about that. His business side was . . . well it was the way he did things. Still does, probably. That's Gareth. I don't think it dawns on him that he is ripping people off or anything like that. Gareth is a rogue. Yes. He knows that. But he's more complex than that. He does have a love for the people he looks after."

And what of the grand deal-maker and money-spinner himself? "To understand all this," Gareth Evans told me, "you have to go back to Spike Island. I mean, firstly, how big was that gig? It was in Widnes and they called it Widstock. It was the defining gig of a generation. No question about that. I was on-stage, that day, with thirty thousand looking on, with Roddy McKenna and Mark Farmer. Now I am an intensely loyal person and, at that point, I would have been perfectly happy to start renegotiating The Stone Roses' contract and that's what had been promised. Zomba always said that, if the band really broke big then they would renegotiate that contract. I was happy with that. I would have entered into a major deal with Zomba.

"Now we got to Spike Island standard. I mean, how big do you want to go? We had done our job, big style. Nobody could have risen faster than us. We pulled it off. Why didn't Roddy McKenna and Mark Farmer go back to Clive Calder at Zomba and say, 'Look, this band are now massive, we *must* renegotiate.' True, McKenna was largely out of the country at that point. But I was waiting for something to happen. Clive Calder wouldn't budge . . . I don't think that Zomba in general understood quite how big it had got. We had evolved beyond the scope of their expertise, really.

"I met with John Fruin, who I still respect, and negotiated that £40,000 bonus for the band. Even that was really difficult and I knew that things were not quite right. We should have been renegotiating on a massive scale, not quibbling over a £40,000 Christmas bonus. And the band got £10,000 each minus tax and National Insurance. That's the truth. They weren't happy with that, to be honest. But it was never anything more than a stopgap, really. We *had* to renegotiate. We had to renegotiate fast. Zomba let us down."

McKenna: "I think the Roses would have been happy to stay with Zomba but they wanted the money from Zomba to come close to the kind of amounts that were being bandied about by all the other companies. But you have to see it from Zomba's point of view as well. What was the point of Steven Howard taking that initial business risk, getting a valid contract with the band and using all the promotional forces at Zomba to get the band into a certain position if, at the end of the day, all the market forces make your contract invalid, or seem too small? You would be working against yourself. No one would do that.

"A footballer's agent wouldn't work like mad to get his man to a point where he has to suddenly compete against lots of other agents. That would be ludicrous. Plus Clive Calder wasn't really a rock man. I'm not sure he understood the parameters. He would say, today, that Zomba got out just at the right time. And he'd be right . . . but I often wonder what would have happened if Zomba had been allowed to continue to nurture the band in their own way. If Gareth had remained happy with the Zomba setup and the band could have been left alone to get on with things. Would they all have fallen out? No one could know."

By the time McKenna had finally come back to the UK for good, the situation had become practically unworkable. Consider McKenna, returning to Manchester, not quite sure what had been going on. He was flushed with pride at the astonishing swell of Madchester and the fact that The Stone Roses had become, to all intents and purposes, the most important band on the planet. But he could see by now that another explosion had also somehow taken place: The Stone Roses had become blown out of proportion, way too fast. Egos were growing, expectations were becoming unreasonable.

★ ★ ★

When Gareth Evans was on business, he would drive along the country lanes of Cheshire – Mobberley, Knutsford, Wilmslow, Alderley Edge – in a battered Ford Escort. One might have expected, given the Evans leaning towards the flash, toward hyperbole, his taste for the outrageous, that he would fall hook, line and sinker, for the trappings of luxury. A Porsche perhaps; after all, even when he had been little more than a grubby low-brow entrepreneur, he had always strived to appear on the cusp of fabulous success. And now he had it. So, why was the manager of the world's hottest rock band, a manager who had finally achieved the power he had always craved, driving through Cheshire in a Ford Escort?

On this particular day, Evans' Ford Escort contained, not only a rather nervous Roddy McKenna but also, lying supine across the back seat, the charismatic, whacked out singer from the Happy Mondays, Shaun Ryder. Ryder had been awake for three days, and now could do little more than gurgle as he stared upwards at the tree tops that flashed by through the car's rear window. Evans was dressed, as ever, in low-grade country wear, caked in mud on this occasion, and looking anything but a successful band manager. Furthermore, Ryder had been forced to share the rear of the car with a giant pot of paste, two fat brushes, and a wodge of posters. Gareth Evans had been flitting around Manchester the previous night, leaping from his car in order to take the concept of 'hands on' management to new and mind-numbingly absurd levels.

"You still postering?" asked McKenna, surprised by this rather unnecessary false economy.

"Gotta keep working," replied Evans, tapping his nose mysteriously.

"You are going around Manchester, with a paste brush, putting up Stone Roses posters?"

"That's the secret. Never forget the grass roots. Never neglect the kids. Better to grab one kid's interest with a poster than be sitting at home getting fat." (Evans' curious and, perhaps old-fashioned, morality can be glimpsed through this particular paradox. Although flash by nature, he feels uncomfortable with an ostentatious vehicle. An Escort also proved much more practical for such 'grass roots' tasks as postering as it would command less attention than a BMW.)

The meeting between McKenna and Evans that followed the car journey was far from easy. Something had changed and Evans' attitude was laced with mild regret.

"Look Roddy," he explained, "a lot has happened here. Your company has done a lot to us . . . I asked your people to give me their best shot. Right back at the beginning, I said come up with the best you can do. I felt that it wasn't going to be a massive deal but that didn't matter as long as the company was fully committed. And this guy came to me and told me it was the best possible deal. He told me it was the best that the company could do at that point. I didn't know, did I? I believed that. But then they came back a week later with a deal that was a vast improvement on the deal that was supposed to be the best they could do.

"That was the moment that Silvertone lost The Stone Roses. It was that early because that was when I realised that these people were jibing me. They thought I was some Cheshire bumpkin. That was when I started to plan ahead. I knew I had to be two steps ahead of Zomba and one step ahead of the band."

That is what Evans told McKenna at the time. At least that's how McKenna remembers it.

"No," says Evans now, "I would have stayed with Zomba if they had shown that they really believed in the band. I admired their marketing. I thought they were better at that aspect than EMI or whoever. Perhaps not better than Geffen, but pretty good in that aspect. But they didn't really have the experience to handle a really major rock act. It's a much more in-depth process than all the pop acts they had been peddling . . . I don't think Zomba had the vision to see things years and years in advance. If you really want to know when Zomba lost The Stone Roses, it was at Spike Island . . .

". . . and I didn't know it at the time because I thought they would hit us with a fantastic new deal. I thought they would rush back to London after Spike Island and immediately start setting up a big new package. It was the disappointment from that. That's what really crushed it. I knew that Spike was the peak. If we couldn't get the new deal immediately after that, we would be finished. That's what killed it for me with Zomba."

* * *

There was now a palpable unrest in the band and those around them concerning their future. Their acclaimed début album had been released almost two years before and it was high time they started recording new material. 'One Love' had been released in July of the previous year; since March 1990, Silvertone had begun re-releasing the band's singles, beginning with 'Made Of Stone'. True, the band had subsequently attempted to start rehearsals for the second album in the spring of 1991. The ideas were there, languishing in the back of their heads, but the work ethic that had powered them through the five years that preceded the release of the first album had started to drain away. In fact, things hadn't been right since Spike Island. The uncertainty over their record company wasn't helping matters, but there was no denying that the unnatural marriage that bonded Brown, Mani, Reni and Squire (and Gareth Evans) so tightly had collapsed into a loose, schoolboyish affair. Hard work and dedication seemed beyond them, now that the gargantuan task of 'making it' had been achieved. They were experiencing the inevitable feeling of anticlimax that greets every new rock star when they have broken through, the deadening realisation that stardom, fame, success . . . none of it really means all that much.

There comes a time, in the life of every great band, when the ball is placed directly at their feet. It's a time fraught with danger for, although the sense of power is intoxicating, that extraordinary feeling that you could sign to any record company in the world for practically any amount of money is the stuff of dreams. But the idea that the artists themselves possess this power is an illusion. In reality, it lies elsewhere.

For a while, Gareth Evans was manager of the most sought after band on the planet. And whatever his shortcomings, Evans wasn't daft. When Warner Brothers sent him tickets to fly to LA, he knew the kind of games they would be playing. Not that he cared. He loved LA. The sheer sense of possibility about the place excited him. If his bluff and bluster could help him to survive in Manchester, what could it achieve in LA, where the hot air of PR is as much a part of the environment as the smog? Evans could feel at home in LA, far from the envious clutches of the Manchester scene, far away from small-time club management, in a different sphere, where smiling men in pastel coloured suits would treat him with a satisfying degree of respect.

With Mathew Cummings, as ever, beside him, Evans checked into the

162

Stadler Hilton. He was provided with his own driver, a bull-necked wall of a man who doubled as a bodyguard. Very impressive, very Mafioso. Very Gareth. When asked if there was anything he wanted to see, Evans replied in the affirmative and was soon being whisked in the direction of San Diego, 90 miles to the south.

"I wanted to see where they made the golf clubs, it was important for me. That might not seem very rock'n'roll but I thought it was fun to see my two worlds, rock'n'roll and golf, collide." On returning to the hotel, he was handed a message.

"Gareth. I would like to have dinner with you tonight. Signed, D. Geffen."

The rise of David Geffen through the American music hierarchy is well charted. Although not a universally loved figure (Frederic Dannen's book, *Hit Men*, covering the dark side of the US music industry, refers to him as ". . . vain, arrogant and an incorrigible gossip"), Geffen's story is nonetheless remarkable. After flunking college, he learned the basics of business from his mother, who manufactured bras and corsets. A spell spent working for the Ashley Famous Management Agency enabled Geffen to learn the basics of the music industry, after which he made the decision to go it alone. His first move was to become manager of idiosyncratic singer-songwriter Laura Nyro, an artist who formed the basis of Geffen's fledgling publishing company. After selling the Nyro rights, he continued on the up escalator by managing the complex careers of Crosby, Stills and Nash, famously signing them to Atlantic Records. As a manager, Geffen was ferocious and was soon regarded as the scourge of the industry, which rebounded much to his credit, of course.

In 1970 he created Asylum Records, the label that signed Joni Mitchell, Jackson Browne, Linda Ronstadt and The Eagles, amongst others. Asylum was a young, aggressive company and Geffen's business skills and ear for new music soon made it a very successful one. Asylum even snared Bob Dylan away from Columbia, albeit for two albums only. After a period of enforced retirement (when Geffen believed that he had cancer), he returned in 1980 to create Geffen Records and strike a distribution deal with Warner Bros. The new label played high stakes with surprisingly low earning signings Elton John and Donna Summer, both of whom left Geffen after disappointing fiscal returns, and, in September of that year, John Lennon and Yoko Ono. All of which added fabulous kudos to his CV, but little weight to his bank account. But his big moves came by linking with the film industry (*Beetlejuice*), financing Broadway shows (Lloyd Webber's dreadful, hugely successful, two song warble-fest, *Cats*) and by signing a string of fantastically lucrative heavy metal acts, including the biggest of the lot, Guns'n'Roses.

Throughout his career Geffen was regarded with disdain by the main body of the industry. A wise-cracking, fast-talking maverick, could he have sensed a strange kinship with this equally eccentric figure from Manchester, Gareth Evans? It would appear so. He loved Evans' openly corny mode of attack. He loved the sheer cheek of the man, and the way the Roses' manager could make extremely intelligent people squirm, struggling to hide their embarrassment when faced with Evans' flamboyance. Evans was great fun.

Evans was equally impressed, both with Geffen and with LA life in general. That night the two entrepreneurs dined at a top Hollywood Italian restaurant. Geffen was flanked by his right-hand man, Ed Rosenberg, and Gary Gersh, the A&R man who had first alerted Geffen to the Roses. The whole meal proved to be a performance, with the chef wandering out to greet Geffen with, "And what can I create for you tonight, Mr Geffen?" Very LA. After a considerable palaver, which Evans loved, the food was duly brought in, served on a silver platter, with a maximum of fuss, though Evans couldn't help noticing that it was, in fact, nothing more than spaghetti with prawns, rather similar to the food served in the Italian restaurant two doors away from International One.

The talk, that night, was of Manchester. Evans: "Manchester was very much the 'in' city and I could tell that Geffen wanted as much of the action as he could get. He was fascinated by my tales of The International Club and, for him, to have someone from the nucleus of the Manchester scene seemed to mean an awful lot to him.

"We talked about the Roses and other bands. I was hot at that time and, I can clearly state now, that both Inspiral Carpets and Happy Mondays asked me to manage them during that period. But I was only concerned with The Stone Roses. It would have been too complicated to diversify. Nevertheless, Geffen's eyes lit up at the mention of all these band names. I fought hard to get the subject back to The Stone Roses. I wasn't about to do lots of PR for all the other bands although sometimes I wonder, when the ball was in our court, exactly what we could have achieved if we had all pushed together. America would have just collapsed before us."

There was, of course, the little problem of Silvertone. Evans painstakingly explained the whole situation, taking great delight in the way that Geffen stiffened with surprise when the comparatively tiny amounts that had originally secured The Stone Roses were brought up. Nobody knows just how impressive Gareth's hard sell was that night and one might conclude that Geffen had already decided to go full out to capture the band before they met but, nevertheless, Evans could justifiably claim that he had delivered a master stroke. During dessert, Geffen handed Evans a cheque for £350,000; a sign of good faith, a loyalty hook. It was Geffen's first indication that he was absolutely serious about getting The Stone Roses for his label. The money was intended to fund the Roses legal case, and wasn't technically supposed to be binding; it was almost a gift. But Evans wasn't stupid. He could feel the strings beginning to tug, and even the natural rush at getting one of the biggest players in the music industry keen to sign the Roses couldn't mask the growing feeling that he was now potentially digging himself into a very deep hole indeed.

As if to emphasise this, on the way out of the restaurant that evening, Ed Rosenberg draped his arm around Evans' shoulders, bending his face close to that of the manager's. His expression was serious.

"Gareth," he informed him, "you do realise we have signed The Stone Roses."

Evans replied to the effect that, as far as he was concerned, the Geffen deal was easily the most superior option. He also liked the notion of moving out to LA, bringing Cummings with him, and branching off into a new direction – the film world.

"Yes . . . I think that's the best option," he repeated, before cautiously adding, "but I'm not the band. It's up to them at the end of the day, obviously. But I will definitely try to persuade them. No doubt about that."

"No!" snapped Rosenberg. "You don't understand. We *have* signed The Stone Roses."

This was the moment when Gareth Evans realised that he had truly started playing with big stakes. There wasn't a great deal of negotiation going on here; Geffen had made his decision, and Evans was expected to fall in with it, period. There was a strange atmosphere between Evans and Cummings on the journey home. For the first time in their business relationship they felt that they had relinquished control of proceedings. This wasn't like Zomba at all. British record companies, it is often stated, are like banks. They are, within reason, content to provide the finance and stand back, if the band so desires, allowing the talent to nurture and only occasionally stepping in when, for instance, the debt becomes too large or the product unpromising. A good record company is, indeed, like a good bank. But that's not the American way and Geffen weren't like any bank that Gareth and Mathew had been involved with. The monster – The Stone Roses – had been created and their original weak contract couldn't continue to tie them down. The band had the potential to become a huge money spinning machine, and there were plenty of vultures in the music industry who were waking up to the fact. Geffen, though amiable, had come in hard, but America was full of such big game players. Who knew who else was hovering around The Stone Roses?

* * *

On May 29, 1991, *The Manchester Evening News* carried the headline: High Court frees band from contract – COURT JOY FOR ROSES. Below it there appeared the following story: "Hit Manchester band The Stone Roses were this afternoon celebrating a High Court victory over their record company. Judge Humphries ruled that the group's contracts with music giant Zomba were unfair and an unjustifiable restraint of trade. The decision leaves the way open for the band to take up a £2m offer from America and frees them from their contract.

"Ruling for The Stone Roses, the judge said, 'Record companies take a considerable risk in spending money supporting comparatively unknown artists. It must be very galling if they cannot share in the vast sums of money if the artists achieve success.'

"He said that in his judgement these considerations did not justify the record company taking such complete and exclusive control of The Stone Roses for seven years.

"The judge described the negotiations and the contract as 'one sided' in favour of Zomba and its Silvertone label. As far as the contract was concerned, he said, 'It's unfair that any competently advised artists would have consented to sign it.'

"The judge spoke of an immense inequality of experience between the record company and the group and its manager. He criticised Zomba for sending a 'deliberately misleading' letter to the band asking for variations in the original contract signed in April 1988. It was then that the manager, Gareth Evans, became suspicious and relations between the two deteriorated.

"The judge awarded costs against Zomba and Silvertone and ordered an enquiry to find out how much, if anything, the band had lost because of the hearing. During the month long case, the band were accused by their record company of saying, 'Boo hoo, we want to get out, after a better offer.' The band said the company was greedy.

"The Stone Roses are planning a massive celebration gig – possibly in Manchester – on the lines of their famous Spike Island rave.

"Their jubilant manager, Gareth Evans, rushed from the court to phone the verdict to Ian Brown and Gary Mounfield in Manchester. Guitarist John Squire and drummer Alan Wren were still in Rotterdam following Manchester United's European triumph. Before going for a victory lunch with the group's legal advisors, Mr Evans said, 'It's been a great week for United and the band. I'm very pleased with the result.' "

Gareth Evans: "Difficult to forget . . . that day. But I always knew it was coming. I always knew that, if Zomba let The Stone Roses down, that it would come to that and that we would win. Again you may debate whether or not I deliberately allowed the band to sign a bad contract in the first place. I think, perhaps, I'd rather regard it as an insurance in case the company failed us. As they did . . .

"You must remember something else here . . . Courts have never scared me. I have been involved in so many court cases, I know that scenario probably better than anyone else . . . although I think we were legally correct, you have to play the courts. I'm comfortable there. I'm involved in cases now (1998). It's part of my work and it's very complex. I communicate well with legal people because I have to. Whether it's in the court or on the golf course. I'm not even sure the Roses understood quite how much effort was put into that victory."

As to whether this is the truth, the whole truth and nothing but the truth . . . No one could doubt that Gareth Evans knew a great deal about court procedure, or that he had often been extremely successful in that arena. But the timing of the Roses/Zomba court case was curious. A few weeks earlier Evans had lost heavily in court over a property squabble and had lost confidence in court procedure, as he confided to Roddy McKenna on the morning that the Zomba case was due to be heard. Immediately prior to walking into court, Gareth, Roddy and Ian Brown had all met outside Embankment Tube Station and had wandered off to have a coffee together.

McKenna: "Yes . . . that was bizarre. They were the band and I was with the company. And yet we had a really good chat. It was so low key. So friendly. As if we were still working together so, clearly, there was nothing personal in this. I tend to think that they saw me as being on their side of the line, in a sense." McKenna was uncomfortable with the idea of appearing in court. On a practical level, he had had to buy a suit. Now he wasn't, and never will be, a 'suit' person, preferring, as he does, denim and motorcycle leathers. But he'd opted for the cheapest suit he could find and was standing there, on the Embankment, shuffling about uncomfortably, when Evans waltzed up to him and announced:

"Nice suit, Roddy. Nice jacket. Look at my jacket."

He opened the side of his jacket to reveal an enormous wad of money pinned to his inner pocket.

"I tell you what. I don't want to appear in court, again. Let's you and me settle something now. Take the money. Concede the case."

McKenna was stunned but he managed a smile, refused the money and, in good cheer, accepted a coffee and a large amount of disarmingly lightweight banter. No tension disturbed the fun. "We were friends . . . and that seemed to lift us beyond the court battle," he says.

Of course, it is not unreasonable to conclude that if Zomba had realised the strength of the bond between the Roses and McKenna, then this sad divorce might have been avoided and, who knows, what would then have become of The Stone Roses?

12

LOVE SPREADS

The vultures were indeed circling around the Halcyon Hotel in Holland Park, one of London's most famously rock'n'roll orientated hotels, as The Stone Roses settled into pre-signing revelry. Gareth Evans, on the other hand, was a worried man. Having met David Geffen, bright and breezy, in the hotel's lobby, he strode down the corridor to be immediately confronted by the MD of Polygram, resplendent in cowboy hat and eye-catching grin.

"Gareth," he greeted Evans. "You are signing for us!"

"Well . . . er . . . Geffen are . . ."

"Gareth, man, you sign for us. OK?"

Evans: "It was really heavy. I was really confused and I had been getting all kinds of strange signals. I proceeded to go and knock on the doors of all the band. I was worried sick, to be honest. I knew that the Roses would soon sack me. I knew that was on the cards, even then, that had been in the undertone for some time and so I had been planning for that as well.

"I mean, that made things even more complicated than they already were. Because I felt unstable. But to have to deal with the might of the American music industry in one ear and have to listen to the band planning my demise in the other . . . it was a pretty precarious position. Years of work lay in the balance. And then to such bigwigs in the same hotel, readying themselves to sign the band. I didn't know they were all going to turn up. I thought, 'I don't need this anymore'."

The whole Roses setup was going to the wire. Bizarrely, in one London hotel there were at least four separate parties, all thinking they were going to sign the band. Half an hour before the actual signing, the band called Evans to their hotel room. Looking worried and slightly lost, they opened their palms, and asked the simple question, "Gareth. This is fucking daft. Who should we sign to?"

"You should sign to Geffen," replied the manager, resisting the temptation to add, "You are already signed to Geffen."

Evans: "The clincher was that Geffen were offering more in terms of money and commitment. It was as simple as that, really. Plus they had already stumped up that £350,000. That meant a lot to me. They had shown belief in the band and I thought there was a certain amount of honour due. But the Roses didn't have any honour, especially not John Squire. He was quite ruthless about it. That £350,000 meant nothing, really, to him. I'm not sure it meant anything to any of them."

The Stone Roses tumbled from the Halcyon Hotel, surrounded by the Geffen top dogs, lawyer John Kennedy and Gareth Evans. Everything had been agreed and those last minute distractions and band doubts, it seems, had been banished. One simple act remained – the signing of the contracts. Maybe it was superstition; maybe The Stone Roses didn't want to repeat themselves – they had, after all, signed the Zomba contract in a hotel and the memory of all that had ensued might have made them reluctant to repeat the experience. More likely though, they were thinking of The Sex Pistols' short-lived signing to A&M outside Buckingham Palace back in 1977. They wanted somewhere blatant and touristy to sign their deal; somewhere daft.

Just then, a red London bus and a black taxi drove by.

"Let's do it on a bus. Let's do it on a bus . . ."

And so, like a gaggle of over-excited schoolchildren, the most sought-after band in the world and the representatives of one of America's top record labels, found themselves waiting at a bus stop. Naturally, it mattered not a jot where the next bus was going, nor how full it was. This was London. People do all kinds of things on buses in London. And the Americans in tow, here, could regard it as a tourist treat.

When the next bus came, the band scampered on board, and headed for the top deck like schoolboys let out early for the afternoon. The other passengers began to exchange curious glances as briefcases were opened, pens were snapped into action, and contracts passed to and fro. Events might have taken an unexpected turn had one particularly uninterested old gentleman, resplendent in his trilby hat, succumbed to Evans' pleadings for him to witness the event. Had this surly and distanced observer obliged, there is a possibility that The Stone Roses story would have taken another direction, perhaps one that would have turned out to be more lucrative for the band. But it was not to be – John Kennedy turned to Evans and insisted, "Gareth. You should witness the contract. In fact, you *must* sign it."

Evans: "I didn't realise the significance of that at the time. I knew, deep down, that the end was on its way. Obviously John Kennedy knew, as he'd been in discussions with the band about it, but he insisted that I should sign. It was like a gift from him to me. A parting gift, if you like, or maybe a little bit of insurance because he'd worked very closely with me and he knew just how hard I'd worked. He also knew that the very existence of my name on that contract, even if only as a witness, would help convince any court that I was obviously working extremely close to the band at the time of signing." Now if and when The Stone Roses decided to wrestle themselves free from Gareth's grip, it would be very difficult for them to prove that they had grown apart from Evans at the point of signing the Geffen contract.

For the record, the Geffen contract provided the Roses with a £2.3 million advance rising, album by album, option by option (record companies always have the option to 'jump ship' on a yearly basis), for ten years with the band receiving an increasingly favourable royalty as the albums skip by. Taken literally, like all such contracts, it looked like a simple route to untold riches; that is, of course, provided the artist, despite increasing wealth and diminishing hunger, can produce ten years of classic work.

* * *

Geffen had signed a band they regarded as a long-term investment, capable of one day achieving global glory. For the first time, The Stone Roses were capable of becoming the world-shattering act they always believed they could become. And yet, like a football team whose season of dominance crumbles during the last few games, everything that made the band special had suddenly stopped working. They were no longer a tight unit of arrogance, talent and inspiration, and at the very moment that they had a platform to deliver on all that promise, things started to fall apart.

The influx of money had imposed an immediate geographical setback. Ian Brown, enchanted with the views of Cardigan Bay backed by Snowdonia, had bought himself a farm in rural North Wales and settled quickly into the kind of unpressured country lifestyle one would normally associate with a richer and more established pop star from an earlier generation. He didn't mind. Unpretentious and intelligent, Brown had grown tired of the twin rat races of the music business and life in the city. A natural gardener, he relished the opportunity to work outdoors in the tranquillity of Wales. Brown had got himself a quiet life though it was not, perhaps, the most inspiring setting for a burgeoning songwriter. Likewise, John Squire had fled Manchester in search of rural calm. Always fond of Cumbria, he forsook Chorlton-cum-Hardy for the fringe of the bay of Morecambe.

By stark contrast, Reni and Mani clung ferociously to their Manchester roots, not wishing to abandon that vital link with the ever-changing youth scene.

Mani: "I ain't never been a country lad. Corny as that. I like going down the town and have always had a very special relationship with the kids in Manchester. I feel safe with them, really, even though, at times, the opposite is true. But I go down to United, down to quite a few pubs, down to the Atlas bar and all that. The Hacienda in those days. What would be the point of staying out in the country? That was more an Ian and John thing, really. Me and Reni, we are big townies . . . always will be, I reckon. If you are away from the action it's like, over, really."

Had The Stone Roses been under the guidance of strong management at the time, the moves to the country might have been thwarted, or at least delayed. One of the problems, however, lay in the relative ages of the band. To Geffen, The Stone Roses looked like young upstarts, ready to challenge the global dominance of the mighty U2 and stake a claim for the new generation. One glance at the band's birth certificates, however, should have been enough to cast a shadow over this belief. The four members of U2 were either 19 or 20 when they signed to Island; indeed, at 29, John Squire was actually older than Paul McCartney and George Harrison were when The Beatles split up. The rest of the Roses, dragging wives, children and mortgages in their wake, were unlikely to spend the next five years trudging the world indulging in rock'n'roll hedonism. Whatever wildness and spirit remained would have to be unleashed in short, sharp bursts. Geffen weren't stupid, however, and they consoled themselves with the thought that The Stone Roses might well flourish in maturity – over the next couple of albums, they were counting on the band evolving from purveyors of a precocious blend of dance and rock to a mature, quality act with international appeal. Whether the band realised it or not, this was Geffen's long-term plan – to put The Stone Roses at the top of the growing roster of hip artists who were also crossing over into AOR territories, acts capable of filling stadiums and happy to promote the product. R.E.M. were the classic example of these acts, were it not for the saving grace of their wilful determination to experiment with music, even at the price of decreasing record sales. The words 'long term' were actually used in a Roses press release of the time; the phrase would soon start to haunt both the label and, indeed, the patient but slowly diminishing body of people who still counted themselves as Roses fans.

One thing was clear: Gareth Evans really was on the way out. The link had been broken somewhere during the Silvertone court case. His work in setting up the Geffen contract was, effectively, his swan song and, despite the band's reliance on him during the day of the signing itself, he was no longer party to the workings of the Roses inner circle. Indeed, he was no longer even welcome. The phones had stopped ringing, and there was a certain distance now in his conversation with each band member.

It hadn't been an easy decision. The band did have their doubts about the cold Evans-free world that awaited them. However, they were being tacitly spurred on by Geffen who had been having trouble dealing with Evans' inconsistencies and doubted the wisdom of having such a loose cannon in control of their leading long term rock hope. In America especially, the fine art of big-time rock management was just one step away from high level accountancy, and regarded very much as a sober affair. Eager to protect their considerable investment, the powers that be at Geffen wouldn't tolerate eccentric rock managers who couldn't be trusted with large amounts of money. Evans didn't fit. Moreover, it seemed obvious that he wouldn't wish to sell the American half of his management responsibilities to a larger, corporate team. Gareth Evans and Mathew Cummings in big-time fiscal America – even now, the thought causes a shudder.

Mercifully for Geffen, The Stone Roses made the decision to part company with Gareth Evans before any real damage could be done to their new deal. It wasn't easy for the four and, whatever one might think of Evans' methods, he had been an awful lot closer to being a member of the Roses than any of the band would later care to admit. What's more, had Gareth not chanced upon the band, and had the audacity to push them through a series of highly idiosyncratic career moves, Blackpool, Ally Pally and Spike Island would never have happened, and The Stone Roses' story would have been completely different. Gareth was hard-working and hands-on, at all times he was fired with an unquenchable enthusiasm and an uncanny knack of keeping the bonds of camaraderie between the band and himself tightly secured. Indeed, it might be argued that his mistreatment of Andy Couzens way back when was due to his sensing a weakness, not in musical terms, but in the way that particular member affected the setup of the band.

Gareth Evans: "I knew that the band would sack me from very early on. I knew what they were like as people, especially John. I knew that, given the chance, he would be a 'user' and I always expected to get the sack. You see, I even played on that a bit. All that Andy Couzens stuff, when I saw how the band reacted against him when it became clear to them that their careers might be affected if he stayed. That 'coldness'. Well, obviously I could use it to my advantage but I was never in any doubt that it would, one day, be my turn.

"This underlying feeling was hardened back in 1989 when Steve Adge made an unbelievable comment to me. He told me that, 'I'm keeping you in a job. If you upset me I'll get the band to sack you.' I knew Adge was vying for the management seat but that's just a normal thing. I didn't blame him. In fact, in telling me that, in asserting his apparent power, he was doing me a big favour. From that moment I had started collecting all the legal stuff. I was determined to be totally ready for the sacking.

"I knew what kind of characters they were. I'd always known that. There was this thing about John working incredibly hard in the studio . . . and he did. He worked tirelessly, all the time and would sometimes complain about it. But what he didn't realise was that, when John Leckie came in and really started working, a lot of Squire's work would be wasted. It was Reni who had an awful lot of musical input. He just worked at a different rate. But John never saw that. He just saw himself, working hard and nurturing, I believe, a desire to use things to his advantage further on down the road. So yes, I watched all this and was ready for the sacking."

The band arranged a meeting with John Kennedy and, at some point during that meeting, it was disclosed that they could sack Evans. Everything funnelled straight back to that original managerial contract, where Gareth had succeeded in pulling the 'equal partners' trick and by pulling Mathew into the equation, had secured 33% for the management team. Although he now insists that this would shrink to a mere 20%, it was still twice the rate that management would normally expect to receive. In short, it meant an awful lot of money was being diverted from the band and, at first glance, it might seem that this meant they could easily free themselves from such a tie.

Evans again: "I think they thought they had cracked it. They had got the major deal, the big contract and they no longer had any need for me . . . [but] they should have stayed with me for another six months to a year. That was their fatal mistake. They got rid of me just a little too early. It now seems obvious that they made the most fundamental mistakes at precisely the wrong time. If only they had kept me for that six months."

Evans backs up his claim by referring to the US dates that were being lined up for the Roses in the wake of the Geffen deal. "We had just set up a series of gigs, centring on dates at Madison Square Garden and the LA Forum and the band wouldn't do them. Bill Graham was going crazy for The Stone Roses at that particular point. If they had done it, they would have been massive in the States and John Squire was totally wrong to pull back from those gigs and decide that he wanted to go with new material. The old Roses stuff was new material in America.

"They upset a lot of people. A lot of very powerful people. The American music business is not like the English at all. I know how it works now. It's not frustrating for me personally because, the way things went, it all worked out just right for me. But the Roses were tilting on the brink of being the biggest British band since The Beatles. No doubt about that. But you can't pull back and then attempt to do it again, later. The moment has gone. But it was amazing to feel that moment in your grasp. They could have played those gigs, got the money, ushered into prime position . . . then they could have sacked me. Then would have been the right time. They were stupid. They got it all horribly wrong."

In a way, Evans' account offers a typical description of Roses behaviour; it's even ironically fitting. They seemed to have the ability to screw things up at the final moment, to snatch defeat from the jaws of victory, though this was screwing up big time. Naturally, opinions vary as to the reasons for what happened next. The much-maligned John Squire has his own version of events: "It's easy to say that we all became lethargic and pulled those big American dates, but we were a band who had got to where we were with a particular body of work, a particular style. Now we had to move onwards. The danger was that we would just continue to play the same set and become very tired, dull. That would never have been a Stone Roses thing, would it? It might have raked in the money for Gareth but it wouldn't have been natural. And we all knew it. We just wanted to do things right."

Evans maintains that the self-belief, so essential to the Roses' success up until this point, had started to cross over into arrogance, a classic rock star pattern and, again, it's difficult not to sympathise with his viewpoint. "They definitely began to believe in themselves to such an extent that, to them, they seemed indestructible. That is very dangerous and very foolish. But it's a classic situation, isn't it? Not just in rock'n'roll, but in all business, in all life. Outrageous fortune arrives, either by luck or skill, it doesn't matter which and it brings with it something incredibly self-destructive. The belief that whatever you do, it will all be for the best because you are so special. I'm telling you. Nobody is special. Nobody. The Roses had a lot going for them but they also lacked a lot. As soon as they lost sight of that fact . . . it was lost."

This period remains tainted by a nasty little incident which took place at Evans' Knutsford Farm after the band had had a meeting with John Kennedy. Presumably firing on an anti-Evans bent, they decided to pull off the motorway, at Knutsford, and, in a dark reminder of the FM Revolver incident, allegedly break into Evans' house.

Evans: "I was at home and my son was upstairs. They pulled out the phones and broke the windows. I was worried about my son. He is a Downs child and had always got really excited whenever The Stone Roses came on TV. We really didn't need this. They were ranting on about how they had wanted more than that £10,000 . . . ranting on but they didn't scare me. I'd been in major situations with the clubs, as you know, and this was nothing.

"I threw Ian out of the house. He's not as tough as he seems. He's quite pathetic. Funny thing is that Ian came back the very next day. I wasn't surprised really. I knew Ian was intelligent and had had time to think about things. He said they didn't want to give me 20%. That was the crunch. He said he didn't want Mathew involved. They still didn't have a clue [about how much work] Mathew did . . . But Ian was running after my car, pleading with me to stop and speak. And of course I would take them to court. It would have been stupid not to. But they did play into my hands a lot. Think about it. How stupid was it to break into my farm at that particular point? How, exactly, would that look in court?"

Although none of The Stone Roses would ever speak about this incident, let alone admit to it, a later statement by Mani might shed some light on the matter. "As a band we worked together, but we were always spontaneous. We always did things on the spur of the moment. The best songs were really written like that. The best gigs were ones where something unexpected happened and all our carefully laid plans counted for nothing. That was the gang-like thing and, as a gang, you can go in any direction. That's what made it exciting and I'd say that was what originally made The Stone Roses a special band. As soon as we became huge, we lost that spontaneity. I suppose that's natural. What can you do? Me and Reni never quite lost it. We'd still have a laugh." Could this trait have resulted in a spur-of-the-moment trip to Evans' farm? It's not hard to see the Roses' maverick attitude, which in many ways made them such a distinctive band, leading them into an unpremeditated act without considering the possible fall-out.

Big management teams were hovering in the background waiting to see what the results of the Evans/Roses confrontation would be. There was significant interest Stateside – Michael Jackson's management were but one of several parties following proceedings closely. In England, most every top level manager had been paying close attention to events for some time, hoping to wrestle the band out of any ensuing scrap. The band themselves opted to put all the legal wrangling to one side, and concentrate on what they knew best – making music. Deciding to use Ian Brown's North Wales home as a base, they began to look for a suitable nearby studio. It was a futile search, for state-of-the-art digital recording complexes are surprisingly thin on the ground in Snowdonia. Nevertheless, with customary arrogance, and with the help of ersatz manager, Steve Adge, The Stone Roses actually pulled off a coup by hiring the much-celebrated Rolling Stones Mobile (a moveable recording studio), plonking it in the hugely unlikely setting of The Old Brewery in Ewloe. The location itself was characteristic of the band – it wouldn't have been at all difficult for The Stone Roses to park the damn thing in a more traditional setting, Geneva perhaps or anywhere in France. But damp, demanding, drizzled-upon Wales, with its greying villages and, on a clear day, stunning vistas, is as evocative as anywhere in Britain; as Led Zeppelin famously testified, the landscape can be a powerful inspiration.

And inspiration is exactly what The Stone Roses needed, as they gathered together, armed with six-and-a-half songs and John Leckie. Without really knowing it, certainly without thinking about it, The Stone Roses were about to launch into one of the strangest periods any top British band has ever experienced. The Roses were a band based on tightness, on ferocious camaraderie; they were four musicians funnelling their different avenues of influence down to one intelligent base, the very process that had so excited Roddy McKenna, four years previously. It has often been said (mainly by Mancunians) that the music which comes from Manchester tends to be good simply because the kids there own vast record collections. The Stone Roses were always the perfect example of that but, unlike Happy Mondays, they had acquired the dexterity to be able to use those sharp influences to the fullest effect, as they had demonstrated on record, especially on their début album. The album that had been greeted with a muted response from nervous critics had, in the time since, come to be regarded as an undisputed classic, one of the greatest début albums of all time.

But the growing esteem of that record was, in itself, beginning to cause immense problems. It was a perfect way to announce the arrival of a band; John Leckie knew instantly that *The Stone Roses* would count among his finest achievements as a producer. As for the new songs, there were six or seven good tunes, with strong melodies, a barrage of great ideas, but the band clearly felt that they were working in the shadow of that first album. Despite the fact that they had arrived in Wales armed with a considerable bunch of tunes, the bonds between them had already loosened considerably. Leckie noted at the time, that when the Roses assembled to start work on the second album, they seemed like a different band. The positive energy, the arrogance, which had so marked them out from the also-rans when they had emerged, had slackened. There was a curious aura of apathy surrounding them and, beneath it, a tumble of insecurities and damaged egos. Nothing unusual in that, of course, every band is an unnatural marriage that often hovers on the edge of disarray. But the Roses hadn't been 'every' band. That was the point. They were different and now, without that self belief, without Gareth too, they suddenly seemed so vulnerable, so lacking in spark. It wasn't hedonism – in fact, had they fallen into any kind of drug-taking, sexually indulgent, booze-guzzling orgy then things might have livened up. It was just a negative, brooding undertone.

The splits within the band were just beginning to show. One between

John Squire and Reni had been growing since the initial sessions for 'Fools Gold', when John Squire played to a drum loop, only consenting to the addition of the real, live Reni afterwards. This was confusing, to say the least. The most celebrated drummer in modern pop had seemingly been pushed aside by an equally celebrated lead guitarist who didn't like playing with him. That could, of course, have been put down to the fragility of band egos when faced with a tight recording schedule. To add insult to injury, the very same thing had happened with 'One Love' and Reni's understandable bitterness began to gnaw away at the band's tightness. This split, which might have only seemed like a minor indentation at the time, proved deeper and more destructive than anyone initially thought. By the time they hit the Rolling Stones Mobile, communication between the two musicians was stifled and professional, their friendship reduced to false gesturing and guarded fooling about.

To lay the blame for this at the feet of Squire would surely be unfair and simplistic. But there is no doubt that the dynamics of the band were now on unsure ground. And Squire's musical confidence no longer seemed to spur on the rest of the band. As the tentative recording progressed, it became clear that The Stone Roses were in danger of becoming a base for his idiosyncratic guitar style. His strange spat with Reni might, indeed, be put down to a simple scramble for power.

In truth, it cut even deeper than that. Slowly Brown started to notice that, in his words, ". . . it was becoming the John Squire Experience . . ." The situation deteriorated during the next twelve months, as Squire's Zeppelin fixation began to guide the songwriting away from their celebrated funky base. During a second spell in the Mobile, they managed to record 'Love Spreads', a mighty roller coaster of a song driven by a monster riff which went some way towards justifying Squire's intention to push the band into rockier territory. 'Breaking Into Heaven', 'Tightrope' and a loose half-formulated, untitled track that would transmute into a second latter-day Roses classic, 'Ten Story Love Song' would also crowd onto the recording.

But Leckie was far from happy. The new material lacked cohesion. Whereas the relationship between the songs on *The Stone Roses* had seemed blatantly obvious from day one, now the material seemed painfully disparate. Brown was also unhappy, sadly noting that the others seemed content to while away the hours ogling Led Zeppelin footage.

"Why are you worshipping that stuff?" he pleaded. "They haven't got what you have got."

"I meant it, too," Brown commented later. "I felt I was the only member of the band who knew how great we were, how much we meant to people. It was stupid, sitting around worshipping lesser bands, really stupid."

Brown, it seemed, was the only one left still carrying the old Roses arrogance. Essential arrogance, too. It didn't matter whether the band were better than Led Zeppelin, just as long as they believed they were. To Brown, this hero worship was a distinct sign of weakness. Also, he couldn't understand, and still can't, quite why they weren't sitting around listening to Augustus Pablo, or Miles Davis, or George Clinton. To take the Led Zep route was, with the greatest of respect, the easy way. Everyone knew that The Stone Roses were fully capable of evolving into a solid, unadventurous, phenomenally successful trad rock act (which is where Oasis would eventually step in and, to a more modest degree, The Seahorses) but they had always collectively despised that kind of emptiness. Leckie knew it. Ian Brown knew it. The sessions stumbled to a halt with the producer informing them that they had only about one third of a good album in their heads. They needed to retreat and regroup. But Leckie wasn't sure that that was possible.

Despite further sessions at the less auspicious Square One Studios in Bury at the start of 1993, the band seemed unable to consolidate their initial burst of songwriting, and continued to float in a directionless, disparate and geographically scattered state. Moreover, the world outside The Stone Roses was changing too, and they were in danger of being left behind. The heady vibe of Madchester was now a thing of the past, to be replaced with a dispiriting and, at times, rather sordid post-rave world. Club owners were apparently unable to hold back the encroaching shadow of the drug gangs and, despite not commanding the headlines of the previous eighteen months, or perhaps because of it, Manchester's criminal ring was tightening. Just around the corner, an unprecedented batch of inspired young bands readied themselves to flood the market under the daft tag, BritPop.

13

LETHARGY

Back in November 1992, Factory Records, for so long the solid heart of Manchester, had, following a domino effect run of bad management and plain bad luck, crashed spectacularly, signifying for many the end of an era. Happy Mondays, post-Factory, were stuttering to a messy and fractured halt and, in truth, had already seen their audience and their inspiration dwindle away rapidly during the course of 1992 following the release of their *Yes Please!* album. The city itself was literally changing fast; for a while it seemed that architecture was the new rock'n'roll, with stylish new architectural superstars such as Ian Simpson transforming whole areas of the city, from rat-infested cavernous warehouses, to media- and design-orientated office space. Metrolink trams cut a swathe from Bury to Altrincham, slipping past the city's new jewels, the Bridgwater Concert Hall, Manchester United's ferocious towering North Stand and the Salford Quays skyline, glistening like Dallas, slap bang in the middle of an area still poverty ridden and patrolled by petty gangsters dealing drugs. In the five years it took for The Stone Roses to release their second album, Manchester had witnessed at least one drive-by killing. (Significantly, many smaller clubs were closing down, often under pressure from drug gangs.) A whole other world, literally within the shadows of those pristine offices.

Nevertheless, Manchester had been scrubbed and revived and there was an undeniable elegance about some of the new constructions. To service the new workforce, off-beat café bars burst into life, to be quickly filled with media slags nibbling sun-dried tomatoes, talking up projects over mineral water and rocket salad, and bellowing haughtily into mobile phones. Scattered amongst this new spread of stylish anti-prole posturing – and surely Factory could share some of the blame for this new style-fixated zeitgeist – was a thin peppering of yesterday's rock stars, all looking distinctly out of time. Mark E Smith could be seen scowling in the corners, diving into a grubby pub, and into caricature, at the first opportunity. Durutti Column's Vini Reilly would sip Cappuccino and jot down songs. Sundry ex-members of The Smiths could be easily spotted, looking embarrassed amid the mass of Armani. The new wave of guitar pop ushered in by the Roses themselves at the end of the previous decade now had raves to compete with, and the nature of live music in the country had undergone a sea-change. "A small band's got to put on a hell of a show these days to compete with a rave," *Manchester Evening News'* Andy Spinoza told *Vox* in 1995. "I'd say it's almost impossible for a band to start small here and build a following slowly." And into this strange new atmosphere came the individual Stone Roses, looking distinctly wide-eyed and lost. Even Reni, forever in and out of the AI music store, had his swagger tempered as he surveyed the new terrain. Baggy was over for good.

Could The Stone Roses be a band of the new designer Manchester? Could The Stone Roses be a band at all? Rumours about them were flooding the city: John Squire had lost himself in a white-powder snowstorm and, perhaps worse, Brown, Reni and Mani had succumbed to a strangulatory apathy. At the time this last, and most powerful, rumour just didn't seem to ring true. This was, after all, the celebrated workaholic Stone Roses we were talking about. The only band in the history of all the practice rooms in Chorlton-cum-Hardy, if not in Britain, who didn't finish in time for last orders. Such dedication; such pride. But time was speeding by at a most alarming rate. Two years after Gareth Evans had departed (re-emerging, as an agent to golf professionals like Mark James, amongst many other roles), the only floppy fringes on the Manchester horizon belonged to the precocious, penniless Gallaghers of Burnage. (There was talk in the pubs of Burnage, Heaton Moor and Levenshulme, that this local band had the potential to grab The Stone Roses' crown but it was mostly taken as daft banter.)

Elements of confusion were creeping in to the framework around the Roses. This became evident when the author asked Anthony Donnelly, one of the infamous and eminently likeable Donnelly Brothers of the Gio Goi street fashion label, who was managing the Roses at the time. "Well . . . it's Adge, really," he offered, ". . . he's more or less the manager but he spends most of his days hanging around our office. We take calls, pass on messages to him about the Roses all the time. Seems the band are being run from within our office, but it's all very loose."

Anthony may have been exaggerating but, nevertheless, the entire operation had clearly run aground. How ironic it was to see the rest of Manchester cleaning up, sharpening its act, moving on, inspired by the momentum which the Roses among others had helped to create in the city, while the band themselves, once so driven by a strong work ethic, had collectively stumbled into an inglorious and unholy hippyish flop.

And then there was Geffen. The label issued statements reiterating that they stood behind the band, that the Roses were the most important band in the world and that it would take time to create a successor to that classic début. Geffen were clearly worried and attempting to buy time until the Roses came up with the goods. But this wasn't Led Zeppelin at the point of *The Song Remains The Same*. This was a band who had only released one album and, wonderful though it was, it had hardly sold in sufficient quantities to justify a dreamy five year hiatus. Let's put this in perspective: Lisa's Stansfield's suburban soul album *Affection*, also released in 1989, had outsold The Stone Roses by three to one.

Geffen, bless 'em, had taken the modern, creative attitude and had given the band enough rope to deliver in their own time. Gary Gersh's replacement at Geffen, Tom Zutaut visited the studio every six months for two years, and evidently didn't see anything to make his company get cold feet: "We heard the beginning of this album a couple of years ago and it was a case of being patient until they were ready to let it go," he told *Vox* in 1995. Ian Brown confirms Geffen's hands-off attitude: "We hardly heard a word out of the record company for two-and-a-half years," he told the same interviewer. "They just kept sending the cheques over."

The facts all seem to back up Tony Wilson's comment in the *Observer* about the Roses: "Working-class bands don't have the work ethic that middle-class acts do. When they got the advance for the record they went away and spent it." Geffen were treating the Roses with kid gloves, convinced that a sympathetic, no-pressure approach from The Man would result in unhindered creativity from the band. Instead, what happened was that all that free time saw the tension that made the band so special drain away. Moreover, any chance that the new friction within the band could be twisted into a creative 'frisson' was equally quashed, due to a seemingly inexhaustible supply of ready money to fritter away, and the geographical separation between members. They simply weren't close enough to each other on a regular basis for creative sparks to fly. In the final analysis, Geffen allowed the band too much respect. If they had insisted on a pre-second album summer single (as they had been promised), which could climb radio playlists during June 1993, and soundtrack a million Mediterranean holidays, then that small release might have carried enough sense of 'event' with it to carry the band through to the album's eventual release.

It could have happened. In March 1993, after being poked and prodded by Geffen's Gary Gersh, the band had called John Leckie who, genuinely astonished that some kind of attitude had been resuscitated, hot-tailed it to Square One Studios where a recording of a new three song demo, including the now amazing 'Ten Storey Love Song', was enough to send the producer scurrying back to Geffen with the encouraging news. It *could* have happened, but the band tensions continued to simmer, with the result that no one seemed willing or even capable of making an actual decision because of the likelihood that someone else wouldn't want to act on it.

'Ten Storey Love Song' would surface, eventually, as a hit single (reaching number 11) but many believe it could have been released sooner, and promoted with more vigour. Strangely, perhaps, it was the crumbling dynamic of the band that seemed to create a lack of confidence in the record company's marketing arm. It can be assumed, and phone calls from this writer to Geffen tend to support this, that the company had already shifted into damage control mode. Certainly, they would fight to recover their money, but would not now provide that extra push – or funds – needed to hurtle The Stone Roses up to the level of R.E.M. or U2. At this point, frankly, the whole damn game was up.

* * *

The music press still kept up a focus of sorts on the band. There was a running, 'We can track down the Roses' feature in *NME*, culminating in Gina Morris famously stalking Square One Studios. Wisely, the Roses refused to be interviewed. A front page at that juncture, without product, without anything solid to offer, would have made for ludicrous reading and could have been potentially damaging for the band. Coverage was the last thing they needed, especially as John Squire was increasingly acquiring a taste for two of rock'n'roll's most damaging indulgences – cocaine and ever-lengthening guitar solos.

John Squire: "There were times, many times actually, when I was simply using cocaine as a tool, as a way of simply getting things done. I knew it was bad, I knew it was wrong but it seemed like the only way to get the creative juices flowing. You fall into this trap and the only thing that gets you up and running is another line . . .

"I wouldn't say it completely took over. I agree that a good deal of narcissistic soloing on *The Second Coming* [sic] is down to coke. This really, really pissed Ian off because he was always against it but it wasn't ever quite as dramatic as some people have made it sound. And, yeah, I got off it by cycling around Monmouth, sixteen miles every morning after doing the Charlie the night before. My heart would be pumping like crazy but, slowly, I pulled away from it. It would return, I'll admit that, but never out of control."

Understandably, Ian Brown's version of events differs from Squire's. "John was on cocaine all the time during the recording of *The Second Coming* [sic].That was obviously a problem for everyone. A man's got cocaine up his nose, he's not saying anything to anybody. You give nothing if you are on coke, all you are doing is taking . . . I loathe and detest coke. If you are on coke you are busted . . . there's something the matter with you. I never did it. I smoked weed. I still do. I don't drink and don't like drink either. Mani used to take all kinds of drugs, anything going really. I don't know about Reni. But none of that was a problem, only John and the coke. It could be said that that killed the Roses. It was certainly a contributing factor."

Later, to *Uncut*, Brown acknowledged the fact that what started out an occasional 'treat' fast became a regular habit. "You are using it in the studio, you are using it at home. Pick the phone up and the next thing four grams are arriving. So you shut yourself in your room, you never come out. I'd go away for a week and come back and no one's talking. *He's* not talking to *him*. *He* thinks *he's* a dick, and *he* thinks *he's* a dick, and I'm trying to be daddy to them all. I'm walking in each room and getting big hugs, but *he* won't work with *him*. Charlie is the devil, simple as that."

Relations between the band and Geffen weakened still further when their A&R man, Gary Gersh, decided to leave the label. This act caused the band to shuffle through their contracts, wondering about the controversial 'key man clause', which links the band to their main contact in the label. Leaving the label wasn't a practical solution although the fact that they were considering it strongly hints at a disfunctioning unit, and quite what signals it sent to poor Geffen remains a matter of some speculation.

Despite this, in June 1993 The Stone Roses gave the company reason to heave hefty sighs of relief as, once again, they booked themselves into Rockfield Studios. Leckie returned, hoping to be swamped with ideas, with tunes, with enthusiasm. Instead, he found a sordid cliché. A band consumed by indecision, smoking themselves deeper and deeper into paranoid apathy, allowing arguments to fester, band members sulking on the couches, still watching Led Zeppelin on the bloody video. Whatever one might say about their shortcomings, Led Zep were undoubtedly the finest band of their generation, a powerhouse act drawing on rock'n'roll, blues and folk music. To achieve their pre-eminent status, they had had to fulfil their own artistic potential. But no band can do that by revering other bands above themselves. Only Ian Brown seemed to be preserving faith in how great The Stone Roses could be themselves. The good taste that had originally powered the band was evaporating.

Squire was chief culprit here; the economical, tuneful approach to lead guitar playing that had made him a genuine, un-clichéd guitar hero for the Nineties was a thing of the past. His work on the new album, while undoubtedly skilful, edged time and time again into solos for their own sake. Brown, perhaps the ultimate rock stylist, knew how sad this was. He knew too, that Squire probably despised his own lack of technique when it came to vocals. Here they were, two of the four powerful forces within The Stone Roses, at artistic loggerheads. They may not have acknowledged this at the time, they may not even have known it, but they were pulling in totally opposite directions. John Squire wanted to be known as a great British guitarist, part of a glorious line that would also include Clapton, Beck, Green, Page and Marr. Brown still existed in the space outside the mainstream, where punk had been born; where guitarists were too amateur to join that elite gang and because of this, rather than despite it, made music that soared beyond stylistic soloing, built on sheer guts and drive.

In all this talk of bad times and failure, bickering and indulgence, it's worth taking time here to remember exactly what made this band so great in the first place, what all four members contributed that marked them out from their peers. No one should ever underestimate the importance of Reni's musical ability in The Stone Roses; here was a multi-instrumentalist, perhaps the heart of the band, capable of delivering a blinding assortment of rhythms while simultaneously supplying tuneful harmonies to complement Ian Brown's lead vocals. In Mani, they had the original vociferous fun-time bassist, quite the antithesis of the sullen bass playing norm. His bass, like his personality, never sat back and moodily pumped away; it had vibrancy, it caught hold of your heartbeat, it snapped away to exquisite effect and, at its best, simply fell from the songs in a heart catching flurry of notes which often complemented one of Squire's tasteful runs. Listen, again, to 'Made Of Stone', how that bass rips from the song; it's unique. As is Reni's effortless drumming; as is Squire's early guitar work; as is Brown's arrogant stance and anti-style.

Back then, they played together; now they were playing for themselves, as the difference in Squire's guitar playing attests. Whether or not this was part fuelled by his cocaine addiction, a source of much of the ill-feeling between Squire and the profoundly anti-coke Brown, remains a moot point. In the final analysis, dabbling with drugs was surely only a symptom; boredom had set in, the band were no longer a unit, and without that discipline of playing together to create something much greater than the sum of its parts, indulgence set in.

John Leckie knew all this. He remains a producer in the most aesthetic sense. He knew a 'diamond' when he saw it – a band who have fallen into a natural state of artistic perfection, when everything they do falls just right. The Stone Roses were no longer such a prospect. They had become a tired parody and, although they would push themselves through a second, worthwhile album, it couldn't possibly challenge their first, less forced effort. As Leckie would, in later years, work with Radiohead and

The Verve, it would seem that his instinct for inspired talent has remained intact. And how significant was it that John Leckie, despite contributing to a couple of the new Roses songs, left Rockfield unfulfilled and unhappy. Apparently, his suggestion that the band should use Led Zeppelin's John Paul Jones as producer hadn't been taken as the joke it was intended to be. One cannot imagine Leckie making a similar suggestion, even in jest after his first meeting with The Stone Roses. How things had changed. With no one new to turn to and with no clue, either, how to attract the perfect producer, the Roses stumbled on under the production guidance of Paul Schroeder, who had been working alongside Leckie and had been engineer on the Roses' début album. Schroeder was to take over co-production with Simon Dawson, a local who had worked at Rockfield for some time (he was house engineer when the Roses recorded 'One Love' at Rockfield back in 1989). When Schroeder too quit the project, it was Dawson who saw the album through to completion.

The choice of Schroeder was not necessarily a bad idea, though he lacked that eccentric spark that might have awakened some of the old Roses spirit. Gareth Evans, one feels, might have plugged a little electricity into the band at this point, when they needed a touch of madness. At one point they tried to escape the deadening atmosphere of the studio by venturing out into the Welsh countryside by day. An understandable desire to break their pattern of non-achievement perhaps, but at a grand a day, the waste of time and money was nothing short of criminal. The band often escaped to Monmouth where they mixed freely with the young locals, enjoying the refreshing beer'n'fags bonhomie of the town, making new and apparently lasting friendships. City boy Mani married a local girl and settled in Monmouth, for a while at least; he even played football occasionally for the town's B-team. Both he and Brown retired their mums with part of their advance too. The summer of 1993 sped past in a bleary haze, with all four band members effectively doing anything to not have to face the awesome blank tape that lay waiting at Rockfield. All enjoyed long holidays. All succeeded in blanking out the tragic fact that The Stone Roses, as a powerful, coherent artistically on-the-edge working unit, were pretty much finished.

Gareth Evans: "It was a waste to hear those stories about coke and Rockfield and a few people did start to wonder if it would have been different if I had stayed . . . But my son, Mark, had gone into Pendlebury Hospital that year, needing 27 operations and needing my time which, of course, I gave him. On a personal level, it worked out perfectly for me . . . because, had it continued, I would have been around the world and that precious time would have been lost in a wave of music business madness. So, for me, I thank the Roses for letting me go at that time. But for them I honestly believe it was a disaster. I could tell what was happening. It had fallen flat for them, then, more than ever before, they needed a spark. They needed someone to make it crazy, to make it work." All great artists have a svengali behind them for at least the most critical years of their career – Brian Epstein, Andrew Loog Oldham, Kit Lambert, Peter Grant and Malcolm McLaren respectively guided The Beatles, The Rolling Stones, The Who, Led Zeppelin and The Sex Pistols to stardom, whatever happened once these acts had made it. In many ways, the Roses were a rock'n'roll test case for what happened if you *didn't* hold on to that guiding light for long enough.

★   ★   ★

It was November 1993 before the band returned to the studio, and even then they famously fell straight back into non-stop party mode, taking the indie band Lush along with them for a while. When they did manage to pop their heads around the studio door, the atmosphere seemed more and more to be dominated by Squire's increasing self-indulgence. The situation became somewhat easier following a meeting with their publicist, Phillip Hall, from Hall Or Nothing. Hall, a former *Record Mirror* writer, was blessed with legendary PR vision and was forging a reputation in the business as a vibrant, innovative industry play-maker. When the band asked Hall to manage them, the only surprise seemed to be that it had taken so long for the connection to be made. Gareth Evans agrees that the band had made a good choice, though inevitably he has different ideas regarding a strategy for the band's future. "Phillip Hall was my best friend. He was the Roses' press agent and we worked brilliantly together. He even name-checked me at an awards ceremony at The Grosvener House. It would have worked well with Phillip and I think the Roses saw him as the logical next step. Although I would have seen it differently. I was actually considering lining them up with a hugely powerful management in America, with a guy who was a top lawyer working with Geffen. That was on the horizon although I didn't let Geffen know that. Perhaps that was my big mistake. I think I would have put them with him and would have had a percentage coming off the whole ball game. The band really need that kind of international push. But, that said, Phillip would have been good for them in a similar way to me. Sadly it wasn't to be."

Indeed not. The universally respected and well-liked Hall tragically died of cancer just at the point where he was about to take hold of the Roses' reins. (The band dedicated their second album to him.) The Roses themselves concur that he would have been a salutary influence on them. Ian Brown: "Phillip Hall was one diamond man. He'd have been good for us, no doubt. I don't think we'd have got into the messes we got in. We didn't have a manager and we were open for anyone to have a poke. At that point we were really vulnerable. We had no inner strength other than a bit of Manc lip, but that was hardly enough for the situation we had found ourselves in."

No manager. Crumbling self-belief. Camaraderie splintering to fractious antipathy. Negative musical despotism. Wounded pride. No direction to speak of. Record company screaming for product. It's a damning litany, and all the while there was a barrage of new bands emerging, a new generation of kids demanding new heroes. One day Ian Brown glanced through the Manchester listing magazine *City Life* and found a vox pop article featuring a 14-year-old pulled from a street in Failsworth who sneered, "The Stoned Bozos? Who the fuck are they?" To some extent, the outrageous length of time the band were taking to make the follow-up album seemed to perversely demonstrate something of their old cool, lifting them above the album-a-year Brit pack. There was something elegant, arrogant, almost regal about 'making everybody wait'; their hardcore fans could still argue that it was further indication that the Roses weren't like everybody else, they made their own rules.

The argument would have held more water had The Stone Roses been able to exert a strict quality control regime over their multitude of songs, some of which were perfectly acceptable, if not world-shaking. But it was clear to everyone close to the band that this was far from being the case. Instead the band were lost in a sordid and desperate scramble to come up with something capable of moving them on from *The Stone Roses*.

As if to intensify the feeling of anti-climax, there was the little matter of attending the funeral of the one man they trusted enough to resurrect their career and guide them into international waters. And here, sadly, we can gauge the cavernous depth of the split in the band. As Ian Brown recalled in *Uncut*, "The kid (Squire) had cut himself off. When Phillip Hall died, John wouldn't come to the funeral. I said, 'At least show his mother and father that he meant something.' No, he wouldn't come to the funeral. The first rock of civilisation is when they bury the dead. I knew there was something the matter with the kid then. Nobody enjoys funerals, but I thought differently about him that day. I thought, 'Little fucker'."

Stunned by this personal tragedy, fractured further by their individual responses to it, The Stone Roses reluctantly succumbed to increasing and wholly understandable pressure from Geffen and, somehow, managed to push through and (almost) complete a full album by the end of the year. Worries that the album sounded 'forced' and lacked the flow of its illustrious predecessor, which would later turn out to be well founded, were somewhat mitigated as Geffen, a label with a hard rock legacy, seemed pleased with the tapes. At one point, the company even leaked a press release stating, "The new guitar orientated direction of The Stone Roses will establish them on a higher international level. It is the sign of one of the world's great rock band's reaching maturity." Whether this was genuine belief, or a spurt of desperate PR optimism fuelled by a label that had sunk millions into what was beginning to look like a white elephant, remains a mystery. One might reasonably conclude, however, that the kind of juggernaut momentum instigated by a record deal of such magnitude is rather difficult to halt.

Alas, one substantial problem remained. Removing the 'almost' from the much-overused phrase, 'the Roses' album is almost ready' would still prove frustratingly difficult for Geffen. A jewel, of sorts, was within their grasp . . . almost! The only hope, really, was to mask the whole affair in mystique, to build on that ludicrous anticipation, the 'elegance' that their silence could be construed to imply, to transform the five-year gap into a valuable marketing ploy. Surprisingly perhaps, this worked – indeed, worked only too well. *NME*, sensing mischief, happily pursued their "Where are the Roses?" line which bubbled away through another summer; vague 'hearings' of the album, already grandiosely titled, *Second Coming*, peppered their reports, like dubious UFO sightings. It was fun, too, and for a while it seemed that the very arrogance of taking five years to produce a follow-up album would be enough to cement the band firmly at the top of the tree, such an album cycle being normally reserved for acts wedged in the upper echelons of rock's hierarchy. Consider Factory Records supremo Tony Wilson's comment, "I think it is fabulous that The Stone Roses have taken five years to produce an album. I think that shows great confidence and a fantastic amount of respect for their own work." It would be nice to have been able to agree with that statement unreservedly. However, the rapidly mounting evidence pointed to a radically different state of affairs, and the band's loyal UK fan base were becoming increasingly worried by Geffen's ongoing allusion to Led Zeppelin in their reports on the Roses' progress.

Moreover, the music press was fast becoming obsessed with another Manchester band. One grey day on a street in Monmouth, Ian Brown met the two Gallagher Brothers, both already well-known devotees of The Stone Roses. It was, in retrospect, a meeting of the past and the future, as if an invisible baton was being passed from Brown to the Gallaghers. Oasis had landed. Two singles in, they were recording their ferocious début album, *Definitely Maybe*, down at Monmouth Valley Studios, an album inspired by the natural flow of a songwriter whose work had been growing prodigiously during his years spent in the shadows. It was now a tumble of infectious tunes, musical brute force and supreme self-confidence, all spiced with the ferocity of arrogant youth. Liam Gallagher

189

had been inspired to become a singer by the sight of Ian Brown on stage. And now Brown was literally staring the new generation straight in the face; he courageously made a joke of it, bonded with the two, gave praise and received the brothers' respect in return.[24] Ian Brown couldn't have guessed at the speed of the oncoming ascent of Oasis, an ascent which would build gloriously on the framework that The Stone Roses had done so much to establish. (And, some might say, by Geffen, who had been sweeping the decks in America, gearing all for the arrival of a new major British rock act.)

Noel Gallagher has never been reluctant to pay tribute to his heroes. "Without The Stone Roses there would definitely never have been an Oasis," he told *Select* magazine. "The fact is that, if Liam hadn't gone to see the Roses that day, he wouldn't have joined Bonehead's group and, subsequently, I wouldn't have joined Liam's group. Something would have happened, I think, but it wouldn't have been the same. We used to sound a lot like The Stone Roses in the early days, mind you, everybody did. I thought John Squire was a brilliant guitarist and, yeah, I'd rip off a load of his stuff.

"The thing is that a lot of people say that we rescued guitar music in the Nineties . . . and we did. I've said it before, we definitely did but it was The Stone Roses and before them, perhaps, The Smiths, who were holding the door open for us. We just came along and nailed it to the wall."

Truth be told, the Roses themselves were under no illusions as to what was happening around them. Mani: "We knew that it had gone on too long. We knew that somebody might nip in and take over. We actually thought it might be Primal Scream, strangely enough, who we knew well and loved, but there was definitely a sense that our groundwork was about to be wasted as far as we were concerned. Perhaps that only served to increase the pressure on us. Who knows . . ."

[24] When asked what the difference was between Oasis and Blur by Q magazine in March 1995, Mani enthused, "Oasis are real. *Proper* real . . . That always shines through." Brown had added, "Oasis just aren't . . . drama students."

14

SECOND COMING

It came on a chill Sunday night. Milling on Manchester's Market Street, over a thousand post-baggies posed for the local press photographers, swilling beer, huddling together to fight the biting December cold, forming two queues which snaked inelegantly from HMV and Virgin. All were awaiting the chimes of midnight, when the new Stone Roses album would finally go on sale. It was a stunt that could have been orchestrated by the ghost of Gareth Evans much, it is to be assumed, to the irritation of the record shop staff. That night in Manchester they passed the album over to three hundred loyal fans, for whom what had for so long seemed an impossibility was about to become true.

Down by Virgin, a local news reporter repeated a simple question and received disturbingly blank looks in return. "Why," he asked, genuinely interested, "are you down here, freezing, tonight, when you can buy the album tomorrow with no hassle?" Although nobody cared to admit it, the answer was obvious. This was the album that had started to rival The Beach Boys' legendary *Smile* in terms of its ever seeing the light of day. Whatever the causes, their enforced absence from the music scene had built up anticipation for new Stone Roses product to a fever pitch; there was now something almost mythic about both band and album. Moreover, such a stunt, surely, wouldn't pass by without at least one of the band coming down to chat to the assembled faithful, and maybe even offload a few freebies! Something would happen. Bound to. As it turned out, it slowly dawned that nothing of note would happen at all. No Roses, just their album. A sense of anti-climax started to descend on the masses, most of whom floated away, clutching their prize, curiosity, mild disappointment on their faces.

It is essential, really, to divorce *Second Coming* as a record from the unique mess of media, hype and expectation which surrounded its eventual release. Few albums could have survived in such a climate and, frankly, after five years and a million stories, anything less than an out-and-out, 14 carat gold classic would fail to satisfy the critics and fans.

191

Moreover, the pop scene had got itself some new heroes. Nothing was going to challenge the rapid ascendancy of Oasis. *Definitely Maybe* had hit number one in August, and would go on to become the fastest-selling début album of all time. The pop scene was being transformed. At the heart of this new phenomenon were the two battling brothers with Beatle haircuts, thick eyebrows and dour expressions. The 'second coming' of Manchester had already happened, and the Roses were shortly to give up their claim to the title of the most important band on the planet.

The sense of anti-climax was immediately apparent to the midnight faithful, who scurried back to their Failsworth bedrooms that night, slapped the CD in place, and heard John Squire's guitar splattered messily across an album full of crevices and cracks and lulls and fevered attempts to beef the whole thing into a Zeppelin-esque *tour de force*. Embarrassingly, there were distinct borrowings from Zep's own back catalogue on the album: an instrumental section in 'Tears' is strongly reminiscent of part of the dreaded 'Stairway To Heaven', and the album version of 'Love Spreads' features something which sounds not unlike the intro to the famous middle bit from 'Whole Lotta Love'. The crisp, tuneful guitar lines which distinguished the Roses' début album were replaced by blues licks *in excelsis*. Moreover, the finished album bore five separate sets of production credits, dividing the honours between Simon Dawson, Paul Schroeder, John Leckie, Mark Tolle and Al "Bongo" Shaw – a tell-tale sign of the procrastination and uncertainty that had formed such a part of the record's troubled genesis.

The Roses had refused to send advance press copies of *Second Coming* to eager hacks across the globe. They also elected to grant their 'come-back' interview exclusively to *The Big Issue*, much to the chagrin of the mainstream music press. "Somebody's going to make money off us coming back, so it was the best thing to do," Ian Brown argued in the interview. "We thought let's put something back. If somebody gets a house just by the four of us talking then it's got to be worth it."[25] Though both moves were in their way admirable, a throwback to the arrogance of old, they were also potentially suicidal. When they finally got their copies, at the same time as everyone else, the music journalists had to somehow make sense of the whole thing, to try to assess the music without taking into account the weight of expectation that came with the album's release. It required a sense of objectivity that was, frankly, impossible to maintain: this was, after all, The Stone Roses we were talking about, and failure to meet the impossible hopes which so many had vested in them was bound to be met with feelings of betrayal and bitterness by the listener. Which is

[25] As it turned out, six homeless people got a place to live as a result of The Stone Roses issue.

why, perhaps, Matt Snow only gave the album two stars in *Q* magazine. In the context of all that anticipation, the record must have seemed like a no hoper.

In a sense, *Second Coming* was as perfect as *The Stone Roses*. It was certainly an honest reflection of the splits and tensions buried deep within the band's dynamic. The tense pull one way, towards Jimmy Page territory, sat awkwardly against the rhythm section's natural tendency to create a glorious funk groove. With respect to John Squire, who enjoys some exquisite moments on *Second Coming*, his often insular work does tend to cloud the beauties that Reni and Mani come up with, and all too frequently, they end up sounding like Squire's backing band. One senses that the bass player is neglecting his natural urges at times and, wishing for an easy life in the studio, falls in line with Squire's direction. That said, if there exists, somewhere, an unfinished tape of this album, minus a couple of months of John Squire overdubs, the author would love to hear it, because, remarkably, it's all there; buried deep, there is a great album in *Second Coming* – maybe not a *classic*, but certainly something worth cherishing. In 1998, Ian Brown observed to *Record Collector* that Reni and Mani had been somewhat buried in the mix on *The Stone Roses* by John Leckie, in favour of the guitar and vocals. "I was hoping *Second Coming* could be the chance to get them two to get themselves through. I still figure they're the best rhythm section to come off this rock – England."

The anti-climax was, if anything, encouraged by the album's lead-off single, the gorgeously titled 'Love Spreads' – mighty, bluesy, addictive and instantly capable of sitting with the Roses' already mighty clutch of classic singles. One could almost sense Geffen's sigh of relief when Bobby Gillespie famously announced in *NME* that the song was, "the greatest comeback single of all time". The single reached number two and, if only for a couple of weeks, effectively crushed everything that surrounded it on British radio.[26] To add to all the fuss, the release of the single was marked by some unexpected controversy. Squire's cover featured a photograph of a cherub, one of a number which formed part of the decorations of a bridge in Newport, South Wales. In January, Stone Roses fans chiselled all the cherubs off, in an act reminiscent of Beatles fans removing the Abbey Road road signs after the eponymous album's release in the Sixties. "People should have more respect for architecture," Ian Brown dead-panned to the *South Wales Echo*.

As a nod towards a new, more USA-orientated Roses, 'Love Spreads'

[26] A live version of 'Love Spreads' was featured on the *Help* charity album released in September 1995, the cover of which had been designed by Squire.

was a sensuous, sprawling miracle. As a precursor for *Second Coming*, however, it was a disaster, for expectations were given one final jolt and could never hope to be satisfied by the mixed bag that was to make up the album. There seems little point in dissecting the entire album again in detail. However, it is pleasing to note that, following the initial disappointment, Stone Roses fans would eventually return a little more fondly to the record.

Four songs in particular stand up with anything the band had previously recorded: 'Love Spreads', of course, to be eventually joined by 'Begging You', 'How Do You Sleep' and, perhaps best of all in retrospect, 'Ten Storey Love Song'. Here are the four corners of *Second Coming*, four songs which hint most strongly at the arguably unparalleled potential of this band. In all of them we discover an unlikely paradox, the curious artistic squabble between Squire and Brown which leads the guitarist to effectively pull the songs back into a reactionary rockist heart. Brown, naturally, adopted a more Maverick approach – and you can hear him fighting in turn to pull the whole thing into some area of experimentalism, and so dub might clash with standard rock, and punk clash against prog rock. In these four songs, that clash is stunningly apparent and it would be mirrored, years later, in the post-Roses careers of both artists. The true crux of this tale is that The Stone Roses managed to glimpse at the full story, the wide screen spectacular: classic, awesome, all encompassing rock perfection. It was almost there, within sight, within reach, and then it was gone. That is what remains so ironic; that, in dysfunctioning, The Stone Roses almost . . . almost grasped the heights scaled by Led Zeppelin. *Undisputed greatness*. The fact that idiots like me and John Robb are prepared to spend time writing books about them may, in itself, be proof of this fact . . . but that's not enough. Then again, as one briefly celebrated Manchester band – The Distractions – once noted, nobody's perfect. Not even the finest band that this fantastic city of Manchester has ever produced. But they almost had it . . .

It is now universally accepted that *Second Coming*, while being obviously flawed, is of far greater merit than anyone seemed to realise back in December 1994. More than that, it would become subsequently cherished as much for its flaws as its glints of brilliance. As Ian Brown would later admit, "I was a bit shocked by the poor reaction to the album. I thought, and I still think, it was a great album. I absolutely did not expect all those bad reviews and I would be lying if I told you that they didn't hurt a little bit.

"We never really cared what journalists thought, but I would agree that our campaign, to not give advance copies, to only speak to *The Big Issue* was naïve. A lot of journalists were seriously pissed off by that. But they shouldn't have been, really. We did it for the best reasons . . . I remember one journalist writing a review that said the album was crap. And six months later he told me that it was his album of the year. That just about sums it up."

January was a hectic month for the Roses. The band came to London on January 9 to remix tracks from the sessions for 'Love Spreads' for future B-sides. A couple of days later, they flew to the US to discuss dates for their long-awaited tour there. At the same time, plans were being made for the UK comeback tour, with the band favouring a series of 'secret' gigs, played under a pseudonym, which would only be announced on the date of the gig itself. Clearly, they were trying to ease themselves back into live performance with the minimum amount of shock. Significantly, in an interview later in the month, Reni had admitted that, "Personally, I'm sick of underachieving." The multi-talented musician had spent the best part of five years with his gifts woefully under-used, and the strain was beginning to show.

* * *

When they weren't shooting themselves in the foot, the band's knack for attracting bad luck remained unparalleled. On February 22, their UK tour was postponed for a month – John Squire had gone down with a vicious bout of pneumonia. It's conceivable that the prolonged wait was building the Roses' fans up into a positive fever of anticipation, making their eventual performances guaranteed sell-outs. But while Squire clearly cannot be blamed for being ill, the band badly needed to get out there and gig, to re-establish themselves with the fans who had waited faithfully for so long to see and hear them again. Such delays, on the back of a five-year absence, were doing The Stone Roses untold damage. (Over the months surrounding the release of the album, Reni was frequently absent from interviews and photo-sessions.) Mani's comment in March – "We're going to do more gigs in a year than we've done in eight. The laziest band in pop finally get stuck into some fucking spade work," was encouraging. This was exactly what the band needed to do, but the bassist's infectious enthusiasm was, unfortunately, not to be backed up by actions.

'Ten Storey Love Song' reached number 11 in February 1995, but significantly, there were more important issues at stake now than just chart performances. The talk in Manchester was of the impending court case between the band and Gareth Evans. The whole thing had seemed easy to resolve, at first. With John Kennedy at their side, the Roses had produced a fat document, containing testaments from a whole range of music business and Manchester personalities, all testifying to the inconsistencies of Gareth's managerial tactics. Plugger Gareth Davies, publicist Philip Hall (approached shortly before his untimely death), Lyndsey Reade and Steve Atherton were all witnesses. Although legal reasons prevent any details of the case being relayed in print, the author has been allowed to read the document and was struck by how weak the overall case seemed. All that is revealed are anecdotes regarding Gareth Evans' methods, most of which are found, in one form or another, elsewhere in this book. Indeed, there are references to Evans' previous court struggles and, obviously, the dark side of his club management days, but the truly striking thing was how insubstantial it all seemed.

The fact is that this document, which one might have presumed would unearth tales of bodies set in concrete, or wild scams resulting in elongated holidays in Marbella, or even deliberate attempts to swindle the band, does not paint Gareth Evans as the unscrupulous con-artist one might have expected. There is a reason for this – most of the witnesses displayed a considerable degree of reluctance when hauled into the tale (a fact that the author confirmed in conversation with Lyndsey Reade and Gareth Davies). Yes, they would have to tell the truth and yes, the truth would be bizarre, but it was no darker than the band already knew. The prevailing feeling was that the band were always aware of the downside of Gareth's eccentricities but had been quite prepared to adopt them for their own purpose. Almost paradoxically, it was Evans who seemed to capture the bulk of the sympathy.

For his part, Gareth Evans had employed Andrew Simpson, the Harbottle & Lewis lawyer who had proved such a solid witness in the Roses vs. Zomba court case. With Simpson he had built a weighty file that testified to the huge amount of work that the manager had injected into The Stone Roses' career. This was solid fact; it couldn't be denied and, since any court in Britain would appreciate that a maverick personality is almost a requisite for anyone wishing to enter into high level rock management, it became suddenly clear that The Stone Roses were not going to win this case. Proceedings were due to begin on 13 March, 1995 at the High Court in The Strand, but the witnesses would never be called. Twenty-four hours before the case was due to start, Gareth Evans' fax rattled into action. The message was starkly simple: "We want to settle out of court." It was practically a *fait accompli*; to settle out of court represented a defeat that would come to haunt the band in the time to come. But ultimately, it was the only thing they could do.

The pay-off was huge – £1,000,000, though it was not paid immediately. There would remain a curious link between Evans and Geffen, and the company set up a bank account for Gareth Evans, in the United States, into which various undisclosed sums filtered. They also agreed to give a priority listen to any Evans-managed acts in the future, a promise which they kept, and still keep, although Evans hasn't subsequently discovered another band blessed with the same talent as the Roses. (He would go on to co-manage The YaYa's with Tony Michaelides, a band who, despite grabbing a great deal of A&R interest, ultimately produced nothing more than a replacement bassist for Oasis when Guigsy was forced to rest up.)

If the traditional rock star trappings such as a regular intake of Charlie were pushing the band slowly towards Spinal Tap territory, then the appointment of a genuine high-powered American rock manager could arguably be seen as the final step in the band's new direction, or the final nail in the coffin of their British credibility, and is worthy of some consideration. At the start of 1995, ex-Guns'n'Roses manager Doug Goldstein, a fast-talking big shot blessed with a devilish sense of humour and, presumably, enough suss to deal with the swathes of ego that came in the form of Axl Rose, appeared on the scene. He knew that The Stone Roses had been having big laughs by winding up the gathering of big-time British rock managers – sober, intelligent Dire Straits supremo Ed Bicknall, hard-line Lisa Stansfield manager Jazz Summers and Simply Red's duo Elliot Rashman and Andy Dodd amongst them – by sending out invitations for the said managers to 'attend auditions'.

Goldstein wouldn't pay heed to any of that. With the blessing of Geffen, perhaps even prompted by them, Goldstein arrived in Manchester armed with a no-nonsense attitude and a single-minded desire to persuade The Stone Roses of his suitability for the job. Ironically perhaps, his first contact with the band would be through Steve Adge who, eager to retain his own managerial credentials, fell into a friendly enough working relationship with Goldstein; as, indeed, did the band. As crazy as it may seem, despite the band's desperate need to acquire a powerful managerial figure, no one else had even bothered to take the personal approach. In short, a huge wad of money was just waiting there, sitting 180 miles up the M6, and no one thought it worthy of taking the lads out for a pint, talking about Manchester United, softening them for the kill. And yet hadn't the extended trauma of the past few years been indication enough of a band screaming for such a thing to happen?

Goldstein certainly thought so, and the personal touch made all the difference; he was duly accepted into the role that so many had coveted but none had made their own. Goldstein immediately realised what a special band the Roses were, and how part of their strength came from the gang-like tightness they had developed over the years. "They have a very cool system," Goldstein told *NME* in 1996. "Although they had their own opinions, they definitely operated as a unit. All outsiders are just that. If you're not actually part of the band, or Steve Atherton . . . you're not part of the decision-making process. I respected that and thought how it was cool that they really leaned on each other." Had he arrived a year, or two years earlier, things would surely have turned out differently. As it was, much to the chagrin of Geffen, his appointment would prove to be a little too late. Goldstein eventually ended up representing the band for about three months, but legal complications – allegedly pertaining to his commitments with Guns'n'Roses – prevented his taking over full-time.

On March 22, the band announced that they would play the Liverpool State Ballroom on April 6, their first UK date for five years. Five more gigs were scheduled in mid-April, followed by a tour of Europe and Japan. Alas, it was not to be. Eight days later, the whole thing was cancelled again, this time because details of the six dates had been published in the music press. It was another disaster. The only hope on the horizon lay in their scheduled appearance as the headline act for that year's Glastonbury Festival. The prestigious Saturday night slot was a towering coup for the band, and seemed to dispel fears that the promoters of England were becoming wary of the Roses; they were, after all, an unfathomable quantity. BritPop was now in full effect – Oasis, Blur and Pulp were clearly the leaders of the field, each gifted with talented individuals – Noel Gallagher, Damon Albarn, Jarvis Cocker – capable of wringing new life out of the grand tradition of great British songwriting. Behind them came the talented Supergrass, the overrated Sleeper and the promising Echobelly.

To call their output 'new' music was a contradiction in terms to many, so enthusiastically did these acts pay homage to the legendary guitar groups of the Sixties, in particular the power-pop of The Small Faces and Ray Davies' beautifully crafted Kinks material. By spring, Pulp's all-encompassing 'Common People', a genuinely classic English pop song, had provided a new anthem for the post-rave generation. And of course, the biggest band of them all – Oasis – openly acknowledged the influence of the biggest band of all time – The Beatles. The Manchester quintet had acquired an awesome reputation as a singles band, scoring their first number one in May with 'Some Might Say'; their second album, *(What's The Story) Morning Glory?,* released in October of that year, would go on to become one of the best-selling albums of all time in the UK. Oasis found themselves at the head of a new Establishment in pop which had been defined with breathtaking pace. How fast must it all have seemed to the Roses, a band from another era? Were they really great enough to be able to stand aloof from this precocious pack?

Despite the worrying signs, the record-buying public made 'Ten Storey

Love Song' a hit, though it was not enough to re-energise the sliding sales of *Second Coming*, which peaked at its entry position of number 4. (Ominously, the video featured a friend wearing a Reni mask behind the drum kit, not the man himself.) Ironically, although the album fell embarrassingly short of the expectations surrounding a band who had commanded such a large record deal, it was turning Squire, and Squire alone, into an extremely wealthy man. For all the criticism *Second Coming* had attracted, it went platinum by mid-January 1995, over 100,000 copies selling in the first week of its release. Squire's dominance over the album was reflected clearly in the song publishing royalties. If the album had performed as well as expected, Squire would have been well on the way to the 'trout farm in Hertfordshire' stage; as it was, even *he* would have to wait a while for that.

Stateside, Geffen were itching to release the album on which so much hope had rested for so long. In February, the band embarked on a US radio tour to whip up enthusiasm for their new record. Pre-Oasis, the Roses were seen as the next great British hope to crack the States, and hopes on both sides of the Atlantic were high. 'Love Spreads' went in at number one in the charts of many US radio stations.[27] Their time in the States was marked by two incidents. After hearing radio ads urging citizens to join up, Ian Brown managed to raise a small storm of protest during a broadcast on a Los Angeles radio station by telling the United States' army to stop killing babies. Lines were jammed by irate callers, furious at this lame English pop star's arrogant put-down of the US military, and the incident made the local press. Secondly, the Roses were told that MTV weren't happy with the fuzzy, monochrome video that the band had made for 'Love Spreads'; they were forced to make another, this time with the director responsible for Beck's 'Loser' video.

Their record company, now a substantial force in the film world, was in no danger of standing or falling on the success of one album, but as several hundred thousand Stone Roses fans in England could have told Geffen at the time, it was now effectively all over. Somewhere during the five year gap between albums, John Squire had effectively left the band. Geffen heard the guitar-heavy sound of *Second Coming* and saw it as a means of selling the act as a classic British rock album; those Led Zep references could cross over very comfortably to a Stateside market. The irony here, of course, is that The Stone Roses had already made a classic British rock album, too British, indeed, to crack the States (*The Stone Roses* peaked at number 89 in the Billboard Hot 100). Furthermore, the inroads they

[27] Trivia note: the tune was also picked as the theme tune to a German quiz show, and as the opening music for an Albanian state TV sports programme!

would make into the US, courtesy of the superbly organised Geffen publicity machine (and make no mistake, giant US record companies do not mess around with selling product) would actually lay the foundations for the oncoming phenomenon of Oasis.

In the US press, Squire acknowledged for the first time that drugs had played their part in delaying the album, and was frank about his own cocaine use. While admitting the band had felt stressed during their time away, Squire refuted the idea that they had been hampered by the pressure of following up that glorious début. "We weren't sitting in the studio wondering what the critics are thinking or even what the fans are thinking," he told the *Los Angeles Times* that February. "I wasn't caught up in thinking of us as the saviours of UK rock'n'roll, or worried about too much time going by." Full points for rock star nonchalance, though one can't help thinking that if the band had maintained a little more perspective on the possible effects of their self-enforced absence from the music scene, it might have been for the better.

Nobody should have been surprised by the failure of The Stone Roses to effectively dent that Stateside armour. This was 1995. Everybody knew that Americans, who preferred to stay true to rock'n'roll tradition, had long since tired of English bands invading their shores, armed with a heady reputation and an irritating line in fey posing. Suede's glaring failure to make it there and the effortless success of their support band, The Cranberries – Irish, of course, and happy to rock out if the occasion merited it – seems the most blatant example of recent times. Even Blur, at their height the Gallaghers' only serious contenders to the pop throne, failed to make a serious impact in the US. Sadly, The Stone Roses, who were to embark on an 11-date tour of the States in mid-1995 on the back of college radio support, succeeded only in providing a stepping stone for later acts such as Bush and Prodigy, who were to achieve extraordinary success there. Many fans in England simply could not fathom how such a turgid rock noise as Bush could succeed in the States while the heart and soul approach of the Roses, not to mention their subtle craftsmanship, had stalled.

Stone Roses purists often cite the spring of 1995 as the time when the band finally fell from grace. It is not the final severing of links with Gareth Evans that prompts this belief, but memories of that fateful day when they read the astonishing *NME* headline, 'RENI QUITS'. Their despair is understandable. This wasn't simply a case of a drummer leaving a major rock band, this was a major part of The Stone Roses tearing itself away. Reni was never merely a drummer. He was a key factor behind the unique dynamic that the band created on their first album. Gareth Evans certainly saw it that way. A year later, discussing the band's by then catastrophic state in *NME*, his praise of Reni was unstinting. "His influence was unbelievable," Evans enthused. "Reni was the most important member of the band. On the music side, he gave the band the ideas and he never got his just reward for the songs because he didn't get his songwriting credits." Reni was the beat that underpinned the Roses' sound, the beat which enabled Ian Brown to willingly push his vocals stylishly back into the mix, the beat that at one time, combined with John Squire's own musicianship, gave the Roses such an advantage over their rivals. Although it caused severe problems between their two personalities – Reni volcanic and lippy, Squire taciturn and introspective – their interaction proved to be the vital element in the complex musical dynamics of this unusual and brilliant rock band.

'RENI QUITS' signified the end of something that many thought might last another decade. But the headline might have run, 'Reni Quits, Squire Wins'. Reni was too proud a musician to put up with repeated clashes with another creative force, and had never got over the hurt of being passed over in favour of a cold electronic backbeat during the recording of tracks for *Second Coming*. His decision to leave, however, would remain one of the most courageous in rock and, although he was seen in the bars of Manchester that week displaying the kind of boozy, cheery delight one might associate with someone who has had an almighty weight lifted from his shoulders, it was difficult to believe that he wasn't suffering from doubt about the decision. And suddenly, it clicked. Perhaps that's why Reni wasn't featured in that photo shoot? Perhaps that's why he hadn't been quoted in any interviews? He left ages ago. The only delay had been in issuing the official statement. As he admitted, initially to *City Life* magazine in Manchester, "It had died for me. I left. I was happy to have gone."

Reni's reasons remained vague – there were rumours of his discontent that Squire and Brown earned more than Mani and himself. There were rumours of drug problems as well as musical differences. The time they had taken over *Second Coming* had clearly taken its toll on the drummer – not being able to utilise his considerable talents had led to frustration and disenchantment. Perhaps Reni had simply moved on – after all, he had a family to consider now – and found it impossible to maintain the drive that had been such a vital part of his contribution to the Roses. The photographs of him on the Roses' re-emergence after their five-year hiatus showed a weightier and slightly worn figure, not the hedonistic rock'n'roll drummer of yore. Whatever the reason or reasons, the gang was splitting up – the band that The Stone Roses now became would prove themselves capable of producing blistering live performances, but they weren't the band that had set the world alight five years before. Like

The Rolling Stones without Brian Jones, or The Who without Keith Moon, Reni's departure made the band a little more like everyone else; suddenly they weren't the impregnable Stone Roses any more. And as with The Who after Moon, there were many who said, in retrospect, that when Reni left, the rest of the band should have called it a day too.

To their credit, the Roses were fighters and they immediately put their minds to finding a replacement; they weren't dead yet. In came Robbie Maddix, 25 and Moss Side-sussed. Maddix was a crisp, hard-edged session drummer, well-known locally and well-liked, who had previously drummed for Rebel MC, Terence Trent D'Arby and Ruby Turner, among others. He was in after playing just one song in an audition – two other candidates were considered, though their names were not disclosed. "We didn't discuss whether I'd go on tour with them or anything," he told *Vox* in July 1995. "I just arrived at their rehearsal room on a Monday afternoon, met them, had a bit of a chat, played 'Daybreak' and that was it." Maddix paid tribute to the lack of rock star pretension in the band: "When I met them, walked into the room, I could see they weren't on a star trip. I just said, 'How ya doin'?' And we started playing." He quickly impressed the remaining Roses by learning the set within the space of half a dozen rehearsals. But he wasn't Reni. It wasn't a question of being as good as; it was just . . . different. He could complement the others, drive the songs along powerfully, but his admirable performance couldn't disguise the fact that this wasn't the same band anymore. It was a question of chemistry. On the Roses' tours of Europe and the USA, Maddix proved himself an effective drummer – and for anyone to adequately replace Reni was an achievement in itself – though the absence of 'Fools Gold' and 'One Love' from the sets seemed to suggest a wobble in the Roses' talent for a funked-up groove. Only Reni could hold that sway, keep that beat simmering at the top of the band's attack.

But it wasn't over yet. The Stone Roses, fragmented and Reni-less, were about to re-discover an unexpected new lease of life. Their European gigs that summer saw a continued improvement in their live performances. In April, their world tour kicked off in Scandinavia, which must have awoken pleasant memories of those ecstatically received live performances all those years ago, before the world went baggy. The first gig was at the Oslo Rockefeller on April 19, and it received mixed reviews (though to be fair, Robbie Maddix had only rehearsed a dozen times with the band before this live baptism of fire). One local paper, *Dabgladet*, called the gig, "a disaster . . . Their stage presence was really bad"; another, *VG*, reported that, "Ian Brown sang awfully out of key almost all the time." In the band's defence, the booking agent, Roar Gulbruandsen argued that they had suffered from a poor sound, but that the set improved as they played, adding praise for Robbie Maddix's performance.

It was becoming apparent to the Roses that there was still a lot of work to do before they would become a strong live act again. Clearly, the realisation was causing tension in the Roses' camp. At a Copenhagen show some days later, the band walked off during 'Love Spreads', leaving Squire on stage alone. The guitarist played on, before taking off his guitar, raising it above his head and smashing it on the stage. Ian Brown's vocals again attracted criticism, and the band, disappointed at their performance, decided to cancel a series of interviews in order to get in some extra rehearsal time. It seemed to do the trick. Stockholm followed, then Germany, Denmark and Madrid, and the band seemed to be picking up momentum as the tour went on. Gigs at Amsterdam Paradiso and E-Werk in Cologne were particularly well received, and by the time they played their last gig of the European leg, in Paris on May 11, the band were becoming a truly special live spectacle once again.

However, backstage all was not well. By the time they toured America, the splits in the band were becoming particularly apparent, with Brown and Squire now travelling in separate tour coaches. Brown dug in with friends and liggers, smoking too much strong Mexican dope, creating a kind of paranoid daze. But things were not, he would tell the music papers, as bad there as they were on the other bus – the rock'n'roll caricature charabanc, in which roadies and toadies gathered around Squire, and chemical indulgence was the order of the day. This was the Charlie bus, an out-and-out and out of it rock cliché extravaganza on wheels, in which the guitar hero would be sycophantically worshipped, and John Squire would soak it all in like a stoned despot.

It struck at the heart of everything Ian Brown held dear about the Roses, everything his punk mentality rebelled against. "I never thought we were destined to become some coked up band", he admitted sadly afterwards. "We were always stronger than that. But then John just became the archetypal regular coked up spoilt brat guitarist. It was pathetic and weak. I don't like weak people. You've got no bottle and no feelings for anyone but yourself. That's exactly how it was. Mani would be gone, too, but in a far more genial, far less sinister way. Just a regular guy, lovely to be around. But with John it became spiteful." During an interview that May, Mani embarked on a striking attack on hard drugs when Reni's name was mentioned. "Why do people get into smack?" he asked. "Because they've got fuck all to do. They've got 24 hours a day to kill." His comment threw more light on the drummer's mysterious departure the previous month, though further details were not forthcoming.

The American tour hinted strongly at something of a return to form for the band. The first date was in Atlanta at a Mid-Town Music Festival gig; the Roses appeared among such luminaries as Scottish MOR rockers Del Amitri and Eighties' icon Adam Ant. There were still signs of the old Roses perversity – a gig in Washington cancelled because the band discovered that it was seated and, hence, wouldn't make for the right atmosphere. But there was clearly a buzz about this odd UK band who had taken five years to make two albums: they broke the box-office record in Toronto at a 3,500-capacity gig which sold out in five minutes. Demand for tickets was refreshingly high, and the LA show had to be scaled up from a 1,200-capacity venue to 3,500 due to escalating public interest. Reports from various dates over the next few weeks, including a gushing piece in *Rolling Stone*, suggested that, at last, the States might be ready to accept a quality English rock band. Especially if that band gave a nod to the days when the Stones, The Who and Led Zeppelin brought rock'n'roll back to the country of its birth and cleaned up in the process. The guitar-centric *Second Coming* was actually creating something of a new audience in the US when, by the same token, it was losing the band fans back in their home country.

By June 2, with the tour over, the band relaxed into the delightfully bohemian atmosphere of San Francisco – a welcome hiatus before the prospect of more live shows in Japan and Australia. John Squire, revelling in the freedom and the sunshine, took to a mountain bike, and made his way over a dusty terrain that was quite the antithesis of the Monmouth countryside. Unfortunately, his ride was to have disastrous and far-reaching consequences. In another example of the ill-luck which seemed to dog the Roses' career, Squire had an accident while cycling, breaking his collarbone in four places and his shoulder blade for good measure. Despite the frantic attentions of physiotherapists and remedial masseurs, the band had to concede that they would have to cancel their upcoming tour of Japan (their equipment had already been shipped and had to be recalled) and, heart-breakingly, withdraw from their headlining role at the 25th Glastonbury Festival, scheduled for the end of the month.[28] It was a desperate situation. Squire had to undergo the frustration of a lengthy recovery programme with the ex-Manchester United physio John McGregor, and an operation at Manchester's Wythenshawe Hospital (he had to have a steel plate and six pins inserted across his collarbone to realign it). Then he had to sit back and simply wait for the damage to heal. There was nothing else to do: doctors had recommended a four- to

---

[28] By way of an apology to festival organiser Michael Eavis, the Roses played the local Pilton Village Fete on September 16, what was to be the first UK live show of their comeback tour.

six-week recuperation period. His enforced break from the Roses did have one positive outcome, though. Squire designed an article of clothing for the charity War Child's Pagan Fun Wear fashion show, which was held at the Saatchi Gallery in West London. His design – a bikini decorated with the infamous cherub and stripes from the 'Love Spreads' sleeve – fetched £600.

But for The Stone Roses, the accident itself had ominous repercussions. Their absence allowed Jarvis Cocker's Pulp to step in at the eleventh hour and claim the Saturday night slot themselves. Pulp had been in the indie hinterland for a dozen years or so, though they had recently gained a more public profile, particularly because of Cocker's witty lyrics and engaging stage presence. Few people who attended the festival that year, or caught the performances on television, will ever forget the glory of that particular Pulp set of June 24. They became the hit of the festival, and when Cocker sang 'Sorted For E's And Wizz', a classic caustic reflection on the rave scene of yesteryear, it could have been the Roses' swan song. It was a new era, indeed.[29]

There was to be one final, glorious Indian summer for The Stone Roses when, for a brief period, it seemed as though they could still confound all the doubters, and even after a five-year gap, re-emerge as the most important band in the world. With Squire now fully recovered, they made a triumphant appearance that August at the Feile Festival in Cork. "It was the most enjoyable gig we've ever done," Mani bubbled afterwards. After a brief period in August recuperating and spending time with their families (Squire, Brown and Maddix all had young children; Mani became the father of a little boy on August 26), the band played Pilton Festival by way of an apology to Michael Eavis for dropping out of Glastonbury. "It was top," Mani commented. "I never saw any tombola indoors. There were no cartons of flowers and vegetables." The band had played well to the hordes who had descended on the little festival, having heard that the Roses were to play, and all save Squire spent time afterwards socialising and signing autographs. On September 4, the band were at Rockfield again, this time to record a new version of 'Love Spreads' for the War Child benefit album *Help*; the sleeve of which had been designed and painted by Squire towards the end of the previous month. To help with promotion, both Brown and Maddix undertook a number of interviews.

After more rehearsal time, the band embarked on their much-delayed

---

[29] Significantly, on June 28 news of a supposed Roses split was announced in the US press, though the band immediately and strenuously denied it.

three-week tour of Japan. They were received rapturously, and played well, regaining enough spirit to suggest that their re-vamped line-up might have a future after all. One could almost sense the relief flowing back into Geffen – their monumental investment in the Roses had dented their standing in the gossipy sections of US trade-sheets *Billboard* and *Cashbox*. Maybe things would work out long-term after all. The band followed up their successes in the East with a brief Australian tour. As with their US appearances earlier in the year, the prodigious demand for tickets necessitated a gratifying scaling-up of venues. In the Australian music press, Mani laid into their contemporaries on the UK music scene with a vengeance: "I hate Blur, Oasis are just repeating themselves with every song, Pulp are a bunch of pussies. There's a lot of people getting away with it at the moment, put it that way."

It was heartening to hear the Roses coming on strong again, to hear something of the old swagger return. Ian Brown's fighting spirit was in fine form, and in an interview with *Select* towards the end of 1995, he too put the pretenders to the Roses' throne in their place. "I never feel we've been overtaken by everyone else," he said, dismissively. "Things've gone back, not forward. There's been a lull. We're here to bring things forward, we do what we want. All these bands who want to sound like Ray Davies or Paul McCartney . . . that's just retro shit." As if to underline his point, 'Begging You' was released on October 30. The song had everything to back up the band's belief in themselves, a storming drumbeat, cut-ups of savage guitar from Squire, and a superbly throbbing bass line from Mani, over which Ian Brown crooned and whispered. (It's worth remembering that for all the criticism Brown's voice has attracted over the years, his lilting sneer remains one of the most instantly recognised, and much-copied, vocals in rock.) This was indeed the sound of a new Roses, a band that were taking up from where they had left off and creating something radically different. The song gave them another top twenty hit (there were eleven mixes of the song, including one by House master Carl Cox), but its significance lay more in its role as a challenge to their contemporaries to come up with something this vital.

The 19-date British tour at the close of 1995 concluded with a succession of legendary appearances. Despite the five-year gap, the mixed reviews for *Second Coming*, the cancelled gigs and the loss of one of their original members, interest in the band remained high, and all 53,000 tickets for the tour sold out within 24 hours. At Leeds Town and Country Club, Liverpool's Royal Court, Manchester's Apollo, Wembley Arena and Brixton Academy, the band gave some of the finest performances of their lives. Wembley, in particular, captured the attention, most notably for a scorching version of 'Love Spreads' captured by chance on the *Roses Live*

In London bootleg which became available at certain record fair counters twelve months later.[30]

"I think in the UK, we played some shows in '95, better than we'd ever been," Brown told *Melody Maker* in 1998. "The love was there, people were willing us. We were smoking." The gig at the Apollo on December 23 was unforgettable. Even a seasoned gig-goer such as the author went into a state of ecstasy at the sight and sound of the Roses in full flight; others in attendance, including Noel Gallagher, were equally stunned by what the band seemed to be pulling off, despite the loss of Reni. It was possible to stare long and hard into the eyes of Ian Brown, a man who appeared to be winning the battle gloriously, although he already knew in his heart that the war had been lost. Strangely, that fact served only to make the atmosphere more intense.

After the gig, rolling down the Apollo steps, tumbling into Ardwick Green and battling for a last gasp pint at the Apsley Cottage, the talk was all about what a revelation the band had been. But for all the joy at seeing a unique magic being created up there on stage against all the odds, there was still a sense that we were witnessing the end of something special.

---

[30] 'Love Spreads' aside, as with most bootlegs, the sound quality is simply atrocious. That said, there is a certain energy which cuts through the murk. Generally speaking, though, this is for ultra completists only.

15

GOING DOWN

One day in the spring of 1996, John Squire received a letter from a lawyer representing the other Roses which began, "Positive noises are being made about the group going into the studio . . ."

Squire was truly stunned, numbed by the obvious chasm that had developed between him and the rest of the band, people he had once counted as his friends. It was so ironic that the band which had once formed such a tight gang, as all truly great groups do, should be reduced to communication via legal letters, approaching an album like two opposites vying over a property transaction. Money, egos and drugs, which often seem specifically designed to scupper the unnatural marriage that is a rock band, had taken away the freshness and fight that had made the Roses so great. The letter was enough to push Squire, who had been dithering for months, finally over the edge.

On March 21, he telephoned Mani, Brown and Robbie Maddix; he told them that, on the last tour, he had felt like a phoney, and that he couldn't do it anymore.

"Do what?" asked Brown.

"Play the guitar . . . can't do it. It's over," came the shaky reply.

Jo Whiley broke the news to her astonished listeners on Radio 1's *Evening Session* on March 25. Crisis meetings were held between all four members of the band in an attempt to find out his reasons for wanting to leave and make Squire change his mind. All in vain. In their April 6 issue, *NME* revealed that the first of these crisis meetings, held on the previous Monday, was the first time Squire had seen the rest of the band since the end of their world tour at Wembley arena on December 29. This gave some idea of the depth of the cracks that had formed in the band. Their future was immediately cast into doubt, for who could imagine a Stone Roses without John Squire? In *NME*, Gareth Evans' sense of frustration at what was happening to his old band was almost palpable: "I'm madly disappointed because every time I switch on the radio now I hear bands who have pinched from them or copied them. Liam's (Gallagher) heroes are the Roses. They should have gone to America, played New York and LA and then stayed in America. They could have flown back every weekend in their own private jet if they'd wanted to."

"It was just the right time to go," Squire now says, rather matter of factly, "there was nothing massively impending. If there was a time. That was it."

In truth, Ian Brown, wasn't shell-shocked by Squire's announcement, a fact which Squire acknowledged in the *NME* interview he gave to discuss his decision. The distance that had grown between the two became all too clear, Squire admitting, "Paradoxically, it was like the first time I'd spoken to him for a good few years. I don't really know who he is now." Brown was, of course, well aware of Squire's increasing state of isolation, especially during their recent tour, and the breach had been widening for all to see. But throughout that February, Brown and the band had been writing songs, indeed six had stacked up, patiently waiting for the deft hand of Squire to introduce that touch of magic. Brown had phoned, several times, leaving long, winding messages on Squire's answerphone, receiving no reply.

"I thought he was busy," says Brown bitterly now, "but was he fuck. He was busy sorting out the rest of his life. He's quite happy for some fat Hollywood guy to give him a schedule for the rest of the year, but I wasn't. 'Cos that's not what the Roses were about. Is that what he wants to be? A pop star?"

Apparently. Squire had witnessed the awe-inspiring rise of Oasis. He'd seen lesser talents skip by him, taking some of the success that the Roses should have had for themselves. He'd also seen The Stone Roses twisting into a nasty knot of negativity. He didn't aspire after greatness any more, he didn't need to be linked with any scene. He was after some genuine success, some solid rewards for the effort and the years he'd put in, and who, in the real world, could blame him?

* * *

Aziz Ibrahim, of Pakistani extraction, was brought up in lively, cosmopolitan Longsight, Manchester. Since the age of 11, Aziz had been an avid guitarist, developing an eclectic interest in all styles of playing, all kinds of music. He developed an eclectic and learned style, ranging from Asian classical to jazz, funk, fusion, soul and rock.

Aziz built up a solid reputation through playing in a bewildering series of reggae and fusion bands in the Manchester area, encountering Simply Red stalwarts Fritz McIntyre and Sylvain Richardson along the way. Often in demand for session work, he was known as a 'walking guitar sound supermarket'. He was the kind of musician not only able to adapt at will, but able to come up with teasingly complimentary solos and ideas, seemingly plucked out of thin air. He was also disarmingly elegant in appearance. Combined with his sharp, professional look, it comes as little surprise that when Simply Red were looking for a guitarist to tour with them, their co-manager Andy Dodd called Aziz to offer him the job, without an audition.

The experience of playing with Simply Red left him somewhat shell-shocked. Monetary considerations aside, Aziz found Mick Hucknall's despotism within the band hard to stomach. "All bands, big and small, have their ego problems, but this was genuinely bizarre," he told the author in conversation. "Hucknall, it seemed to me, had no concern for anyone other than himself. Not only did he expect everyone around him to agree with him all the time, on everything, which drove me fucking insane, he'd dictate whether some band we were watching were good or not . . . they'd wait, test his reaction and agree. It was the most horrendous thing I had ever come across." It ended, of course, with a silent phone. A whole mass of live work and suddenly, he was back at home, waiting for the phone to ring.

Throughout his career, Aziz always had a number of projects on the go and a number of bands to play in all at once. The notion of being confined to one tightly guarded musical unit seemed like hell to him. A musical prison, no less. He had to be a free spirit and he remained quite the antithesis of the kind of musician Squire would seek out for his post-Roses project. And, that same disparate quality would make him, eventually, perfect for the looser, open-minded Ian Brown.

Summer 1996, and the music press had been rife with rumours about the man who would replace John Squire. The prospect was rather like asking someone to replace Pete Townshend in The Who: quite impossible. In retrospect, the decision to carry on as The Stone Roses can quite possibly be counted as the most ludicrous decision in rock since that fateful day when, if only fleetingly, Jimmy Pursey was asked to replace Johnny Rotten in The Sex Pistols. That said, Aziz would prove to be an inspired choice as guitar wielding catalyst for Brown's sullen muse and as advisor and fellow music obsessive, and would play a significant part in the singer's future musical career.

The 1996 Reading Festival will forever be remembered as the event that finally killed The Stone Roses. How unwise was it to headline the Sunday night, to deliberately attract that level of attention? As the weekend wore on, as Shaun Ryder's Black Grape, Garbage, Dodgy and Billy Bragg thundered through their respective sets, the talk was all of the new Roses. Reports that the band hadn't managed to get beyond that proverbial 'third gig sound' caused a certain amount of anxiety in the crowd. There seemed to be a lingering loyalty among the masses, a tangible fear that a much-loved band might crumble up there on stage in front of their very eyes.

Ian Brown's reasons for continuing were solid enough. He strongly needed to shake off any traces of mystique and, for better or worse, have

The Stone Roses accepted as a real band again. Perhaps the Roses would still be respected for their honesty, their courage in carrying on despite the blows they had already received? That was the theory but perhaps, on the Saturday night, the nerves began to dig in. For Ian Brown, acting quite out of character, decided to spend the entire night raging and ranting with Cressa, sinking deeper and deeper into an alcohol and dope daze, talking up the excitement of the next day . . . and physically splintering his already precariously pitched voice. It was out-of-character behaviour for him, and desperately unwise, but Brown's confidence had been boosted by five apparently seamless shows in Europe where Squire's absence was less blatantly obvious than one might think. He genuinely felt the band to be ready.

As did Mani, who, like a kid ripping open a pile of Christmas presents, eagerly soaked up the Reading experience, happy to be regarded as a pop star once more, to flit around backstage chatting amiably to any journos, Radio One DJs or giggly fanzine scribblers bent on discovering his favourite colour. Brown, too, was seen backstage, somewhat the worse for wear. Out front, Black Grape thundered through their ramshackle party set; after the demise of the Mondays, Shaun Ryder had, against all the odds, re-emerged with a storming new band, who cooked up a fiery mixture of punk energy and funky beats. The whole heady brew was topped off with Ryder's off-beat lyrics, delivered with a Lydon-esque sneer. Ryder had performed a miraculous resurrection. Ian Brown was smiling as the hoards clamoured for more: tomorrow it would be his day.

There was, of course, the obligatory daft press conference, with Roses new and old standing before the colourful Reading posters. They lorded it above Sonic Youth, sniggered into their microphones, and hurled empty verbal assaults at John Squire, in a sordid display of shallow braggadocio. Aziz was even moved to comment, "This is the big one for me. It has been waiting for me. Some of the things I have done in the past haven't been for the right reasons. This is."

In retrospect, the press were kinder than they might have been. For it was blatantly obvious, at that press conference, that whatever charismatic arrogance the band had possessed even during their ill-advised Spike Island press conference, had faded away. In its wake was a gaggle of self-obsessed has-beens, too flushed with past glories to notice the glaringly obvious: the magic had gone. It now seems implausible that Ian Brown, normally as cool as Mark E Smith at a Showaddywaddy gig, could not realise what exactly had happened.

If the press conference was dire, the gig was worse. Stumbling on stage amid rock foolery dry ice, with Brown sidling around like a latter-day Chris Eubank, shadow boxing, trying to build up a sense of confidence in himself and his band, a dim growl rolled into 'I Wanna Be Adored', the old understated classic, though this version was rock-driven and showbizzy. As well as Robbie Maddix and Mani, this last Rose line-up featured Aziz Ibrahim on guitar and one Nigel Ippinson, the Roses' first and only keyboard player. The crowd was noticeably divided. Terrifyingly young Liam-ites squinted curiously towards Brown, probably longing for 'Roll With It'. Older heads bounced effortlessly to the rhythm which was still infectious and still, potentially, hypnotic. Then came the sudden shock of Ian Brown's voice from the speakers, seemingly dislodged from the bulk of the music. The effect was startling. Think back to the worst live television broadcast you've ever seen, when the television used to separate the sound, throwing the lead vocals seemingly beyond the scope of the backing. Think of New Order singing 'Blue Monday' live on *Top Of The Pops*. With Brown's voice unable to settle into the backbeat, and Brown unable to allow his voice to drift along, the vocals were nothing more – or less –than an arrogant undertone, and the whole point of The Stone Roses was lost, completely undermined by that sound. The fact was that the voice, normally controlled, cool and assured, if not technically excellent, was now heard to 'wander' across the sound. It lacked the very arrogance that made Brown so special.

Mani tried heroically to introduce some of the Roses' old swagger, but his gargantuan bass lines failed to save the songs. Aziz coped superbly but not for one moment did he seem anything other than a supremely confident session player. It was glaringly obvious: Aziz was capable of taking Brown to a different level, but punching through a set full of Stone Roses greatest hits, which is how it seemed and the cabaret implication is quite intentional, was contrary to everything this band had previously believed in.

After the initial disbelief, punters started to flow from the main stage in their droves. One could almost hear the scribblings of a hundred writers, striving to describe the appalling spectacle they were witnessing. It was over long before the final insult – dancing girls on-stage.

Here's where the story ended. Ian Brown's post-Reading statement of October 29, 1996, made music press, broadsheets and tabloids alike. The tone betrayed sadness and sarcasm in equal measure: "Having spent the last ten years in the filthiest business in the universe it's a pleasure to announce the end of The Stone Roses. May God bless all those who gave us their love and supported us throughout this time. Special thanks to the people of Manchester who sent us on our way. Peace be upon you."

Aftermath

A RESURRECTION . . . OF SORTS

Mani was the first to hit the ground running. His beaming face soon graced the line-up of Primal Scream who, he would repeatedly and enthusiastically assert, were "the best band in the world". An over-the-top claim, of course, but his characteristic drive helped to rejuvenate the Scream when their career seemed to have stalled. Along with his exemplary bass-playing skills, Mani brought an infectious enthusiasm and a boundless energy – it was in his nature, although the frustrations of the Roses' recent history must have made him long to belong to a band who simply went out and played music. Admittedly, Mani only managed to sneak in at the tail end of the sessions for their splendid 1997 return to form, *Vanishing Point*, and to perform in front of somewhat disappointing crowds in Europe. Still, there was no doubt that the leap, from one legendary band to another, was as effortless as it was unlikely and Mani, understandably grateful to be granted a second bite of the cherry, grasped his new position with aplomb. He remains impossible to dislike.

With the numbing hedonism of Primal Scream a seemingly part-time occupation, during the following eighteen months Mani would fall into a likeable huddle of Mancunian musicians of cultural and historical importance, or ex-pop star status, depending on one's point of view. Whatever, local 'celebrity' is there to be milked and Mani would often be seen in close proximity to former Smiths' bassist Andy Rourke, or former Inspiral Carpet man Clint Boon, attending café bar openings, guesting as DJs, hovering around free bars or cinema previews or even making fleeting cameo appearances in local band's pop videos.[31] Not that there's anything wrong with that. On the contrary, Manchester's musical heritage is so strong now that it is difficult to wander into one of its café bars without falling over some ex pop idol reflecting over his ciabatta.

[31] Check The Filthy Three's *Sweeney* pastiche video for a clear sight of Mani, Rourke, Mark E Smith and Frank Sidebottom.

Mani continued to live unspectacularly in a semi in Heaton Chapel, Stockport.

★ ★ ★

Squire had made that final phone call to Ian Brown from York, where he was staying with his trusty guitar technician, Martin. Together the pair had talked through Squire's predicament, subsequently deciding to take a walk into the ancient city's tight little centre for a drink. It's a strange place, York, maybe because of its shadowy mediaeval heart, or because many of its busking youngsters hail from the wealthy greenbelt which surrounds the city. Whatever the cause, it's one of the few cities in Britain where folk culture is still an influence, infecting even the sharper, trendier kids. York is also full of pubs. Not just tacky theme pubs, or trendy bars filled with poseurs and ear-bleeding house music, but genuine, oak and glass pubs. There may be something old-fashioned about a pub where people chat, play darts and sip cask-conditioned ales, but York's pubs also provide venues for spirited young local bands to run through a set free of egocentric posing and dreams of distant record contracts.

John and Martin, perhaps exhilarated by the heady sense of freedom brought about by Squire's departure from the Roses, strayed into one of them and settled, beer'n'fags in hand at the back of a room in which a pub rock band, The Blueflies, were busily setting up their meagre equipment. Anyone who has seen British pub rock in action would have recognised The Blueflies' set. It was rock'n'roll covers pulled through the veil of pumping R&B and spiced by hints of funk – a James Brown cover, in this instance. The band were well into their fourth pints of the evening by the time they hit their Chuck Berry-esque closer. As it happens, their regular bass player, rather implausibly perhaps, had fallen foul of RSI. His replacement, 20-year-old Stuart Fletcher, had been performing in York-based bands since the age of 11. As such he carried with him a confidence, a serenity that belied his youth – partly because his playing had kept him in the company of older, wiser owls than himself. By the age of nineteen, after performing in supporting roles to many touring bands, as well as the embryonic Shed Seven, he had gained enough experience to wander comfortably into any live gig situation. But he was more than merely a jobbing bassist.

"As soon as I saw him," says Squire, "I knew he'd be great to play with, and that was before I'd really thought too much about the band personnel." Such, it seems, was the strength of this disarming young man's on-stage charisma.

After the gig, amid the smoke and torrid banter, both John and Martin attempted to congratulate the bemused Fletcher on his playing abilities. At

214

this point he was, of course, fuzzed by the alcohol, dizzied by the post-gig buzz and had no idea that the man standing in front of him, offering a warm hand of congratulations, was John Squire, now an ex-Stone Rose. As he left the pub afterwards, Squire hit his head on a five-foot tall fibreglass seahorse, which was hanging above the exit sign.

It was Martin, however, who managed to prise a phone number from the amiable goateed bassist and talked up the idea of Stuart helping John form a post-Roses band. It was a loose meeting, to say the least. And strange too, with Martin supplying Stuart with a demo of songs to listen to. Five songs, all roughly recorded, including 'Standing On Your Head' and 'Happiness Is Egg Shaped'. It was difficult for Stuart to sense any kind of direction in these songs, songs that could so easily have become part of a third Stone Roses album, but he had to admit feeling incredibly honoured. John Squire had laid down some basic requirements for inclusion in his new project: candidates should be independent and flexible. Fletcher believed he fitted the bill and so, much to his delight, did Squire.

Chris Helme, 24, from the York suburb of Oswaldkirk, might be forgiven for believing that fate had dealt him a few absurd cards, especially during the autumn of 1995 and the spring of 1996. As a buoyantly confident singer/guitarist, 1995 had seen him bouncing through a chaotic busking trip through rural France with his band Chutzpah (nice name!), after which he returned to embark on four months of crippling poverty, living with his girlfriend in Brighton. In retrospect, this might sound like a romantic interlude. It didn't seem so quaint at the time, though (Helme was forced to steal his food from the local supermarket) and, dulled by the grim realities of gutter life, he returned to York as the easiest option.

Easy indeed, to be performing one-off gigs in York's less salubrious pubs, or busking outside Woolworths on dead Sunday afternoons. Fate is an enigmatic force at the best of times, but the heavily inebriated man who staggered past that day, heard something in Helme's version of the Stones' 'No Expectations' that fired his imagination; he staggered back to demand a demo tape. The man's name was Dennis; he was a friend of Martin's. He knew, of course, about Squire's search for band members, and convinced Helme that it might be worth his while to send him a tape and passport photograph.

Squire, intrigued rather than impressed with the tape, went to see Chris play at a York bar called Fibbers. It was a strained, nervous outing for Helme, who had become well drunk by the time Squire arrived, and now had only two strings left on his guitar. Bravely, he performed 'No Expectations' *a capella*, his eyes firmly shut (a habit which singularly failed to impress Squire).

Helme: "I was really nervous . . . and can you blame me? Two days before I had been busking and suddenly I'm supposed to be doing this audition. I couldn't even afford a pint and there was a chance in a million on offer. But it was the most scared I'd been which is why I kept my eyes shut. I didn't want to see John Squire standing at the back of the room. That would have just made me fumble even more."

Squire was reticent. After the gig his congratulatory chat seemed, to the eager Helme at least, strangely reserved. As a front man, Helme would be the visual focus of the new band, once Squire's curiosity appeal had worn thin. But those eyes? That folksy urchin appeal? Helme looked, and still looks, like a throwback to the days when Fotheringay were considered the cutting edge of the underground scene. Significantly, this faint retro-look actually appealed to Squire, whose vague idea for the new band would be to trim away the funky edges of latter-day Roses, and return to a more basic, rock approach.

And so the Squire camp devised a test. They would wrench Helme from the homely environs of York and plunge him into the very heart of Manchester: The Roadhouse. A blackened cellar venue, refreshingly lacking in any trace of Nineties' club chic. Wandering into The Roadhouse is rather like stepping back to 1978, to the kind of venues which serviced the swell of post-punk pop hopefuls. It's an evocative sweat pit, teeming with bedenimed beer slurpers and off-beat non-clubbers, a lifeline for young bands, astutely run (by music fans, believe it or not) and capable of building an atmosphere with less than a couple of dozen punters. If, reasoned Squire, Helme could survive intact in this little hot spot, he would be in. John Squire: "It was a really arduous test. I knew at the time that, if it had been me on that stage, I'd have been really scared. That's a tough gig, really, for someone to be thrown into. But he responded to it really well."

John, Chris and Stuart now rented a cottage in Coniston, Cumbria, for a four-month period that spanned the hot summer of 1996. Gradually, the three began to bond, fusing Helme's folk-edged songs with Squire's sophisticated blues attack. The combination was sublimely captured on the band's first single, 'Love Is The Law', which sounded like Jon Anderson singing over a Jeff Beck Group rehearsal – a concept which couldn't be anything less than intriguing. The period spent in Cumbrian isolation was a time well spent, resulting in a setful of new songs and an increased sense of camaraderie; the process cannot have been harmed by the awareness that elsewhere what was left of The Stone Roses was self-destructing at an alarming rate.

Coniston suited Squire. Here he was detached from the rest of the music scene and could work at his own rate, undisturbed. Moreover, the area had an attractive dramatic and literary heritage which appealed to him.[32] Although the fine summer saw the area inundated by Berghaus-garbed hoards and Day-Glo coloured water sport posers, it still retained an atmosphere of aloofness, with profoundly unpretentious pubs still decorated in pre-Sixties dark oak beams and stools, red vinyl benches and thick syrupy real ale. In many ways, this retreat was reminiscent of the Roses' move to Wales to record their second album; this time, however, the eyes of the music world were not trained so keenly on Squire, and the atmosphere, not to mention his own head, was much more conducive to creativity. In 1997, Squire told American fanzine, *Squirm* that, "It was always great to get out . . . to Wales or Cumbria. You could live there and completely forget about all that rat race Manchester or London stuff. It just feels fantastic to step out of it, to wander in shops where no one knows you or, even if they did, they couldn't care less. It's very refreshing and quite inspiring." Where better, then, to establish the roots of the band Squire had decided to call The Seahorses? Undoubtedly, had they started to swan about the pubs and cafés of Didsbury, they would have fallen straight back into the gossipy swirl and been open to the influence of the prevailing local music. This way the music came straight from them.

The rehearsals sandwiched a famous appearance, by Squire, with Oasis at Knebworth. A harmless touch of fun, or an indication that a Johnny Marr-style future of guesting with his peers beckoned for Squire? Many, without knowing about The Seahorses, believed the latter, and couldn't see a route for Squire beyond endless snatches of celebrity riffing. Well, it did look that way at first, as Liam Gallagher's spiky intro, "It's John Squire . . . with Oasis," preceded two songs – 'Champagne Supernova' and 'I Am The Walrus' – both of which spiralled into a cacophonous frenzy. 'Supernova' in particular saw Squire in full Zep mode: as Noel Gallagher confessed to *Select* afterwards, "He was playing all this mad fucking Jimmy Page stuff . . . I'm thinking, this is another *moment* in my life . . ."

During 'I Am The Walrus', the musical chaos increased, perhaps appropriately, as Squire, unable to hear anything other than Noel's guitar and "a bit of Alan [White, Oasis' drummer]" launched into wild psychedelic solos that leapt away precariously from the central sound. To some, down the front, lost in a trance, the effect was orgasmic, judging from their faces. To others, further back and, therefore, more able to separate Squire's guitar from the main thrust of the band, it merely

---

[32] The area's literary past seems almost unparalleled. One thinks not only of Coleridge and Wordsworth, but of Elizabeth Gaskell, De Quincy and WH Auden. One glance in Grevel Lindop's *A Literary Guide To The Lake District* will add a multitude of minor poets and novelists to the list.

sounded disjointed. Bravely, Oasis would allow the legendary Knebworth version of 'Champagne Supernova' to grace the three track CD that came with the *There And Then* video.[33]

The final addition to The Seahorses' initial line-up came in the bearded and bespectacled form of drummer Andy Watts. Watts was London-born although brought up in a Nomadic spree of house-hopping which took him to Formby, Nottingham, Dublin, Durham, the Yorkshire Dales and York. Hence, he retains an accent that sways wildly across the country and fools just about everybody. He met Stuart Fletcher in York, and spent a short spell drumming in the same band, punching out fairly shaky Hendrix and Yardbirds songs on the pub rock scene. On Friday nights, amid fog like smoke and the apathy of hardened beer drinkers, a regular event would take place: during the Hendrix covers, an inebriated figure would lurch from the crowd, clutching a bottle in the manner of Manchester punk legend, Jon The Postman, and launch into impromptu vocals. This figure was Chris Helme.

The invitation for Andy to join The Seahorses came out of the blue. The band, having auditioned countless hapless sticksmen, had fallen into despair – presumably because Squire had only previously worked with the mighty Reni, one in a million to say the least. Reni, of course, could not only play drums (and guitar, and bass as it happens) but could sing as well. It was only when Squire was musing about this, that Chris suddenly started to think about Andy Watts. Andy used to sing. He had fronted bands. He had nous, too, attitude by the bucketful and, to John Squire's absolute delight, had never been much of a Stone Roses fan – so he wouldn't sit through his entire audition casting inane admiring grins in Squire's direction.

The first live performance by The Seahorses came, not in a flurry of Evans-style publicity, but amid a soft hush of secrecy, at the infamous rockist heart of Deeside, the Buckley Tivoli, spawning ground for Mansun and spiritual home for parochial mix'n'match rock cross dressing. Squire was astute in his choice of venue, knowing just how comfortably easy it would be for his band-mates to ignite the crowd who regularly attended this remarkable little hall. Suitably distant from both Liverpool and Manchester, it is that rarity, a club with a built-in audience who were, for the large part, uncritical. Squire used to visit the Tivoli regularly during the Roses' record-ing sessions nearby and often marvelled at how the place seemed like an echo of a bygone age. In the large cities, today, the intense competition of clubland has all but killed the small music venue. Not in Buckley, mate.

---

[33] Needless to say, 'I Am The Walrus' was considered too far out for even the most perverse of marketing people to consider.

There are still bands in Manchester who regularly gig at the Tivoli just to feel what it is like to play before something more than a cavernous shell echoing with deadening apathy. The Seahorses' gig passed by, an effective if unspectacular performance centring on the striking guitar spiral perfected by Squire in 'Love Me Or Leave Me'. The dangers of dusting off the old cult of guitar hero worship were blatantly obvious.

A second gig, at Rico's in Greenock might, at first glance, seem to be a tentative stab at playing the sticks. But Squire knew that Greenock was staunch Roses country; it was another way to ease his band in gently, to bolster their self-confidence. The set, a surprising nod back to an era one might tastefully define as 'underground' (rather than progressive), received rapturous enthusiasm from a Greenock crowd receptive to something familiar and undemanding. The Seahorses were a perfect nip'n'tuck rock outfit, whose most courageous move was to plunder from singularly unfashionable areas of rock's history. And yet, if Greenock and Buckley were indications of a world-wide audience (as they would prove to be), then the world really was waiting to hear echoes of Anderson's Ian and Jon, and the distant growl of Greenslade. How strange that, twenty years after punk, people seemed rather fond of that early Seventies' penchant for bluesy guitar solos and plodding drums after all. The Seahorses were a homely blast of the familiar, a safe retreat from the bewildering new world of sampling and brain-battering beats per minute. John Squire's pared down, uncomplicated dream of rock stardom saw him relax into a hit band built around his playing, which could score reasonably high-selling singles and avoid the ego clashes of a democratic band, or the pressures of a band seeking to produce something truly innovative. It all came to lucrative fruition in the form of the globally successful album *Do It Yourself*. To Squire's credit, he allowed Helme's not inconsiderable melodic talents to push to the fore, and the album featured tunes which had a knack of lodging in the head for weeks, which allowed Squire the freedom to indulge himself in playing guitar.

A safe bet, then, and one that romped home in some style. Although The Seahorses looked awkward – check out John Squire's brief penchant for leaving the cardboard tags on his Levi jacket and jeans – they slipped into place with cynical ease. 'Love Me Or Leave Me' and 'Blinded By The Sun' both nudged into the top fives of Europe and the top ten of America, effectively ensuring that the album, *Do It Yourself*, released June 1997, would spend lengthy spells languishing in top twenties across the world. Everyone, it seemed, enjoyed The Seahorses although few, it might be noted, would actually love the band. Technically, it could be said that they would become instantly more successful than the Roses, certainly an easier sell. But never would they, or indeed could they, attempt a

Spike Island. Seek them out and find them eternally third on the bill at Reading and Glastonbury. It's unfair to discount *Do It Yourself* too quickly. Tony Visconti's production would be particularly effective on two notable performances, 'Suicide Drive' and 'I Want You To Know', two tracks that faintly recall Jimmy Page and Robert Plant, especially Page, whose distant ghost haunts almost the entire album.

★ ★ ★

By the time of Ian Brown's post-Reading statement in October 1996, which marked the formal end of The Stone Roses, John Squire's re-emergence was already the stuff of music press whispers. There was little indication that Brown himself was contemplating any further involvement in the 'filthiest business in the universe'. Indeed, in interviews of the time, Brown was enthusing about the glories of . . . gardening. With the physical and psychological demands of being in the Roses behind him, it seemed that Ian Brown was ready to indulge his more idiosyncratic whims. At the time, he talked of "doing old ladies' gardens, messing about with a Transit, toiling the earth. Most people do this when they are 60 or 70 . . . I may just do it now."

After years of brain-twisting ego-battering in The Stone Roses, clinging to that troubled beast as if nothing else mattered in the world, the simplicity of rural life that he'd experienced in Wales really did begin to seem attractive to Ian Brown. He could leave the music business behind him for good, start a new life on his own terms, which need have nothing to do with his past. However, although a life in the shadows might have seemed appealing to Ian Brown in those dark post-Reading days, it was never really a possibility. He may not have wanted to think about it at the time, but the Roses really had been special; and Brown had been a major part of the equation. He had managed to touch people in a way that most contemporary rock stars cannot. Ian Brown was loved, and during the twelve months which followed, he would be constantly harangued by unlikely locals, besuited bankers and grubby oiks alike. "Kids were saying to me, 'Who are these jokers? Do your thing,' " he told *Melody Maker* in January 1998. Such comments doubtless helped to save Ian Brown from potential obscurity. Moreover, so many connections with his past were still in place, that music never completely disappeared from Ian Brown's horizon. The link with Aziz Ibrahim was far too refreshing and held far too much potential to ignore. Something would happen around Ian. Bound to.

In the wake of Mani's departure, and somewhat contrary to rumours of Brown's horticultural plans, Brown, Nigel Ippinson, Ibrahim and Robbie Maddix reputedly used the proceeds from their Reading appearance –

thought to be around £200,000 – to buy the aptly named Rose Garden Studios in Bury. And it was in Rose Garden that Brown and buddies slapped together a demo tape, though it was only an echo of the kind of material that would appear on Brown's solo album, released two years later. The tape, which featured titles such as 'High Time' and 'Ice Cold Cube', was abruptly, one might say aggressively, knocked back by Geffen. Possibly stunned by the Reading disaster, the company wasted no time in flushing Brown from their roster, though they held on to Squire with enthusiasm. This was a knee-jerk reaction after the experience of shelling out a huge advance on the Roses. Geffen were playing it safe – there was clearly money to be made from the trad rock of The Seahorses; Brown was considered too experimental, too much of a risk. And no one, really, could blame Geffen for adopting a tougher attitude at this stage. After all, these musicians had single-handedly exposed major flaws in the company's A&R system. But by March 1997, Brown appeared to be floating alone.

There was no doubt that he was in retreat. In 1995, Brown's actual income barely rose above £9,000. Court costs and light-fingered Stone Roses' employees had stripped the singer's income to the bare minimum. Throughout 1996, writs flooded through Brown's front door and, eventually, numbed by the genuine unfairness of it all, or perhaps provoked by it, he retreated into his bedroom (literally) and remained holed up with a bass guitar, an acoustic guitar and a drum machine, at all of which he was a complete novice. Whether motivated by desperation or inspiration, it matters not; Brown had shed himself of any excess baggage. In choosing to start from scratch, learning how to play instruments in which he had no previous experience, and use them to compose new material, he was boldly and deliberately adopting a musically naïve approach. He bought a Bob Marley songbook and a blues songbook and, recalling that Otis Redding had written on an acoustic guitar, settled down for the winter.

Although his new freedom was refreshing, and certainly hinted at some kind of 'new beginning', it rapidly became clear that Brown needed a foil, a catalyst for songwriting, somebody to fill the role that John Squire had vacated. It wasn't difficult to find the right man. Aziz was ready, willing and able to work on the songs and see where things lead – he brought no ego baggage with him and was by now well-versed in the idiocies of pop stardom. Indeed, after the twin horrors of his two excursions into the limelight, he was not particularly interested in becoming a star anymore. Quite perfect, for Brown. Not only did Aziz, like Brown, refuse to drown his muse with alcohol, he showed little interest in drugs – and Brown, while happy to indulge in spliff, was famously wont to thunder against any kind of white powder: for one thing, he saw it as one of the factors behind the deterioration of his relationship with John Squire and, hence, of the

Roses themselves. Eventually, Aziz's Eastern-flavoured guitar graced six songs on Brown's solo album, for which he was given co-authorship.

Brown really was skint by now, and had to move back from idyllic Wales to a very ordinary house in Lymm, Cheshire, fleeing the grabbing hands of one close acquaintance in particular, who had been filtering money from him on a monthly basis. He could, he knew, alleviate the immediate problem by travelling, cap in hand, to London, stirring up interest in his old contacts and accepting a small advance. But it would have been too undignified for Brown to be seen as the kind of has-been artist that a label holds for a brief spell simply to fuel the look of their roster. Far better surely, to hit them later, with a completed album.

Encouragement overwhelmed Brown. People everywhere, in Lymm, in Manchester, in Liverpool and London, were forever coming up to him, giving him respect, asking when his next record was coming up. Why? What did it matter to them? They had college courses to cope with, or crushing nine-to-fives to battle through. They cared for the same reason the young Brown had cared about The Clash. It had seemed the world to him, back then; it had seemed so essential. And it's difficult for anyone aged 32 plus, to recall such spirit. For Brown it was genuinely bewildering, touching even and, fighting back the trepidation, he talked it through with Aziz, whose own enthusiasm hadn't diminished one iota. Aziz wanted the music – stuff the trappings, stuff all that negative Hucknall stuff. The trick was to create something, anything, that would somehow enrich the lives of these kids. Conquer that, as The Stone Roses had done, and you are genuinely a rock star of worth.

It wasn't about chocolate brown Roll Royces and Caribbean island studios. It wasn't about opening bars, hotels and clubs in Manchester and Florida, or posing with Alex Ferguson or delivering Brits speeches. Only one successful band in a hundred rise above such things. Ian Brown was beginning to understand his own worth. Of course he couldn't sing. But that was the true point. Had he been blessed with the voice of Hucknall, had he been able to relax into professional musician mode like John Squire, then he wouldn't have been so special to so many. It wasn't about virtuosity, it wasn't about prowess. It was about confidence. If you could demonstrate the kind of potential that lay within the reach of the everyday kid on the street, rather than superhuman vocal gymnastics or guitar soloing, and prove to those kids what was genuinely achievable given an average amount of talent, then you would soar effortlessly beyond the Hucknalls of this world.

Reni was still around. Aziz would still catch him drifting around Manchester's A1 music shop, dreaming, forever forming new bands, hanging out. Reni would clearly be happy to work with Ian, even loosely.

And looseness was the key, as in lo-fi Trojan/punk/dub looseness, and eight-track demo looseness. The kind of 'naïve' musical approach which didn't allow the notes to get in the way of the heart and soul – there is actually a kind of beauty and real achievement in creating songs when you're restricted to a handful of chords. When he'd captured what he wanted on eight-track, Brown duly took the material to a larger studio, to be fed through the mixing desk, to be dubbed rather than polished. The engineers were bound by Brown's insistence that no reverbs, no echoes, no techno trickery should clutter this album. His drive, perhaps, was to create the antithesis of the slick Squire overdubs that had bogged down *Second Coming*, he wanted a record that sounded honest. It was music for himself, to prove to himself that he could do it. Until this time, Ian Brown had no idea at all that he was, in the true sense of the word, musical. He knew that Ian Brown, as a name, as an image, could feasibly be enough to set the record company marketing men into overdrive. But that wouldn't be enough. He had to know, for better or worse, whether he could actually make it on his own terms. No frills.

The album's genesis was suitably ragged. In the summer of 1996, Nigel Ippinson and Robbie Maddix, living together in a cottage called The Tawny House, had written and recorded 'Nah Nah' and 'Ice Cold Cube', the latter re-worked by Brown and Aziz. From late '96 to March '97, Aziz and Brown worked on more songwriting and recording at each other's houses. During this period, Ian rescued 'Can't See Me', which had been recorded during the Roses' sessions for *Second Coming* but vetoed by John Squire, adding more guitar and a bass. There was further recording and mixing in May at Chiswick Reach Studios. Chiswick Reach is a very old studio which uses valve equipment; this, along with the fact that the Trojan reggae singles were recorded there, proved a major attraction to Brown. The final mixes were completed in the summer at The Forge Studios, in Oswestry.

True to his maverick spirit, Ian Brown had made an album on his own terms. "I wasn't in the music business when I made that album," he said later. "I had no label, no lawyer, no manager, no one knew what I was doing. They say it's experimental but I had a pretty clear idea of what sounds I liked. I'm creative and the only thing that's stopping me is the musical ability to get my ideas across. All it is is rhythms and tones and lyrics put together in a nice way." It is to Polydor's immense credit that they understood this. When Brown presented them with a patchy, tentative album, sprinkled with glittering brilliance though marred by obvious dips in quality, their first instinct was probably to push the entire thing under the nose of a producer whose notion of quality might lie in the lushness of sound, rather than scattering of half-formed ideas. (Such is the norm: get the sound right, worry about the songs, later.) But, incredibly they bowed to Brown's insistence that this was, indeed, the finished product.

It would have a fitting title, too. A title that would pre-empt the obvious response, that the listener was in fact, hearing a pile of demos. *Unfinished Monkey Business*. Perfect. The epithet 'King Monkey' began as nothing more than an off-the-cuff joke from Dodgy's Mathew Priest, back in the days when broadsheets and music press alike were hunting down The Stone Roses for taking eons to produce their second album. "If you speak to Ian," Priest told a gullible *Guardian* hackette, "you have to refer to him as King Monkey." She did, and the nickname made it into the article. Far from taking offence, Brown was amused and saw no reason not to take the nickname on board. The self-explanatory 'Unfinished' tag hinted that he was aiming for a certain freshness in the tracks, by consciously resisting the temptation to polish them off too cleanly. Ian Brown wanted to make an album that, perhaps, might nod back to The Clash circa *Sandinista* and would also strike a kinship with the posthumous, half-finished Jeff Buckley album, *Sketches For My Sweetheart The Drunk* which, although it might never have had the blessing of the artist, seemed all the more precious for its rough demo approach. The album included contributions from Mani, Reni, Robbie Maddix, Nigel Ippinson and Aziz – in fact, all the personnel who had passed through the ranks of the Roses, with one obvious exception.

Unfinished Monkey Business will never be accepted as a classic. There are too many lulls, it's too messy and unfocused – at times, the album's pacing seems stunningly ill-conceived. So much so, in fact, that it would become known for its 'love it or hate it' quality. If nothing else, however, the record proves that Ian Brown still burned with a passion for music and a flair for innovation. In many ways, the record he created was caught on the cusp between The Stone Roses and Happy Mondays – the gift for a tuneful melody played by musicians with more heart than musical qualifications. But there are also splendid, simple moments on the album that could have settled comfortably alongside the songs on *The Stone Roses*. The understated, drifting 'My Star', which even survived a naff egg crushing sequence, wherein Brown would strangely smash a tray of harmless eggs to pieces, on *Top Of The Pops*, seemed omnipresent on our radios through the winter of '97/'98, and awoke distant echoes of 'I Wanna Be Adored'. An intriguing taster for the album, the song opened with astronaut samples from a NASA video Brown owned, kicking into a glorious groove, highlighted by a 'Dear Prudence'-esque riff from Aziz. A typical Brown vocal – half-whispered, half-sneered – featured some playful space imagery, including a memorable line about astronauts being 'the new conquistadors', and gave Ian Brown his first top five solo hit. The lilting genius of 'Corpses' which paired ugly imagery with the prettiest melody of 1998 provided another hit later in the year, and suddenly Ian Brown had a solo career well and truly off the ground.

Unfinished Monkey Business was released in February 1998, entering the charts encouragingly at number 4 (the peak position of *Second Coming*, ironically), though it quickly dropped off thereafter. The publicity campaign ushered in a new dimension in saturation marketing. Polydor, wise to the fact that Ian Brown was visually still as striking an icon as he had been ten years previously, pasted the cover everywhere. The one-time pretty boy of baggy had matured – his face now was gaunt, lived in, a bristling of stubble catching the harsh light in the photo. King Monkey's cheekbones graced walls from Newcastle to Newquay, his eyes lost in the shadows of his heavy brows; it was a strong image, the mouth firmly set, more of a mask than a face. Ian Brown still looked disarmingly cool and unreadable; intent on business.

The flood of press interviews that he engaged in during the weeks before the album's release found Ian Brown in positive mood. He even managed to find something to cherish in the infamous Reading performance. "They can write what they want about it," he told *Melody Maker* dismissively in January. "I've heard the tape, the singing was poor but no one can take away from me the love that was given to me and the feeling of seeing smiling faces." Brown made the point that his singing was never about note-perfection anyway: it was about soul (a comment also made by Embrace's Danny McNamara, who had also recently been criticised for vocal weaknesses). He also let rip some stinging criticism about his estranged partner, accusing Squire of preventing him from having adequate vocal monitors on stage: "My guitarist on stage just wanted to hear his guitar so you try hearing yourself above all that when he's got four amps on 11." There were even a couple of flashes of the old arrogance. Commenting on Noel Gallagher's enthusiastic presence in the audience at the Roses' storming Manchester Apollo gig in 1995, Brown admitted he found it somewhat surprising, as *he* wouldn't go to an Oasis show. And when asked about his views on Verve's recent rise, his initial words of support were somewhat thrown into context by his comment that, "They sound a bit like Echo and The Bunnymen to me and the Bunnymen always depressed me."

Overall, Brown gave the impression of being on top of things again, happy to have survived the pressure of being lead singer in one of the most influential bands of all time, and willing to acknowledge their status: "With the Roses I knew we were good, I knew we were going to do it, you know. When I said we were the greatest, I meant it. Now I'm happy just to be alive."

Like all the best pop stars, Brown is unpredictable; indeed, if anything, his behaviour is becoming more unpredictable as time goes on. Witness the events of April 1998. Brown had guested as *Melody Maker*'s singles reviewer, chatting with journalist Ian Watson, loosely adopting panto critic mode and throwing in the odd bit of verbal spice. In this lightweight arena, Brown lobbed in an unexpected bombshell during his comments on the Divine Comedy's cover version of Noel Coward's 'Marvellous Party'. "I don't trust the British fascination with homosexuals," Brown stated casually, adding for good measure, "Violence comes from Romans, Nazis, Greeks – they were all homosexual. And I've got gay friends that will back me up." The logic in Brown's argument was hard to follow, though his motivation seemed to be down to an anti-monarchist stance – "For a start, Noel Coward was a good friend of the Queen Mother's, so I can't give that record anything" – as anything else.[34]

Watson lost his initial tape but had the honesty and presence of mind to admit this, and go through the interview on the phone, a second time, though this didn't help to clarify the motivation behind what had been said. Nor did it stem the flow of damnation from such figures as Pet Shop Boy Neil Tennant and journalist Jon Savage, both condemning Brown's seemingly homophobic leanings. Of course, and Jon Savage certainly knew this, Brown had always openly supported gays. One only has to think back to the celebrated anti-Clause 28 gig at International Two, to Ian Brown, John Squire and Reni marching through the streets of Manchester in 1987 in total support of gay condemnation of Clause 28, despite being taunted for their actions by some of the less enlightened in their inner circle. Moreover, the first Roses front cover was on *Gay News*. Anyone who has more than a passing acquaintance with Ian Brown would understand completely that it would be unjustifiable to call him a homophobe.

Gareth Evans concurs, though points out that Brown has demonstrated a mysterious, more aggressive side from time to time. "Ian Brown is not homophobic. Not at all . . . but . . . when I saw that article it did ring a few bells. That old dark side to Ian . . . and John. Ian is not right wing but he always had a fascination for the extreme right and I think that was to blame for his right-wing thing back in his scooter days. It was a fascination and a strange obsession with history, with religion, with war."

Interestingly, when asked by Ian Watson who his idea of a hero was, Brown replied: "Moses. Follow the path of Moses and you won't go

[34] The track 'Elizabeth My Dear' from *The Stone Roses* was an early example of Brown's socialist leanings – 'I'll not rest till she's lost her throne . . . It's curtains for you, Elizabeth my dear'.

wrong. Don't follow Noel Coward." This touches on a common theme to Brown's work over the years: much of his lyrical inspiration has come directly from the Bible. Early songs borrowed biblical ideas and phrases with a verve that bordered on blasphemy – 'I Am The Resurrection' springs immediately to mind, but 'I Wanna Be Adored' also cleverly combined teen dreams with arrogant aspirations to be god-like. Then there was the fact that the Roses called their comeback album *Second Coming*, a typical touch of rock'n'roll cheek, as was the lead-off track 'Breaking Into Heaven' – a bold statement of intent which, alas, was not supported by the strength of many of the following tracks. In the following week's *Melody Maker*, John Robb drew attention to this aspect of the man, tying it in with Brown's well-known love for reggae and dub: "I know he's very into his Old Testament stuff, you know, like how old dub reggae guys are into the Bible." Ian Brown is clearly a complex character, bright and gifted enough to research his history and to see beyond the history books, though one can't help feeling that the different parts of his philosophy don't quite add up at times.

Predictably, the response was immediate and damning. Inevitable castigations followed, not just by indignant gay artists and writers, but by friends and family too. In June, *Melody Maker* printed an interview in which Brown attempted to contextualise his comments. The interviewer pointed out that Brown's ideas were not new – the argument that there were homosexual power structures in Ancient Greece, Rome and Nazi Germany is put forward by William Shirer in *The Rise & Fall Of The Third Reich*. But his comments still left a bad taste in the mouth, and he proved evasive when called on to justify them. Maintaining that he didn't 'trust' transvestism, Brown added, "Gay people who are super-camp, exhibitionist . . . It comes from insecurities. You know, fine and dandy, that's you, great! But you know, pack it in. Behave!" What did he mean? "I just don't like exhibitionism, people who think they're shocking when they're not. If you've got it, flaunt it. But there's nothing worse than someone showing out who hasn't got it. It's embarrassing." Was that it, then? Did he say what he said because he found the tendency to show off among some gays 'embarrassing'? Despite the desire to believe him, Ian Brown's decision to float such heavy concepts through a lightweight pop medium, such as *Melody Maker* had become, seemed rather inappropriate to say the least, and came across as half-baked right-wing philosophy which Brown himself seemed uncomfortable about clarifying.

Perhaps it was inevitable that the indignant, stubborn, sober, careful Brown would, at various times, be misinterpreted as arrogant. Amid the slosh and mud of Glastonbury – particularly sodden, that year – he had been interviewed by a journalist from *Select* magazine. The resulting article wasn't particularly slanted in any way although the curious phrase, "Ian Brown's oft-remarked manly odour wasn't present today . . ." caught the attention of the casual reader, not to mention that of Brown himself. A confrontation ensued between Brown and the journo, during which she admitted she was referring to the contents of just one letter sent to her which coyly mentioned Brown's alleged aromatic state. Brown saw red, verbally attacking her and banning her from his tour bus. By all accounts, Brown's fury was, let's say, passionate although later, speaking to *The Independent On Sunday,* he would show mild remorse, admitting ". . . you shouldn't speak to people like that, but the fact is she wanted a cheap laugh."

You shouldn't speak to people like that! This is the reflective Ian Brown. Brown the gardener. Brown the guide perhaps, offering the kids that still attended his shows a glimpse of a more mature outlook. Whatever, there is no doubt that as he trudged around a necklace of UK dates, enlivened by spirited sets at three festivals, Glastonbury, T In The Park and V98, another irony became apparent. Here he was, surrounded by a band who he had never intended to exist, who fell together in the wake of the album's success, pulling off relaxed, quietly triumphant performances at British pop festivals. As Brown observed to *NME* in November 1997, "After Reading ('96) I never thought I would ever play another festival again. I never thought anyone would ask me back, I never thought I'd have the guts to do them and I never thought they could possibly be so enjoyable. I felt so honoured to be offered them. In 1996 I couldn't have wished for it."

Heartwarming stuff. Unfortunately, his comeback was not to be the only significant feature of 1998 for Ian Brown. Another incident had rather more serious consequences. On a flight from Paris on February 13, 1998, there was a mid-air disturbance between Brown and a stewardess. According to the stewardess, Ms Christine Cooper, she had stopped by Brown with the duty free trolley, thinking that he had gestured to attract her attention. Realising he had only been reaching into his pocket, she apologised with an 'open hands' gesture. To which Brown, allegedly, replied, "Don't you wave your fucking hands at me. I will chop your fucking hands off." Attempts to pacify Brown apparently met with further abuse; when the captain, Martin Drake, was called, Brown (again, allegedly) told him that he would do what he liked, finishing off by telling Drake to "piss off and have a shave". He was also accused of leaving his seat and hammering on the cockpit door as the plane was in preparation for landing, at which the captain radioed for police assistance. Ian Brown's version – that a misunderstanding had been blown out of all proportion, that it was the captain who had been aggressive, not him – was disregarded by the judge who, on October 23, jailed the singer for four months. A subsequent appeal failed and Brown went down for four months, firstly to a minimum security jail then, in November, to Strangeways.

His re-emergence into the pop arena has been rewarded by a trickle of hits and a big-selling album. How long, one might ask, before Brown, once again, longed to spend his days doing little more than dead-heading the flowers in his small garden? "I am happy in my ex-council house," he stated flatly, though while it is possible to catch him wandering dreamily up Pepper Road in Lymm, he tends to spend more time in New York, listening to front-line hip hop with his Mexican girlfriend.

For all the controversy which has dogged his time in the public eye, Ian Brown remains refreshingly humble about his career. As he explained to *City Life* magazine, "I know how lucky I am. I'm grateful . . . It's more than anyone could reasonably dream of. Just think how the Roses were loved world-wide. Really loved. I don't expect to ever get back to that level again. But that doesn't matter. That's been more than enough for me. I cannot contemplate the amount of love throughout my life that people have given to me. I feel like I've done something. I have nothing to prove."

* * *

The International One is a sad sight to behold these days. It's a warehouse now, and seems to sag in dismay amid its deadening row of shops and restaurants, ignored and seemingly in the wrong part of town. Gigs today arrive neatly packaged, in the pristine and purpose-built Manchester Academy, a perfect rectangular slab set slap bang in the centre of studentland, and a venue that contains all the soul and feel of a Wimpy starter home. But it's a safe, clean venue with a crisp sound. In the city centre a thousand café bars bristle for business, offering students and post-graduates a mind-boggling choice of export lagers, before they move on to the streets and into clubland. It's a whole different world now. In 1998, beatings and murders, shootings and knife fights may have dented the night-time economy, but the breezy sophistication of those café bars, enlivened by the ferocious energy of the 'gay village', continues to fight back.

By night, cosmopolitan Manchester is now softly lit and warmly intoxicating. When The Stone Roses played their groundbreaking dates at The International One it still felt as if the gigs were housed in a building set among the dark satanic mills of a gritty northern city. Much has been gained, for all that has been lost. The old mobsters who would surround Evans in his clubland days now laze on Majorcan beaches, or open theme pubs in Cheadle; their activities have been infamously usurped by drug dealing gangs who scavenge the city centre. Drugs'n'guns are the stuff of a new urban folklore.

Gareth Evans lives in a different world now, a world as far removed from rock'n'roll as it is possible to get. Take a car, perhaps, to the Knutsford turn-off on the M6 and head right, sliding past Tatton Park, on the link to the M56. This is Mere – cheerily described as the 'wealthiest area of Britain' in a 1997 *Guardian* article. Mancunians have, for many years, known the strip of detached housing splendour that lines this road as 'millionaire's row', and each gravelled driveway seems to boast a collection of automobile finery.

If you turn left at the sign proclaiming 'High Lea Garden Centre', you will find yourself heading towards the strange new world of Gareth Evans. To the right sprawls a twenty-seven-hole golf course, featuring American standard greens and a clubhouse designed by the renowned architect, Stephen Hodder. In 1998, as this book was being written, the clubhouse was rising from the ground in a mass of bricks and beams. To the left a Portakabin office served as a venue for a site meeting – a table surrounded by Cheshire set movers and shakers, and chaired by a cheery Mathew Cummings.

Cummings' role in the story of The Stone Roses is a subject of considerable speculation. In conversation with the author back in 1985, he seemed extremely personable and unerringly polite. But when Gareth introduced me to him, in the summer of 1998, his face seemed to darken in recognition. It's clear that both men have had to dredge around a few unsavoury quarters. So what? To run The Internationals, you would have to, wouldn't you? Surely, to survive all that and thrive in a world of scratch handicaps rather than smashed kneecaps, is something to be proud of. But clearly Matthew Cummings would prefer the past to remain another country.

Nowhere on earth could seem more removed from the beery stench of an early Stone Roses gig than the High Lea Garden Centre, but this unlikely venue is near to the heart of Gareth's empire. Resplendent in Prince of Wales jacket and pink golf shirt, the 1998 version of Gareth Evans is flushed with health and affluence. He skims around the outside of the café, offering breezy greetings here and there, before snatching a clasp of wooden flowers from a fixture and striding cheekily up to the coffee bar and presenting them coyly to the girls behind the counter. Gareth Evans has kept his roguish charm, and is well-liked here, though the pat cosiness of the scene is mitigated rather refreshingly by the fact that he currently manages a hardcore Liverpool punk band called La Dog Flambe.

Evans drives me to the golf course, and then on to his farm cottage, squatting in a hail of ivy, apparently abandoned. This is an eerie experience. Gareth no longer lives here, but the entire career of The Stone Roses seems to be lying around the place, in the form of records, Xeroxed articles, legal documents, gold discs, videos, demo-tapes, posters and accountancy files, all resting among a scattering of golfing paraphernalia. There is much dust, and desks overflowing with legal documents, with newspapers apparently swiftly read and discarded. A fax rattles in the corner of the room: an invitation for Gareth's golfing pro Mark James, to attend some function or other. The farmhouse sits in a fat swathe of land – Gareth's – and he surveys it quickly before climbing back into his black Ford, a car seemingly modest in this environment, where pristine BMWs regularly flash past. Later in the day, a meeting with one of the clubhouse builders requires him to travel the two thin miles which separate the golf course from the centre of the village of Lymm. Very Cheshire set and neatly perched betwixt Manchester and Liverpool, Lymm swirls with footballers, popsters, architects and high level PR directors.

The meeting with his builder lasts five minutes. As he turns away, Evans notices a ghostly figure, waving at him from the upper front room of a modest ex-council semi-detached. For a second he thinks he recognises the face, and then he turns back to his car. A knock on the window forces him to spin around. This time he knows there is no mistake. The figure gesticulating in the window is that of Ian Brown. And how strange he looks, and how unlikely, framed in that space, shadowy behind a row of dog-eared books. Panning back, Gareth takes in the full view of the house. Small and pebble splattered, surrounded by an unkempt garden, rickety gate. Fine, one might think, for Ian Brown had he not, a few short years before, signed one of the most famously lucrative record contracts of recent years. And now, in 1998, here he is, a hit solo album under his belt, about to enjoy his third solo hit single and, this very night, jetting to New York. In two weeks time he'll return, apparently as happy as ever, performing on Chris Evans' *TFI Friday* . . . and yet his house seems so disarmingly ordinary!

In a minute, Ian Brown is standing in front of us both, a smile flashing across his taught face. "Hey . . . hey great to see you . . ." he begins, offering his hand as if nothing had ever changed between Evans and himself. As if the split from management had been effortlessly amiable; as if he had never raided Evans' house; as if they had actually held one single conversation during the intervening years.

Evans refuses to shake Brown's hand.

"Ah, come on man, it's all in the past now," laughs Brown, before continuing, "You know, I never wanted to leave you . . . I was never up for that split." There is something strange about Brown. He stands here, flicking up the collar on his jacket, poking a cigarette into his mouth and lighting it, cupping his hands around the flame like a schoolboy behind the bike shed, like a scally at a football match. Then Evans notices something else. While Brown acknowledges his neighbours as they trundle by, openly demonstrating a lack of affectation, there seems to be something curiously sad about this angular figure, now a genuine pop star in his own right. He wants to talk. Ian Brown, whose features have flashed passed Evans a thousand times during the past month, from magazines, from billboards, from advertisements posted to the rear end of local buses, and whose voice had been seemingly omnipresent on the car radio, wants to get something off his chest.

He tells Evans that he isn't presently living with his wife or his two children, though he does see his kids occasionally. He stresses that he is being managed by Noel – a likeable old acquaintance of Evans' from Moss Side; that, following the departure of Squire from the Roses, he had wanted to get back in touch with Evans, but didn't have the bottle. Bitterness fuels his words. He tells Evans that he had just paid £33,000 for this house and that the transaction had got rid of his last remaining £15,000; that things may seem hunky-dory on the outside, but his was a house filled with writs – most tellingly, a demand from Geffen for a £100,000 repayment fee, apparently against the Roses' advance.

Much of this comes as a shock to Evans, who had genuinely believed that Brown's recent successes would have raised him above such worries. (Maybe, by the time this book is published, they will have.) But this wasn't a triumphant Ian Brown at all. He spoke long and hard, about John Squire, about Steve Adge, surprising facts spilling from him with curiously careless abandon, although they remain too personal to repeat here. At the end of the meeting, he spins away and strides briskly back to his front door. Evans regrets not proffering that handshake. He drives away, still in a state of mild shock. Ten minutes later he is back in his own world, asking a greenkeeper if he would run a mower over his own Knutsford lawn.

* * *

Thirty miles away, still within the expanse of Cheshire's leafiness, John Squire settles into his new house, a pristine £400,000 sprawl in the village of Morton, Macclesfield.

In Manchester, a weightier Reni – now resplendent with a sinister beard – sits with his manager, John Nuttall, auditioning guitarists for his optimistic new project, a band featuring Reni, not on drums as one might reasonably presume, but on lead guitar. It's a necessary musical escape for Reni, who still lives on Grosvener Road, Whalley Range, an infamous area of leafy decay, bustling with students, and once famously celebrated by Morrissey. It's a strange place, perhaps, for a pop star who had actually 'made it' in the traditional sense, but life goes on and Reni, despite everything, remains the Stone Rose with his feet most firmly planted in reality. He did have problems. In June 1998 he was actually sent to prison for seven long days after apparently being rude to Manchester stipendiary, Derrick Fairclough. It was an interesting exchange. Reni, charged with having no car insurance, apparently lost his temper when the magistrate started to quiz him about his earnings. It was an odd outburst, but one which seems to parallel the pointless explosion that occurred when this writer, ever so tentatively, approached the drummer in regard to this book. "I'm terrified of this book coming out," he has reportedly told members of his new band but no one . . . not one person from The Stone Roses inner circle can explain why he might react in such a way.

Mani, as previously noted, doesn't seem to care about much, but floats happily on as celebrity bassist with Primal Scream.

* * *

A neat ending? It will never happen. The Stone Roses story remains a messy one, with lines of distrust and deceit persisting in the wake of The Seahorses and Ian Brown's solo career. For all its worthy aims, the new material from Squire and Brown is, by and large, a pale shadow of past glories. It has little resonance or depth. It is a mere distraction, not something to believe in. To really believe in, and live a little, whether at Spike Island or Blackpool.

* * *

November 1998. It's strange how things are: Mani the townie, John the country Squire, Reni deep in the rehearsal studio and Ian Brown sadly, and somewhat harshly, slammed inside the echoey horror of Strangeways. Most people feel that Brown was used as some kind of example, a scapegoat to soothe a prevailing judicial mood and a prevailing media mood, too. It wasn't his fault that bad behaviour on aeroplanes suddenly became a *cause célèbre* just when he happened to have a misunderstanding with a flight stewardess that escalated a bit; bad timing, that's all. Whatever, it remains difficult to wander past the ironic posters that now line our city walls, enticing us down to the now defunct 'Ian Brown Tour, December 1998!' However, it is even possible to catch a faint whiff of victory here. Ian Brown, the only non-musician from The Stone Roses, undeniably emerged as the most loved of that particular gang. Furthermore, despite his temporary incarceration, and possibly because of it, one can sense that fondness strengthening, day by day.

233

DISCOGRAPHY

PRE-SILVERTONE Singles
So Young/Tell Me
(Thin Line LINE 001, 12″) September 1985

Sally Cinnamon/Here It Comes/All Across The Sand
(Revolver/Black 12REV 36, 12″) May 1987

Sally Cinnamon/Here It Comes/All Across The Sand
(Revolver/Black 12REV 36, 12″ reissue, different versions of Sally Cinnamon and All Across The Sand) February 1989

Sally Cinnamon/Here It Comes
(Revolver/Black REV 36, 7″) December 1989

Sally Cinnamon (single mix)/Sally Cinnamon (12″ single mix)/Here It Comes/All Across The Sand
(Revolver/Black REV XD36, CD, thick jewel case with picture booklet) December 1989

Sally Cinnamon (single mix)/Sally Cinnamon (12″ single mix)/Here It Comes/All Across The Sand
(Revolver/Black REV XD36, CD reissue, slim jewel case. no picture booklet) 1990

Sally Cinnamon (single mix)/Sally Cinnamon (12″ single mix)/Here It Comes/All Across The Sand
(Revolver/Black REC XD36, CD second reissue, thick jewel case with picture booklet) 1990

Sally Cinnamon (single mix)/Sally Cinnamon (12″ single mix)/All Across The Sand/Here It Comes
(Revolver/Black REV MC 36, cassette) December 1989

SILVERTONE Singles
Elephant Stone/The Hardest Thing In The World
(Silvertone ORE 1, 7″) October 1988, reissued February 1990

234

Elephant Stone (7″ version)/Full Fathom Five/The Hardest Thing In The World
(Silvertone ORET 1, 12″) October 1988, reissued February 1990

Elephant Stone/Full Fathom Five/The Hardest Thing In The World/ Elephant
Stone (7″ version)
(Silvertone ORECD 1, CD) February 1990

Elephant Stone/Full Fathom Five/The Hardest Thing In The World/ Elephant
Stone (7″ version)
(Silvertone OREC 1, cassette) February 1990

Made Of Stone/Going Down
(Silvertone ORE 2, 7″) February 1989, reissued March 1990

Made Of Stone/Going Down/Guernica
(Silvertone ORE 2T, 12″) February 1989, reissued March 1990

Made Of Stone/Going Down/Guernica
(Silvertone OREC 2, cassette) March 1990

Made Of Stone/Going Down/Guernica CD
(Silvertone ORECD 2, CD) March 1990

She Bangs The Drums/Standing Here
(Silvertone ORE 6, 7″, 1st 3000 with postcard – OREX 6) July 1989

She Bangs The Drums/Mersey Paradise/Standing Here
(Silvertone ORET 6, 12″, 1st 5,000 with colour print OREZ 6) July 1989

She Bangs The Drums/Mersey Paradise/Standing Here/Simone
(Silvertone ORECD 6, CD) July 1989

She Bangs The Drums/Mersey Paradise/Standing Here/Simone
(Silvertone OREC 6, cassette) July 1989

What The World Is Waiting For/Fools Gold 4.15
(Silvertone ORE 13, 7″) November 1989

Fools Gold 4.15/What The World Is Waiting For 7″ repressing
(Silvertone ORE 13, 7″ repressing with titles 'flipped') November 1989

What The World Is Waiting For/Fools Gold 9.35
(Silvertone ORET 13, 12″) November 1989

Fools Gold 9.35/What The World Is Waiting For/Fools Gold 4.15
(Silvertone ORET 13, 12″ repressing with titles 'flipped') November 1989

Fools Gold 9.35/What The World Is Waiting For/Fools Gold 4.15
(Silvertone ORECD 13, CD) November 1989

Fools Gold 9.35/What The World Is Waiting For/Fools Gold 4.15
(Silvertone OREC 13, cassette) November 1989

Fools Gold (The Top Won mix)/Fools Gold (The Bottom Won mix)
(Silvertone ORECD 13, Gold CD) 1990

One Love/Something's Burning
(Silvertone ORE 17, 7") July 1990

One Love/Something's Burning
(Silvertone ORET 17, 12") July 1990

One Love (Paul Schroeder mix)/Something's Burning
(Silvertone OREZ 17, 12") July 1990

One Love/Something's Burning CD
(Silvertone ORECD 17) July 1990

I Wanna Be Adored/Where Angels Play
(Silvertone ORE 31, 7") September 1991

I Wanna Be Adored/Where Angels Play/Sally Cinnamon (Live At The Hacienda)
(Silvertone OREZ 31, 12" stickered with colour print) September 1991

I Wanna Be Adored/Where Angels Play/Sally Cinnamon (Live At The Hacienda)
(Silvertone ORET 31, 12") September 1991

I Wanna Be Adored/Where Angels Play/I Wanna Be Adored/Sally Cinnamon (Live
At The Hacienda)
(Silvertone ORECD 31) September 1991

Waterfall (7" version)/One Love (7" version)
(Silvertone ORE 35, 7") January 1992

Waterfall (12" version)/One Love (Adrian Sherwood Version)
(Silvertone OREZT 35, 12") January 1992

Waterfall (7" version)/One Love (7" version)/Waterfall (12" version)/One Love (12"
version)
(Silvertone ORECD 35, CD) January 1992

Waterfall(7" version)/One Love (7" version)
(Silvertone OREC 35, cassette) January 1992

I Am The Resurrection (Pan and Scan Radio Version)/I Am The Resurrection
(Highly Resurrected Dub)
(Silvertone ORE 40, 7") April 1992

I Am The Resurrection (Pan and Scan Radio version)/I Am The Resurrection
(Highly Resurrected Dub)
(Silvertone OREC 40, cassette) April 1992

I Am The Resurrection (Pan and Scan Radio version)/I Am The Resurrection
(Highly Resurrected Dub)
(Silvertone OREC 40, cassette) April 1992

I Am The Resurrection (Extended Radio Club mix)/ I Am The Resurrection
(Stoned Out Club mix)/ I Am The Resurrection (LP version)/Fools Gold (Bottom
Won mix)
(Silvertone ORECD 40, CD) April 1992

Fools Gold '95/Fools Gold (The Tall Paul mix)/Fools Gold (Cricklewood Ballroom
mix) 12″
(Silvertone ORET 71) April 1995

Fools Gold '95: Fools Gold 4.15/Fools Gold 9.53/Fools Gold (Tall Paul remix)/Fools
Gold (Cricklewood Ballroom mix)
(Silvertone ORECD 71, CD) April 1995

Fools Gold 4.15/Fools Gold (Tall Paul remix)
(Silvertone OREC 71, cassette) April 1995

GEFFEN Singles
Love Spreads/Your Star Will Shine
(Geffen GFS 84, 7″) November 1994

Love Spreads (LP version)/Your Star Will Shine (LP version)/Breakout/Groove Harder
(Geffen GFSTD 84, 12″) November 1994

Love Spreads (LP version)/Your Star Will Shine (LP version)/Breakout
(Geffen GFSTD 84, CD) November 1994

Love Spreads/Your Star Will Shine
(Geffen GFSC 84, cassette) November 1994

Ten Storey Love Song (LP version)/Ride On
(Geffen GFS 87, 7″) March 1995

Ten Storey Love Song (LP version)/Moses/Ride On
(Geffen GFST 87, 12″) March 1995

Ten Storey Love Song (LP version)/Moses/Ride On
(Geffen GFSTD 87, CD) March 1995

Ten Storey Love Song/Ride On
(Geffen GFSC 87, cassette) March 1995

Begging You (album version)/Begging You (Chic mix)/Begging You (Cox's
Ultimate mix)/Begging You (Stone Corporation Vox)
(Geffen GFST 22060, 12″) November 1995

Begging You (album version)/Begging You (Larota mix)/Begging You (Stone
Corporation Vox)/Begging You (Young American Primitive remix)
(Geffen GFSTD 22060, CD) November 1995

Begging You (album version)/Begging You (Chic mix)
(Geffen GFSC 22060, cassette) November 1995

Albums
THE STONE ROSES
I Wanna Be Adored/She Bangs The Drums/Waterfall/Don't Stop/Bye Bye
Badman/ Elizabeth My Dear/(Song For My) Sugar Spun Sister/Made Of
Stone/Shoot You Down/This Is The One/I Am The Resurrection
(Silvertone ORE LP 502, LP) March 1989
(Silvertone ORE CD 502, CD)
(As above with added track 'Elephant Stone' Silvertone ORE LP 502) November
1989
Subsequent resissues contained other bonus tracks

THE SECOND COMING
Breaking Into Heaven/Driving South/Ten Storey Love Song/Daybreak/Your Star
Will Shine/Straight To The Man/Begging You/Tightrope/Good Times/Tears/
How Do You Sleep/Love Spreads
(Geffen GEF 24503, 2 LP Gatefold Sleeve) December 1994
(CD has added hidden track 'The Fox')

Compilation Albums
TURNS INTO STONE
Elephant Stone/The Hardest Thing In The World/Going Down/Mersey Paradise/
Standing Here/Where Angels Play/Simone/Fools Gold/What The World Is
Waiting For/One Love/Something's Burning
(Silvertone ORELP 521, LP) June 1992
(Silvertone ORE CD 521, CD)

THE COMPLETE STONE ROSES
So Young/Tell Me/Sally Cinnamon/Here It Comes/All Across The Sand/Elephant
Stone/Full Fathom Five/Hardest Thing In The World/Made Of Stone/Going
Down/She Bangs The Drums/Mersey Paradise/Standing Here/I Wanna Be
Adored/Waterfall/I Am The Resurrection/Where Angels Play/Fools Gold/What
The World Is Waiting For/One Love
(Silvertone ORELP 521, 2LP) May 1995
(Silvertone ORECD 521, 2 CD, bonus disc features two exclusive tracks: 'I'm
Without Shoes' and 'Groove')
(Silvertone ORECD535, 2 CD, includes a different version of 'I Am The
Resurrection')

GARAGE FLOWER
Getting Plenty/Here It Cokes/Trust A Fox/Tradjic Roundabout/All I Want/Heart
On The Staves/I Wanna Be Adored/This Is The One/Fall/So Young/Tell
Me/Haddock/Just A Little Bit/Mission Impossible
(Garage LP1, LP) November 1996
(Garage CD1, CD)
A compilation of early demos

Videos
BLACKPOOL LIVE
(Windsong WIV 006) November 1991

THE COMPLETE STONE ROSES
(Wiener World WNR 2057) November 1995

Box Sets
CD SINGLES COLLECTION
Elephant Stone/Made Of Stone/She Bangs The Drums/Fools Gold/ One Love/I
Wanna Be Adored/Waterfall/So Young
(Silvertone SRBX 1, 8 x CD singles) February 1993

12" SINGLES COLLECTION
Elephant Stone/Made Of Stone/She Bangs The Drums/Fools Gold/One Love/I
Wanna Be Adored/Waterfall/I Am The Resurrection/The Stone Roses LP (2 discs)
(Silvertone SRBX 2, 10 x 12"s) February 1993

IAN BROWN Singles
My Star/See The Dawn/Fourteen
(Polydor 571 987-1, 7")

My Star/See The Dawn/Fourteen
(Polydor 571 987-2, CD)

My Star/See The Dawn/ Fourteen
(Polydor 571 987-4, cassette)

Corpses/Jesus On The Move/Lions (With Denise)
(Polydor 582 987-1, 7")

Corpses/Jesus On The Move/Lions (With Denise)
(Polydor 582 987-2, CD)

Corpses/Jesus On The Move/Lions (With Denise)
(Polydor 582 987-4, cassette)

Can't See Me (Bacon and Quarmby Vocal Dub)/Come Again/My Star
(Polydor 586 946, 12")

Cant See Me (Bacon And Quarmby Vocal Dub)/Come Again/My Star
(Polydor 586 946CD, CD ROM)

Album
UNFINISHED MONKEY BUSINESS
Intro. Under The Paving Stones/The Beach/My Star/Can't See Me/Ice Cold
Cube/Sunshine/Lions/Corpses/What Happened To You Parts 1 & 2/Nah
Nah/Deep Piles
1998

SEAHORSES Singles
Love Is The Law/Dreamer/Sale Of The Century
(Geffen GFS 98, CD)

Love Is The Law/Dreamer/Sale Of The Century
(GFS 98, cassette)

Blinded By The Sun/Kill Pussycat Kill/Moving On
(Geffen GFS 102, CD)

Blinded By The Sun/Kill Pussycat Kill/Moving On
(Geffen GFS 102C, cassette)

Album
DO IT YOURSELF
I Want You To Know/Blinded By The Sun/Suicide Driver/The Boy In The
Picture/Love/Happiness Is Egg Shaped/Love Is The Law/1999/Standing On Your
Head/Hello
(Geffen) June 1998

PRIMAL SCREAM (featuring 'Mani')
Album
VANISHING POINT
(Creation CRECD 178)